This is Our Story

This is Our Story
Free Church Women's Ministry

Edited by
Janet Wootton

WIPF & STOCK · Eugene, Oregon

Wipf and Stock Publishers
199 W 8th Ave, Suite 3
Eugene, OR 97401

This is Our Story
Free Church Women's Ministry
By Wootton, Janet
Copyright©2007 by Wootton, Janet
ISBN 13: 978-1-62032-128-7
Publication date 3/1/2012
Previously published by Epworth Press, 2007

Contents

Notes on the Contributors	vii
Foreword by Kathleen Richardson	xi
Introduction Janet Wootton	1
1 **The Grounds of Dispute: Theologies of Leadership, Ministry and Ordination – and Women's Ministry** Jane Craske	11
2 **Women's Ministry – a Developing Story** Kirsty Thorpe	30
3 **Worship and Preaching** John Drane and Olive M. Fleming Drane	50
4 **Are there Traditional Women's Ministries?** Cham Kaur-Mann	68
5 **Women's Leadership in the Church and Feminist Theology** Janet Wootton	82
6 **The Ordination of Women and the Ecumenical Movement** Jean Mayland	105

CONTENTS

Stories
Kate Cotterill	129
Susan Durber	135
Fleur Houston	142
Jane Leach	150
Margaret Mwailu	160
Suzanne Nockels	167
Ann Peart	173
Angela Robinson	180
Madge Saunders	187
Nezlin Sterling	193
Pauline Webb	196
Afterword	202
Bibliography	206
Index of Names and Subjects	216

Notes on the Contributors

Jane Craske is British and a 'southerner' by birth and upbringing, though she has now lived in at least six different locations within the UK for a significant period of time. She is Methodist by background and choice. She was a secondary school teacher for three years, teaching English and drama, before training for Methodist presbyteral ministry. During that period of training, she studied for a PhD, exploring issues to do with women, peace and violence from a feminist theological perspective. Following training, she ministered for three years in a Methodist circuit in central London, then moved to Manchester to serve a circuit in the south of the city at the same time as taking a post in theological education at Hartley Victoria College within the Partnership for Theological Education in Manchester. The theological education post has been full-time for the past five years. She is to move on to ministry in Leeds in summer 2007. She is currently Chair of the British Methodist Faith and Order Committee.

Jane Craske is co-editor of *Methodism and the Future: Facing the Challenge* (Cassell, 1999) and author of *A Woman's Perspective on Preaching* (Foundery Press, 2001). She is married to John Overton and pursues interests in singing, reading, theatre and supporting a football team.

Kirsty Thorpe is a minister in the United Reformed Church, married to fellow minister Martin Smith. She was brought up in Portsmouth, studied Modern History at Oxford, and trained for journalism on the *South Wales Echo* newspaper in Cardiff. While on a journalism course in Canada she encountered Christian feminist ideas. In 1981 she reported on the World Council of Churches' conference on 'The Community of Women and Men in the Church' in Sheffield.

She trained for ministry after her two sons were born, completing a theology degree at the University of Wales, Cardiff. After a year of practical training in a United Reformed Church/Methodist pastorate she did a Masters degree in Pastoral Theology at Heythrop College in the University of London.

NOTES ON THE CONTRIBUTORS

Her interest in church history and feminism led to her authorship of *Daughters of Dissent* (URC, 2004) with Dr Elaine Kaye and the Revd Janet Lees, two United Reformed Church colleagues. This is an account of women's ministry within the denomination and its predecessor traditions. Her PhD, awarded by the University of Manchester in 2005, is on the background and early history of women's ordained ministry in Congregationalism in England and Wales.

She was secretary of a URC working group on Ordination and Human Sexuality from 1998 to 1999 and secretary of the denomination's Doctrine, Prayer and Worship Committee from 2000 to 2005. Now she serves as convenor of the URC's national Editorial and Communications Committee. She currently lives in Blackburn and ministers within two congregations in Bolton.

John Drane and Olive M. Fleming Drane have shared a passion for each other and for a radical approach to Christian discipleship since they were teenagers. Forty years on, they have had extensive experience of ministry in many different contexts, in the local church as well as on the national and international scene, where they have found wide acceptance among Christians of many different traditions. They both have postgraduate degrees in theology, and for part of the year work as professors in the School of Theology at Fuller Seminary, Pasadena, California, though their home base is in Scotland. While in the UK, Olive works as a mission consultant to the Baptist Union of Scotland, and both are regular speakers at church conferences and seminars. They also teach at Cliff College on the MA in Emerging Church (which was the subject of Olive's dissertation). John is co-chair of the Mission Theological Advisory Group (a partnership between the Church of England and the Global Mission Network of CTBI). Their books include (John) *The McDonaldization of the Church* (Darton, Longman & Todd, 2000) and *Do Christians Know How to be Spiritual?* (Darton, Longman & Todd, 2005); (Olive) *Clowns, Storytellers, Disciples* (BRF, 2002) and *Spirituality to Go: Rituals and Reflections for Everyday Living* (Darton, Longman & Todd, 2006); – and together, *Family Fortunes: Faith-full Caring for Today's Families* (Darton, Longman & Todd, 2004).

They have three adult children (lawyer, architect, and medical doctor), and two grandchildren. Favourite recreations include snow skiing, rollerblading, gardening, DIY, and travel.

Cham Kaur-Mann is a second generation British Asian Indian convert to Christ. She was born in Birmingham, lived in Smethwick, and later left to study English at Sussex University (a decision influenced by the proximity of the sea!). She then studied Theology at the London School of Theology and completed her Masters in Contextual Theology at

Manchester. She has no ambition to study further and now prefers to read from picture books!

Cham is the first and, at present, only Asian woman minister within the Baptist Union of Great Britain. She hopes that one day there will be many more women of Asian heritage in accredited ministry. Cham wants to encourage and promote women in ministry and particularly those exercising leadership roles within the Church and society. Cham has served as a minister in Leicester and is currently in Birmingham, where she serves as co-pastor of The Regeneration Centre, an innovative church plant based on cell church principles.

Cham's ambition is to star in the Bollywood version of *Tomb Raider* (playing none other than Lara Croft) and to have a stunt double!

Janet Wootton is Director of Studies for the Congregational Federation. Prior to that, she was minister of Congregational churches in rural and inner city locations for more than 25 years. She was minister of Union Chapel Islington from 1986 to 2003, a church which built up a community and arts project, including two performance spaces and a homelessness project.

She read Greats at St Hilda's College, Oxford, and Theology at Mansfield College, Oxford. Her doctorate, gained at King's College London in 1988, was a comparison between John Scotus Eriugena and Alfred North Whitehead's Process Thought.

She has held various offices in Women in Theology, the Society for the Ministry of Women in the Church and the Ecumenical Forum of European Christian Women. She is a former President of the Congregational Federation, President of the National Free Church Women's Council and Moderator of the International Congregational Fellowship. She is currently co-chair of the International Congregational Theological Commission, and on the editorial team for the *International Congregational Journal*, *Feminist Theology*, and *Worship Live*. She is a published hymn-writer and has been involved in producing a number of liturgical resources.

She has written and spoken widely on liturgical development, mission, and feminist theology and praxis. Her own hymns and writing for worship, *Eagles' Wings and Lesser Things*, will be published by Stainer & Bell in 2007.

With her husband, Chris, she lives in Bedford, and enjoys attending Bunyan Meeting Congregational/Baptist Church.

Jean Mayland was born at home in Stoke on Trent on 17 May 1936. She gained a degree in Modern History and a diploma in Theology at Lady Margaret Hall, Oxford.

She was accepted to train as a parish worker in the Church of England but could not cope with the system as it then was and so went to teach. She taught in schools in Ashton-under-Lyne, London and Sheffield, lectured at a teacher training college in Doncaster, and became a tutor and lecturer in Old Testament and Liturgy on the Northern Ordination Course.

She was a lay member of General Synod for 25 years and served on the Liturgical Commission, the Board for Mission and Unity, the British Council of Churches and its Executive Committee, the Central Committee of the World Council of Churches, the Study Committee of the Conference of European Churches and the Ecumenical Forum of European Christian Women.

She was ordained deacon in 1991 and priest in 1994. In 1995 she became Associate Secretary for the Community of Women and Men in the Church at CTBI and then in 1999 the Co-Coordinating Secretary for Church Life. She retired in 2004.

She was Vice President of the Society for the Ministry of Women in the Church (SMWC), a founder member of the Movement for the Ordination of Women in the Church (MOW) and later of Women and the Church (WATCH)

In her retirement she is involved with WATCH in the struggle for women bishops. She is also Patron and Trustee of Changing Attitude (CA), which works for the full inclusion of gay, lesbian, bisexual and transgendered people in the Anglican Church.

She is married and has two daughters and three granddaughters.

Foreword

The stories and commentary in this book arise out of the experience of women in ministry in the Free Churches. They are personal and each speaks from their own perspective, but there is also communality about that experience that enables the title of the book. It is *our* story and I am privileged to belong to it as well.

I suppose each of us who has experienced the struggle for acceptance and recognition has her own favourite anecdote about it. Mine is of walking out from a cathedral where I had been preaching to hear a male cleric say to his companion, 'If you can forget she's a woman, she's not bad.' The one thing that no writer in this book wishes to forget is that she is made in the image of God in the female gender and that God looks at all that God has made, says it is good and invites from that creation both glory and service.

The book spells out in detail the history, sociology, theology and practice of women's ministry in the Free Churches of England and Wales. For those who read this book whose tradition of Christian experience comes from outside those churches there may be some surprises, for that ministry has not been as widely recognized as it deserves within British society. The story is told of unfriendly hierarchy, of outright prejudice, of intimidating and patronizing superiority, of ignorant biblical interpretation that have sought to keep women from exercising the ministry to which they are called. But it is also a story of brave women and men who perceived what God was doing among them and welcomed it.

It is a story moreover that seeks to go beyond gender parity into the more relevant question of how the ministry of women brings new insights into what it means to be a child of God growing up into full maturity. In this it is not simply informative, but inspirational. It requires each of us to reach deeper into the springs of our being and to perceive those things that nourish but do not confine and to learn not to despise the femaleness within ourselves.

This book allows voices that are so often heard only within their own circles to reach a wider audience. It will be of inestimable value to a

FOREWORD

new generation of women and men who move into a landscape that is continuing to change as we seek God's purposes.

The Reverend Baroness Richardson of Calow, OBE

Introduction

JANET WOOTTON

If you visit that part of any English or Welsh town which was built during the nineteenth century, you will at some point come across a quintessentially English/Welsh building of the time, a chapel. They are as much part of the country's built heritage as are the village parish churches and grand city cathedrals, which are often regarded as representative of Englishness, at least.

In some towns, rival chapels were built facing each other on opposing sides of a crossroads. Often, they represented the height of hypocritical arrogance, petty division and middle-class snobbery. But they were also, in their time, at the radical edge of mission and social care during the torrent of sociological change that marked the industrial revolution and the urbanization of Britain.

As Welsh pit villages spread, to take up the expanding population of miners and their families, Nonconformist chapels offered spiritual resources alongside education, welfare and sobriety. In England, the awakening evangelical spirit led to a building boom of chapels and meeting houses in towns and villages, peaking in 1798, with a 60 per cent rise on the previous year.[1] In the developing conurbations, it was the Nonconformists, not the Church of England, that first responded to the spiritual and social needs of the industrial and working classes.

The development of dissenting and Nonconformist[2] churches from street corner missions to great preaching houses, from persecution and political exclusion to reforming political influence, through the changing religious and political climate, is part of the consciousness that has formed our national life. It is too easily forgotten or overlooked, at least in England, in a country with a dominant Established Church.

This book focuses on the Free Churches in England and Wales. The story in Scotland is different, as is that of Ireland, north and south. Specifically, this is the area covered by the Free Church Federal Council (FCFC), and I have defined 'Free Church' with the breadth of that Council's membership and membership policies. The term 'Free

Church' describes the non-Anglican Churches of the Reformation and the eighteenth- and nineteenth-century revivals, together with the Pentecostal and black majority Churches: the 'big three' (United Reformed Church, Baptist and Methodist), a group of smaller bodies, including the Congregational Federation after 1971, the Wesleyan Reform Union, the Countess of Huntingdon's Connexion, the Pentecostal Assemblies of God, Council of African and Caribbean Churches, and New Testament Assembly, among others.

The title 'Free Church' was enshrined in a number of ecumenical organizations through which the Free Churches worked together. In 1940, the Federal Council of the Evangelical Free Churches of England and the National Council of Evangelical Free Churches came together to form the FCFC, with its women's organization, the National Free Church Women's Council (NFCWC), as a federation of Free Churches in England and Wales. The FCFC stood alongside the Church of England and Roman Catholic Church in representing the Christians of England and Wales (the representation was always slightly anomalous as the Church of England never represented Wales). The annually elected Moderator of the FCFC was regarded as the representative of that body of Christians in the same way as the Archbishop of Canterbury and Cardinal Archbishop of Westminster for their constituencies.

The ecumenical field is by no means static. There was a major shift with the demise of the British Council of Churches and the formation of the 'Ecumenical Instruments' in 1990. The great triumph of the Council of Churches for Britain and Ireland (CCBI, later Churches Together in Britain and Ireland (CTBI)), and the national bodies in England, Ireland, Scotland and Wales, was their flexibility. Because of their openness to 'legitimate diversity',[3] more of the Free Churches were able to take part. And, for the first time in an ecumenical organization of this kind, the Roman Catholic Church was in full membership.

As part of this change, the FCFC was open to receive new members, who wished to have a sense of ecumenical fellowship without commitment to the institutions of ecumenism, or who saw the FCFC as a natural home within the ecumenical movement. These included the Pentecostal Assemblies of God, and a number of groups of black majority Churches. These came to play an important role in shaping the ecumenical vision of Britain and Ireland. As well as acting as a 'bridge' into the ecumenical movement for some Churches and groups, the FCFC carried out a valuable role, maintaining the presence of the smaller Free Churches, which did not have the resources to participate fully on their own. More recently, the FCFC has become a 'group' within Churches Together in England.[4] This led to something of an anomaly for the Welsh Churches in membership of FCFC.

During all this reorganization, the question of women's ministry has hovered uneasily between the 'Church Life' desk, or in issues of 'Faith and Order', where it can be regarded as a barrier to greater church unity, and 'Human Rights' or 'Social Justice', where it jostles with issues of racism, poverty and others that are often seen as more deserving. Staff provision for what came to be known as 'The Community of Women and Men' was often peripheral, hard-won where it existed, and the first to be cut when the going got tough.

The other great event of the 1990s, of course, was the ordination of women in the Church of England. This story is well documented, but the longer, more complex story of women's ordination and leadership in the Free Churches is less well known. This book tells 'our story', a story which has been doubly silenced. The story of the women who led independent congregations in the seventeenth century, whose preaching helped to bring the gospel to so many in the early Methodist movement, who did cellar, garret and gutter work in the Salvation Army and who won the right to ordination in the early twentieth century in Congregational, Unitarian and Baptist Churches and are now ordained in most Free Church denominations, has remained largely untold because they were women. But it was also untold because of an assumption of identity between English Christianity and the Church of England.

Carol McCarthy, a Baptist minister in London in the 1980s, expresses a rage which mirrors my own, over the same period of time. Before women were ordained in the Church of England, Free Church ministers were treated as oddities and largely ignored:

> I try to face my own sense of rejection and resulting anger. And when I examine this anger, I find it strong and deep. I am tired of being patronised and I am tired of surprising people. I am tired of being treated as a peculiarity in the churches, and in banks, shops or anywhere I cash a cheque. I am tired of the way conversations stop when I 'admit' to being a minister . . . And, in truth, I am angry and disappointed sometimes, when men cannot cope.[5]

But the debate over ordination of women in the Church of England, which should have given rise to a sense of solidarity, only served to exacerbate the situation:

> I am impatient with media coverage of the ordination of women (and I have said so). They talk as if no woman has ever before been ordained and what makes me most indignant is the way they ignore the Free Churches.[6]

The Free Churches have their roots in the Reformation and the period of developing unrest that led up to it, and in the great Evangelical Revival and the Holiness Movement. Congregational, Baptist, United Reformed,

Quaker, Presbyterian and other Nonconformist Churches were born in the maelstrom of Reformation Europe. They called for 'Reformation without tarying for anie',[7] and were impatient at the legal requirement to conform to the Church of England, which was seen as aping Rome.

The Methodist Churches and the Churches of the Holiness Movement go back to the evangelical fervour of the eighteenth and nineteenth centuries, with the Salvation Army finding its calling in the desperate social needs of the new urban underclass, and Pentecostal Churches offering a call to Spirit-filled life and worship.

These Churches vary considerably in their organization. Some are congregationally ordered, that is, each local church, each congregation, is independent and free to order its own life. This power is vested in the Church Meeting, which gathers the covenanted members of the church on a regular basis to seek the mind of Christ in such matters as the calling of a minister, the ordering of worship, and any initiatives the church might take. Generally independence is balanced by interdependence, and such churches work together in associations of churches, to share resources and express a common witness.

As we will see, the power of a local church to call its own minister was significant in the early development of women's ministry.

Others have stronger central bodies, which exercise more authority. The Presbyterian Church is organized in a series of Synods, a pattern which was interwoven with the congregational system in the United Reformed Church. The Methodist Church brings local churches into circuits, served by circuit ministry. In the UK, the Methodist Church is not episcopal, as it is in the USA, though the issue is under debate within the Methodist Church in Great Britain. However, some of the African and Caribbean Churches are served by bishops, including, in some denominations, women bishops.

Most of the Free Churches hold an annual Assembly or Conference, at which an annual President or Moderator is elected. These positions hold no authority, but rather have a representative function, both within the denomination and outside. For the most part, these national positions are open to women as well as men, though far fewer women than men have held them. Some are open to ordained men and women only. In the Methodist Church, there is an ordained President and lay Vice President, so until the ordination of women in the 1970s, the higher position was open to men only. The first woman to hold the position of Vice President was Mildred Clarissa Lewis in 1948.

The FCFC also traditionally had an annually elected Moderator, though this pattern was changed in 1990 to a four-yearly term, to match the terms for Presidents of the Ecumenical Instruments. The first woman Moderator of the FCFC, the Revd Dr (now Baroness) Kathleen Richardson, OBE, became the first ordained woman in the House of Lords following her period in this office (1995–9). We are honoured by her contribution of the Foreword to this book.

While women have had limited, and occasionally celebrated, access to the largely figurehead role of President or Moderator, there are very few women at the head of the administration of Free Churches. The post of General Secretary, often, in a loosely structured body, a central and powerful role, has been almost without exception held by men. I am delighted that one of our stories is that of the General Secretary of the New Testament Assembly, unusually, a woman holding such a role.

Styles of worship also differ between the Free Churches, though the nineteenth century saw the development of a measure of conformity, as they struggled for respectability alongside the Established Church.[8] The major denominations began to publish hymn books, which, though they had characters distinctive to their own constituencies, did contain a core of hymnody by authors across the denominational spectrum.

Preaching, rather than the sacraments, is at the heart of much Free Church worship, and most churches have a large central pulpit, with pews arranged for ease of hearing and seeing the preacher. Many nineteenth-century churches are great 'preaching boxes', offering very little in the way of visual stimulus (since imagery was generally considered idolatrous), and allowing little scope for any movement or interaction between members of the congregation.

At its height, this form of worship was extremely powerful. Great preachers drew huge crowds, to listen to lengthy, learned and inspiring sermons. Hymn books gave access to the wealth of the centuries. Translations of the Psalms, of early Greek and Syriac liturgies and medieval Latin and Reformation German hymnody opened up huge spiritual resources. And hymn-writers such as Isaac Watts and Charles Wesley provided the opportunity for the singing congregation to share in the expression and extension of their faith.

The title of this book is adapted from a hymn written in the nineteenth century by a woman, Frances van Alstyne, also known as Fanny Crosby (1820–1915). Although she was blind from early childhood, she was an enormously prolific hymn-writer, whose hymns carry a passionate personal Christian faith, and had a tremendous influence on evangelical spirituality. The 'perfect submission' of the second verse of the hymn 'Blessed assurance' may not be to the taste of modern and postmodern worshippers, but it defines a kind of theology which we will see, in the pages of this book, served to liberate and also confine women in their aspirations to leadership in the Churches. The chorus, 'This is my story, this is my song, praising my Saviour all the day long', gives rise to the title of the book, and also expresses the dedication and faith shown in the stories of women in leadership, which form the second part of the book.

Hymn-writing was an area in which women's voices could also be heard in great abundance. Women were not admitted to the scholarly and ecclesiastical institutions that created the great translations of the Bible for use in worship, or compiled prayer books or authorized liturgical resources. But hymnody gave women an avenue for creating material for congregations to sing. For a generation, Anna Laetitia Barbauld's hymns were as well known as those of Isaac Watts. Catherine Winkworth was instrumental in bringing German hymnody into common use in Britain through her translations. And there were many others who helped shape the spirituality of the Free Churches, and of the nation.

A new generation of hymn books in the second half of the twentieth century recognized the impact of women's hymn-writing and hymn-writing in general on the worshipping life of the Churches. The Methodist and ecumenical *Hymns and Psalms*, on whose editorial committee I sat, held a discussion with a group from Women in Theology about the introduction of inclusive language. The Preface states, 'As far as possible . . . the compilers have endeavoured to offer hymnody which takes equal account of the place of both women and men in the life of the church.'[9] Current women writers such as Jan Berry, Judith Driver and June Boyce Tillman, among whom I include myself, consciously seek to express the spirituality of women alongside men in their texts.

Patterns of ministry and leadership also vary between the Free Churches. Many adhere to the tradition of an ordained minister in pastoral charge of a congregation. Ordination is seen differently in different contexts, particularly with regard to presidency at Communion. In the Methodist Church, it is unusual for a lay person to preside. In Congregational churches, the Church Meeting may invite, and in some cases is encouraged to invite, lay persons to preside at Communion. In the Salvation Army, it is not uncommon for a married couple to work with a corps, and other kinds of team ministries operate in Pentecostal and some new Churches.[10]

Importantly, in most of the Free Churches, the minister does not generally have the priestly function that s/he has in the Anglican, Catholic and Orthodox Churches. This means that arguments about women's ministry have not dealt with issues of priestly representation. The minister is not a representative of Christ except insofar as every member of the congregation seeks to express the mind of Christ, and the church as a whole is seen as the body of Christ.

Nor is the ministry of most Free Churches seen in terms of an apostolic succession.[11] This means that the tradition that there were twelve male apostles is not often used as an argument against women's ministry. The tradition itself can be challenged, of course, with the view of Mary Magdalene as an apostle, even 'the apostle to the apostles', as we will see in the following pages.

INTRODUCTION

Arguments about women's ministry and women's leadership have rather focused on the scriptural propriety of women having authority, and being allowed to speak, or have a voice, in church. As we will see, there exist many challenges to those passages in the Epistles of the New Testament which ascribe 'headship' to men over women, and proscribe women's authority to teach, or, in some instances, even to speak.

However, many of these discussions presuppose traditional forms of leadership. As the debate widens, feminist theology has challenged those forms as inherently patriarchal. The predominance of a professional, ordained leader can be profoundly disempowering of those who are by the same definition 'lay'. Feminist theology has explored radical new ecclesiologies with new patterns of service and leadership.

The argument has taken place over the centuries, and now finds its place amid a wider range of theologies, including feminist, womanist, mujerista and other liberation theologies. While many, perhaps most, ordained women or women in church leadership do not see their role as changing church language or structures, a few do. Others attempt to engage in these debates from within new patterns of Church, or new religious movements. The challenge to patriarchal language and structures, and the dream of a new fully inclusive, fully human society, comes from a great variety of sources.

This book seeks to tell 'our story'. It is important that this is done not only in essay form, but also in the form of actual stories. To have told 'our story' in a book of essays only, would be something of a betrayal, since one of the gifts of counter-patriarchal ways of thinking is interaction between narrative and reflection. One of the aims of *Feminist Theology* journal is, 'to encourage writers and artists in these areas (including reflective and experiential writing) to value their work and to contribute'.[12] The same challenge comes from other non-western, non-patriarchal sources. Isabel Phiri is the Coordinator of the Circle of Concerned African Women Theologians, which she describes as 'a community of African women theologians who come together to theologise from the experience of African women'.[13]

In both fields, one of the aims is to 'hear people into speech'; not only to hear the voices of professional and academic writers, but also to empower those who are not usually heard to enter the debate. It has the great advantage of widening and at the same time earthing the debate in more people's lives.

The book contains eleven autobiographical stories of women in different kinds of church leadership. They are placed in alphabetical order of surname: a relatively unimaginative structure though, of course, women's surnames traditionally tell their own story, as they change, or stand against change with the vicissitudes of life and relationships. The order gives rise to some serendipity. The series begins with the arresting story of service in the Salvation Army, throwing us in at the deep end of pastoral and social ministry. Two women who have served as missionaries abroad come together. One is an English woman teaching in Bangladesh; the other came as a missionary to England from Jamaica, beginning a pattern of partnership between Churches that has challenged traditional ways of thinking – and about time too! The last story is told by someone who has never been an ordained minister of a church, but who has exercised a worldwide ministry through a long career, while campaigning vigorously for ordination for women.

We have women at the beginning of their ministries, and others well through their careers. Some of those careers have included academic and administrative positions at different levels. Many speak of the impact on their lives of motherhood, and changing relationships and sexuality. For some, their gender has hardly been an issue, while others have gone through bitter struggles to recognize and convince others to recognize their call. Many have grown in their awareness of gender as a factor, both in the injustice of societal and ecclesial restrictions and as a joyous element in their personality, released and engaged through the exercise of their calling.

I am delighted that we have achieved such a variety of stories, though I heartily regret the inevitable gaps. Despite our best endeavours, there is no story from a Baptist woman. Some were too busy, but one, tragically, felt that it would jeopardize her position to tell her story honestly! We approached several women in Wales, and the lack of a story from west of that border is serious. Sadly, again, no story was forthcoming. I apologize from my heart for both these lacks, and others that will be only too evident. In a sense, any gathering of stories would leave gaps, and those contained here must be allowed to speak for many others.

The six chapters by experts in various fields draw out the themes of women's ordination and ministry, telling not a little of their own stories in the process. Again, I was delighted that scholars of such standing and experience were willing to be part of this enterprise and to enter into the spirit of working collaboratively, to a certain extent. Olive and John Drane produced their chapter together, and I met with three of the other authors during the process of bringing the book together.

This is our story. It is a story that has not been much told, because we are women and the histories and biographies of church life have been mainly about men. When stories were told about women, it was the explosive fact of the ordination of women in the Church of England that held the high ground, hiding behind it a century or more of women's leadership in other Churches. It is time for our story to be told.

INTRODUCTION

Notes

1. Janet Wootton, 'English Congregationalism and its Relation to Ownership of Property and Land', *International Congregational Journal* 2.2 (August 2002), pp. 179–200, p. 192.

2. 'Nonconformist' technically describes all those who did not conform to the rule of the Church of England as required by the Act of Conformity (1559). A 'dissenter' is similarly one who dissents from the Established Church in England.

3. The *Reports on the Working Parties on Ecumenical Instruments* (London: British Council of Churches and Catholic Truth Society, 1987) included the aim, for England, at least, 'to be sufficiently flexible to allow participation by smaller churches and the Black-led churches', p. 8.

4. More information on the Free Churches Group can be found at http://www.churches-together.org.uk, by following the link to the Group.

5. Carol McCarthy, 'Ordained and Female', *The Baptist Quarterly* 31.7 (July 1986), pp. 334–6, p. 336.

6. McCarthy, 'Ordained and Female', p. 336.

7. The title of a pamphlet published by Robert Browne, a leading Separatist, in 1582.

8. Wootton, 'English Congregationalism', pp. 191–6.

9. *Hymns and Psalms: A Methodist and Ecumenical Hymn Book* (London: Methodist Publishing House, 1983), p. viii.

10. For an overview of Free Church positions on leadership and ordination, in the wider ecumenical context of Churches Together in England, see *Called to be One* (London: CTE Publications, 1996), pp. 24–5, 28 and 75–8.

11. *Called to be One* also sets issues of apostolicity in an ecumenical context, see pp. 76–7.

12. *Feminist Theology* (London: SAGE Publications), title page.

13. Isabel Apawo Phiri, Beverley Hadda and Madipoane Masenya (eds), *African Women, HIV/AIDS and Faith Communities* (Pietermaritzburg: Cluster Publications, 2003), p. 5.

1. The Grounds of Dispute: Theologies of Leadership, Ministry and Ordination – and Women's Ministry

JANE CRASKE

In the discussion of any subject in the Christian Church or Christian faith, we must start from the point of view of what people believe – Christian theology. Behind what the Church is and does is a structure of belief about God, what God does for human beings and what God wants of human beings. One area of Christian belief about what God has done in Christ is reflection on the community of disciples of Jesus after the resurrection. As it developed, that became reflection on the way the Church should be structured and ordered. The kind of leadership that is appropriate for the Church is one aspect of that reflection.

Leadership in the Church, or how ministry is exercised within and by the Church, are, of course, subjects that have filled many books. In one short chapter, I shall first survey some of the elements in churches' very varied beliefs about leadership, ministry and ordination. In this initial section I name the issues that are raised when theologies about church leadership are applied not just to men but also to women. I shall concentrate, in line with the focus of this book, on Free Churches in Britain, but will need to compare their emphases with those of other churches as well. Then in the second part of the chapter, I give examples of how those theologies of leadership, ministry and ordination have been used, questioned, changed or ignored in particular discussions around the leadership of women in the Free Churches. While Kirsty Thorpe's chapter deals with beliefs and practices to do with women's ministry over a broad sweep of Christian history, I shall concentrate on the more recent debates of the twentieth and twenty-first centuries.

Throughout this chapter I use the terms 'leadership', 'ministry' and 'ordination'. Debates about what roles women may play in churches can arise around all three of these words. The broadest, most clearly sociological term is 'leadership'. That is the broad canvas on which these debates take place. It is women's leadership in the Church which is at stake: never their *membership* of the Church, but only whether they can appropriately be leaders or what kinds of leadership role they may undertake. The term 'ministry' crosses a number of boundaries. In some churches' usage, it is almost synonymous with 'ordination'; in others it is a much more functional word referring to certain activities undertaken in the service of others. Underlying the word 'ministry' is the Greek term 'diakonia' which is also often rendered 'service'.[1] 'Ordination' is the narrowest of the three words, referring to a specific ceremony authorizing people as leaders within the Church. The terms 'ministry' and 'ordination' are not self-explanatory. In each case the context in which the words are used needs to be clarified before any particular usage can be fully understood.

The broad context: the ministry of the whole people of God

In the World Council of Churches' document *Baptism, Eucharist and Ministry* (*BEM*)[2] published in 1982, one of the key emphases was that any discussion about specialized ministries had to be rooted in an understanding of the ministry of the whole people of God, itself rooted in Christ's ministry. The work of the whole Church is to continue the ministry of Christ in the world, and only when that has been appreciated should we think about the (therefore theologically less important) place of specialized ministries. However, history shows that the Church's reflections on specialized ministries have generally taken much more time and space – and therefore importance – than any discussion on the ministry of the whole people of God. That remains true unfortunately, even in *BEM* and in other ecumenical documents.[3] What is interesting, however, is how many British Free Churches responded to *BEM* very positively on this particular point,[4] affirming how important is that theological statement of the ministry of all God's people.

Not quite interchangeably, a similar theological statement is being made by those who base any discussion of ministry in the doctrine of the *priesthood of all believers*. As a Christian doctrine, the phrase refers first and foremost to Reformation teaching that no Christian has to have another mediator between themselves and God (in contradiction to the practice of the medieval Church of requiring priestly mediation). It has also been a rallying cry for those opposed to the special status given to priests, in the medieval Church and since, who also believed that there should be relatively few specialist functions given to any leaders in the churches. In that sense, potentially any member of the Church could minister to others. The churches which sprang from the Reformation, however, clearly developed specialized, structured leadership of various kinds. It was rarely, if ever, a case of anyone being able to do anything. The 'priesthood of all believers' is better expounded as a priesthood which is held by the whole body of believers together: it is not to do with the rights and duties of individuals but with the way in which the whole Church acts together.[5] What is key, though, is the emphasis in these concepts on *all* the people and the potential for any to minister, in opposition to some special status of the few.

Women are clearly part of the people of God, the believers who share priesthood together. For those who believe in the ministry of the whole people of God, women must be ministers within that broad understanding of ministry. The theological disputes are over what kinds of ministry and service can be exercised under this dispensation, and which are more restricted, whether for women, or for both women and men.

Beyond this broad context, church traditions vary. In the short sections below I name some of the elements that make up theologies of leadership, ministry and ordination. Though I have separated, and grouped, these elements for the sake of clarity and analysis, no church or denomination would look for only one of them in their selection of people for leadership roles. However, certain elements are more characteristic of some churches than of others. Churches of Roman Catholic and Orthodox traditions, and some Anglicans, are likely to stress priestly imagery, with the notion of the 'representative' particularly important and closely linked to presidency at the Eucharist. Because that is less of a tradition among British Free Churches, it is not an element to which I shall give much attention later in the chapter, though it has been a significant part of the debate about women's ministry in other denominations. Debates in British Free Churches over the last century or so have more usually been conducted in the areas of call, gifting, biblical interpretation (often combined with interpretations of early church tradition), theological learning and social factors.

The essentials: call, gifting and learning

Most churches insist that only someone who is called by God can fulfil ministerial roles in the Church. The notion of God's initiative in calling someone into a particular role, or into a particular relationship with God's people, has important biblical precedents in stories about the calling of Old Testament prophets (Isa. 6.1–8; Jer. 1.4–10), or the calling of the first disciples of Jesus (Mark 1.16–20; John 1.35–42). It is not necessarily easy to describe how the call of God comes to people or how it is to be understood, but it is a key prerequisite for leadership in many churches. In Methodism, for example, the question of call is asked of many roles within the Church[6] and no-one can be authorized to preaching ministry who is not able to speak of a call from God. For those traditions which focus on the call to leadership and ministry, and then ask questions about women's ministry, the issue may be whether God has called a particular woman to this particular ministry, or it may be the bigger question of whether God ever calls women to particular forms of ministry.[7]

Common to appointment in many roles in the world and in the Church is the recognition of a person's gifts as suitable to the roles that they will be undertaking. In theological terms, however, there is a particular understanding of gifting: gifts suitable for roles in church life and beyond it are given by the Holy Spirit. Within that basic framework, distinctions may be drawn or not between 'natural talents' and 'supernatural gifts'. In the Pentecostal tradition, there is a theological emphasis on the fundamental gift of baptism in the Spirit interpreted as a specific anointing for further ministry.[8] Behind these ideas is the claim that leadership in the Church is resourced by God's Spirit and cannot be undertaken apart from that resourcing. Recognition of gifts already given is important for some churches in selecting people for particular ministries. In all, there would be acknowledgement that continuing gifting is necessary.

Where women's ministry is concerned, the debates may touch on what women's gifts might be in general. There are in some arguments clearly gendered expectations: that women's gifts are in caring for people, or in relationships generally. Alternatively the question may be whether a particular woman is correct in believing herself to be gifted or anointed by the Spirit, and whether that gifting should be expressed in a particular form of ministry.

In all traditions leaders, as well as being gifted by God, are seen to need varying degrees of education or training. For some traditions, this takes place over a substantial period of time before people actually engage in leadership. Other traditions emphasize the development that is needed once leaders begin to engage in their ministries. Reformed traditions have had a particular regard for 'the learned minister'.[9] Even in the early twentieth century there were debates as to whether it was possible or suitable for women to undertake the kind of training which had become customary for men. Sometimes the debate was as basic as whether residential facilities were suitable for women as well as men (see later section on Independent traditions). More seriously, theological interpretations of 'women's nature' were involved in these debates. There has been debate in theological circles in many fields over assertions made about 'human nature'; in feminist theological circles there has been particular critique of arguments asserted on the basis of 'women's nature'.

Areas of dispute: biblical interpretation, early church models and tradition

Many belligerent debates about women's ministry centre on the interpretation of the Bible. These debates, as so many others among Christians, are not simply about the importance of particular texts: Christians dispute because they disagree more fundamentally on how to interpret Scripture in general.

Disputes may focus on how to understand particular stories in Genesis (particularly the creation of human beings, Gen. 1.26–7; the creation of Eve, Gen. 2.18–24; the fall and its consequences, Gen. 3), or particular New Testament texts: usually 1 Cor. 11.3–16 and 14.33b–36, and 1 Tim. 2.11–15. However, there are also underlying issues about attitudes to modern biblical criticism, as well as which parts of Scripture are used as key resources for interpreting other parts. Some use principles from the Timothy or Corinthians texts cited above as the key for understanding. They then interpret stories about women's activities in the New Testament Church in the light of those principles – so that, for instance, references to women's prophesying in the New Testament are understood as very different from authoritative teaching, or as a ministry exercised in private. For others, the primary material is the examples of women's activities as evidence of a wide range of public ministries in which women were involved. Texts restricting women's activities are then interpreted as instructions for particular congregations, aimed at solving particular, local difficulties, but not intended to be principles for all time.[10]

Two major strands of twenty-first-century Christianity refer to aspects of tradition in their discussions of leadership in the Church. There are those who see themselves 'returning' to the purity of the New Testament Church, intending to follow the patterns of church order and organization, including leadership, which they understand from the Bible to be the oldest and closest to the time of Jesus. Clearly not all those who have that principle end up with the same understanding of the kind of leadership that was exercised in the earliest churches.[11] Where women are concerned, the debate in this strand of the Church is similar to the debate over biblical interpretation, though perhaps more simply stated: were women involved in leadership in the early years of the Church? The answer is given as 'yes' by some Christian groups and as 'no' by others.

Apparently in contrast to this, yet also I would argue significantly connected to it, is the emphasis on the unchanging nature of Christian tradition as key to church order. For Orthodox and Roman Catholic traditions in particular, the patterns of church order were set by Jesus through the earliest apostolic tradition. Central to this interpretation of tradition is the stress on a succession of church leaders through whom unity has been maintained and true teaching given from the beginnings of Christianity to today. These churches interpret 'the Tradition' in such a way that they play down changes and developments over the centuries and are hostile to what might look like a major change of direction, such as the ordination of women. As with biblical interpretation, there are assumptions made about the uniformity of the Christian tradition in this reading of Christian history.

The setting apart of some

The attention, and sometimes the status, given to various ministries in the Church has often been related to the extent to which those who exercise them are 'set apart' to do so. Some ministries of teaching and preaching and pastoral care are engaged in by a large number of people in any one tradition (Sunday School teaching, pastoral visiting, speaking to fellowship groups, leading worship and preaching). But there is often a step change when a person is set aside by the church (often financially supported) to devote all their time or a considerable proportion of it to particular ministries. 'Being set apart' may refer in some traditions specifically to ordination, in others to another form of recognized leadership. This element of a theology of ministry may apply to a life-long commitment on the part of the leader; or to a specific task or period of time.

In the debates over women's ministry, the practice of many churches in Britain followed that of other sectors in society for a long time, supporting women economically to a lesser extent than men, out of beliefs about a man's earnings supporting a whole family, and a woman's earnings supporting only herself and married women not being expected or even allowed to work or earn in certain roles.[12]

Many Christian traditions and denominations have as one element of their understanding of ministry and leadership the notion that the church leader is a representative person. The leader may be seen as representative of the particular congregation within the community at large, or as acting on behalf of the whole congregation, including in presiding at the celebration of the Eucharist by the whole congregation. The leader may be representative of one part of the Church to another: in British Methodism the ordained person is spoken of as a 'connexional person', since they have a particular role in linking together the local church with its fuller life in the circuit and in the Methodist Church connexionally (nationally). There are ways of expressing a similar 'linking' role in other traditions. Beyond and often inclusive of this understanding, the word 'representative' for some Christians more readily refers to the leader as representing God in Christ. That representation is often attached closely to presidency at the Eucharist, but may also refer to a prophetic ministry and to aspects of authority and discipline. What is at stake in many continuing debates about women's ministry is whether women can act as 'representative' of Christ – often interpreted as a restricted 'physical' representation.

Many churches refer to some of their church leaders as 'ministers of word and sacrament'. There is for most a particularly close link between ordination and sacramental ministry, whether 'sacramental' is understood to refer to two sacraments or to more than that.[13] In many traditions, presiding at the Eucharist is reserved entirely to those ordained to a particular ministry, and their theology of ordination is predominantly explored in relation to sacramental ministry. For some, this element of a theology of ordination extends into specific imagery about priesthood, related to but distinct from the priesthood of all believers discussed earlier. In such an understanding the president at the Eucharist is the priest who has a particular relation to Christ whose sacrifice is recalled in this central act of the Church's worship. Priestly imagery, with the notion of the minister as representative of Christ, may lead to a strong emphasis on the necessity of the minister as a physical 'icon' of Christ and the impossibility of a woman representing the male Christ.

The social context of Christian discussion

One crucial area in exploring theologies of leadership, ministry and ordination is the most difficult to untangle. Christians may think of their beliefs about leadership and their theologies of ordination as solely a Christian matter, but invariably they will have been influenced by models of leadership and notions of authority in many cultures over the centuries. Ideas about clergy status and even forms of dress (such as the use of 'imperial purple') were in some cases modelled on leadership in the Roman empire in the early centuries of Christian history. Of significance for this book, notions of appropriate roles for women in society, in leadership or more usually out of it, have influenced what has been said about women's ministry. That is true both for the centuries when patriarchal assumptions ruled that women should not have, were not capable of, public leadership roles and also for the much more recent moves towards equality for women.

This factor in the debate still becomes most apparent in questions about what is appropriate for married women as opposed to single women, and in the sense throughout the twentieth century, though in varying ways, that family and home are the primary sphere of activity for women in a way they never are for men. In the early years of the twentieth century, in both church and society at large, the expectation was that a woman would resign from her occupation when she married (though see note 11). Untangling how these beliefs emerged, what part Christian theology had to play in shaping them over centuries and to what extent twentieth-century British churches followed (behind) society as expectations changed is a bigger task than I have space for here.[14]

But how do those general factors play out in the debates of particular churches and groupings of churches about the leadership and ministry of women? The rest of this chapter is designed to show that. For reasons of space, this is a survey by theme and example rather than a fully comprehensive discussion.

Equality: The Religious Society of Friends and the Salvation Army

Two Christian groups within the broad umbrella of the 'Free Church' label have been known for their positive commitment to women's ministry from their foundation: the Religious Society of Friends (Quakers) and the Salvation Army. Interestingly, they are both non-sacramental traditions and do not use the term 'ordination'. The acceptance of women's leadership in both began with the acceptance that particular women were being called by God to preach, particularly Margaret Fell for the Quakers and Catherine Booth for the Salvation Army. That experiential base, interpreted as the calling and gifting of God, led to the re-examination of received interpretations of Scripture which appeared to bar women from preaching. In these two cases, the women themselves wrote the arguments that helped to make sense of their experience.[15] Women's ministry in these traditions, in contrast to so many others, was not simply pushed into the background over time, perhaps because the process of institutionalization and organization resulted in different patterns from the traditional structures of the Church.

Yet even in these Christian groups, the pattern of male leadership as the norm asserts itself in surprising ways. The website for Quakers in Britain, in its introduction to Britain Yearly Meeting,[16] notes: 'The chief executive officer has the title Recording Clerk. Since July 1998 the post has been held by Elsa Dicks, the twentieth in this office (and the first woman) since Ellis Hookes (c. 1630–1681) was appointed about 1657 as "clerk to Friends".' The first woman – in more than 400 years of commitment to equality in leadership! Informal conversation with a Quaker member confirms that the social pattern of women doing much of the work and men being in the 'top' paid positions has still been evident in recent Quaker organizational history.

As for the Salvation Army, Kate Cotterill's story in this volume affirms the equality of leadership that has been expressed particularly in husband and wife officer teams. Yet she notes that William Booth's observation from 1888[17] about the priority given to the husband in such teams still has resonance, since it is attitudes to women's and men's relationship in marriage that is often given attention over and above their leadership roles or officer status. The rule until relatively recently that on marriage a woman took the rank of her husband but not the other way round was a sign of the same thing. In the case of both the Quakers and the Salvation Army, a predominant theological commitment to the equality of women and men in leadership on the basis of calling and gifting was sometimes compromised by expected gender patterns in social roles and particularly in marriage.[18]

A learned ministry and the call of a congregation: the heritage of Independent and Baptist traditions

In 1917, Constance Coltman was ordained as a Congregational minister. She had completed a course of theological study, accepted into the training college at Oxford by permission of the Principal. In a tradition where 'a learned ministry' was particularly valued, the openings offered or restrictions imposed by the institutions of theological learning which prepared people for ordained ministry were very important. In an era when opportunities in higher education were beginning to be opened to a few women, inroads into various professions were made by one or two prominent women prising their way into education for those professions, often through the support of men who were the 'gatekeepers' for those opportunities. *Daughters of Dissent*[19] tells the story in more detail, putting the story of women in ordained ministry in the churches which preceded the United Reformed Church (URC) into the context of women in other forms of ministry, from preaching to the ministry of elders and deacons. The story of women and theological institutions reveals that the restrictions imposed were often not about theological factors or questions about educational abilities, but to do with residence: whether it was acceptable for women and men to live together in one institution, or whether the residential facilities were 'suitable' for women.[20] This is a clear example of the social order of the day being a key factor in the development of women's ministries.

In the model of church organization embodied in many Reformed and Baptist traditions, the call of a particular congregation is critical to the ministry of any individual. Theologically, all church traditions have ways of testing and affirming a call from God through discernment processes which issue in a call from the Church. Differing understandings of what the Church is mean that the call comes from a range of places within the Church. Some Free Churches have national selection processes; some rely on the call of a particular congregation; some operate a system which combines the two. The process will also vary depending on the ministry concerned. So, in the URC, the authorization of lay preachers or of elders rests chiefly with the local congregation. While the call of a congregation is also key to the placement of ordained ministers in the URC, this is combined with selection and training operated on a denominational basis. All this builds on the initial key recognition of a call from God to an individual.

The call of the Church in these traditions has been both an opening factor and an inhibiting factor where women's ministry is concerned. Particular congregations can choose whether or not to call women into leadership. Where decisions are by vote of the Church Meeting, there will be an unidentifiable range of reasons why someone votes for or against any particular candidate, within the process of discernment. Here is one of the places where it is extremely difficult to separate out theological and social factors in debates about women's leadership, ministry and ordination. But for some individuals, and sometimes for churches which see themselves within particular theological traditions, there is a spoken or unspoken decision-making line: women should not be in certain forms of ministry, therefore a call should not (cannot) be issued to them.

For the Baptist tradition, Ruth Gouldbourne's Whitley Lecture, 'Re-inventing the Wheel', demonstrates that twentieth-century developments in the recognition of women's ministry were pragmatically driven by the call of particular congregations, in an ecclesiastical context where a central body does not make binding decisions on local congregations.[21] So, for instance, in 1918, Edith Gates was called as the pastor of Little Tew and Clevely, in Oxfordshire, and put on the list as a probationer minister, after training, in 1922. Gouldbourne notes the way 'the list' of various ministries in the Baptist Union has functioned to highlight or downplay women's ministries: 'women pastors' were separately listed from 1927 to 1956, then listed as 'women ministers' for a time. In 1975, one ministerial list was created of women and men. Variety in local church decisions, for theological reasons or not (though recognizing the difficulty of separating the two), in practice still constitutes women's ministry in Baptist churches as a minority. Despite a statement in 1925 that Baptists did not see any objection to women ministers,[22] Gouldbourne notes that there was no major debate in the twentieth century in Baptist circles around women's ministry, but the consequence is that there has been no facing of the key issues and little discussion of what many believe to be true: that there are clearly 'no-go' areas for Baptist women in leadership – churches to which women will not be called.[23]

An emphasis in theology on calling and learning marking out those who are suitable for ministry has opened up opportunities for women. Even in those traditions which value calling and learning, however, these can be downplayed in favour of other factors, inhibiting women's ministry.

What are we waiting for? The Methodist Church

Since the union of various Methodist denominations in 1932, Methodism's primary statements on the theology of ordained ministry have derived from the Deed of Union.[24] In that statement there is a basic hostility to the language of priesthood if it would separate the ordained from those who are not ordained. In 1974[25] a statement on ordination was accepted by the Methodist Conference which highlighted the representative aspect of the minister's role (though without explicitly clarifying what that meant). Since the 1990s, the British Methodist Church has explicitly recognized two separate orders of ordained ministry, presbyters and deacons. Presbyters are called to a representative, ordained ministry of word, sacrament and pastoral responsibility; deacons are called to a representative, ordained ministry of witness through service. Yet none of these terms was really at issue in Methodism's debate about women being ordained to the ministry of word and sacrament.

As in many other denominations, the history of Methodism's decision to ordain women is one of numerous reports and almost as many delays.[26] Wesleyan Methodism decided by 1925 that there was no function of ministry that could not be undertaken by women. In the newly united Methodist Church, a 1933 report stated: 'The Committee cannot find that there is any function of the ordained ministry, as now exercised by men, for which a woman is disqualified by reason of her sex, and ... there is no longer any sufficient reason for withholding from women the full privileges and responsibilities which are proper to the work they perform.'[27] This judgement was repeated in a series of later reports. It was, however, practical issues that were seen as problematic. Methodism has a strong emphasis on itinerancy for its ordained ministers, and many of the proposals for women ministers concentrated on itinerancy as a problem for women. This relates to the debates already mentioned about women, home and family, but also to reluctance to appoint women in the face of expected opposition from local circuits. It was assumed in the proposals of the 1920s–1940s that women would resign from ministry on marriage. The debate changed only as society's expectations for and about women changed, leading to the clearest affirmation of women's ministry in the 1960s, before women were actually ordained in 1974. This feature of the delays was much more to do with social factors than theological, though some local opposition might well have reflected other factors than were affirmed at a national level.

The other issue behind the delay was ecumenical concern, in both the early 1930s and the 1960s. From 1929, Wesleyan Methodism postponed any decision in favour of joint work among the soon-to-be-united Methodist denominations. In 1961[28] a thorough report went over many of the arguments about the ordination of women which would be familiar from a range of traditions. But the committee which produced the report was still divided on whether to recommend accepting women into ordained ministry in part because of the practical considerations. Further discussions became enmeshed with the Anglican–Methodist conversations which were high on the Methodist Church's agenda. In 1966 it was decided that no further moves would be made pending the outcome and the consequences of those conversations. The Methodist Conference did, however, pass an amendment affirming the Methodist conviction that women could be ordained. Only with the failure of the Church of England to endorse the conversations' proposals did Methodism actually ordain women. Commitment to women's ministry has become more explicit and stronger in very recent years. That is now being expressed again in the ecumenical sphere. It was clearly stated in *An Anglican–Methodist Covenant*.[29]

Of course, the issue has moved on, as ongoing conversations between the Church of England and the Methodist Church encounter the failure of the Church of England to ordain women to the episcopate and the unwillingness of Methodism to incorporate the historic episcopate into its structures at this time. It is noteworthy that the balance of the argument has shifted slightly. The 2005 report *In the Spirit of the Covenant* argues that the Methodist Church's position is clear, while the Church of England is debating the matter.[30] The ordination of women bishops in the Church of England is described as a step which 'would transform the prospects for closer visible unity'. However, it is noted that there is 'opposition to such a step among a significant minority within the Church of England'.[31] This demonstrates a greater Methodist confidence in the rightness of the ordination of women, which was not evident in the earlier discussion, where the issue of equality was subordinated to discussions about unity. In other similar discussions, though, the ordination of women is still seen as 'the problem' standing in the way of a unity which would be achievable without it.

Anointing, gifting and the Bible: from Pentecostalism to the new churches

In his history of the rise of Pentecostalism, Harvey Cox makes an unequivocal statement about women's role: 'Pentecostalism is unthinkable without women.' He continues, 'women have continued to play a disproportionately prominent place in the Pentecostal movement'[32] – though the question 'disproportionate to what?' comes to mind. But he also notes that Pentecostalism has not always stuck to the practice of supporting women's leadership. Diana Chapman finds the same pattern in the early years of Pentecostalism in Britain.[33] The focus of the revival which grew into Pentecostalism was on experience of the Holy Spirit, analogous to the day of Pentecost, poured out on women and men alike. Therefore, Pentecostal theology has focused its understanding of ministry on the Spirit's gifting, and particularly the experiences that follow baptism in the Spirit as the necessary anointing for many forms of ministry. Early on, the gifts of the Spirit were recognized in women's preaching and testimony. But almost from the beginning also – Chapman traces this to a major debate at the Sunderland convention in 1914 – questions were asked about women's prominence and public ministry on the grounds of 'scriptural limitations'.[34] That basic tension between those who see the Spirit's gifting as allowing women's ministry and leadership and others who insist on particular limitations on women's ministry because of their interpretations of Scripture has remained in many of the movements and churches which owe their beginnings to the Pentecostal tradition – various Pentecostal denominations, many churches which in Britain are black-led and black majority churches, and also those new churches influenced by the more recent charismatic movement.

The result of that in some churches which do limit women's ministries is shown in examples given by Elaine Foster in her research on some of Britain's black-led churches. She describes the significant ministries undertaken by women, within the context of women's exclusion from the 'top tiers' of decision-making and governance. 'The concept of women running the church, but men leading it, seems common in Caribbean women's understanding of the dynamics of their relationship with their men.'[35] She notes this is often justified by the women she interviewed through their interpretation of Scripture.

The issues of biblical interpretation are examined from a Pentecostal perspective by Janet Everts Powers in her article on 1 Corinthians 11.3–16. She describes the school of evangelical biblical interpretation expressed in John Piper and Wayne Grudem's work which argues for a clear differentiation between women and men, and the inappropriateness of women ever having oversight roles over men.[36] Powers discusses the particular use of the Bible in Grudem's work, showing how Paul's letters and passages of teaching are prioritized over the narratives of Acts (and the Gospels) and the stories that are told there of women's involvement in leadership and ministry in the earliest Christian communities.[37] Ultimately she argues that interpretations such as Grudem's do not give sufficient authority to the biblical texts and stories which are key for Pentecostal theology.[38]

The analysis of evangelical interpretations of the Bible which make use of arguments about male headship is pursued also in Fran Porter's research on the experiences of evangelical women in Northern Ireland.[39] She traces helpfully the way in which the arguments about headship have changed in response to serious debates among evangelicals. Debates which were about 'hierarchy' versus 'liberation' are more likely now to be between 'complementarian' and 'egalitarian' positions. Those who argue for male headship, she notes, are now likely to stress male responsibility more than male rule and have taken seriously the necessity to deal with abuses of the headship/submission model of relating between women and men.[40] Like Powers, she notes the distinctions in interpretation of Scripture between those who focus on particular texts and those who concentrate on the context of particular texts within what they see as the whole 'sweep' of biblical teaching.[41]

The distinctions discussed by Powers and Porter are vividly illustrated by the contrast between two of the 'umbrella groups' for new churches. The website of the New Frontiers movement tackles head-on that movement's understanding of women's ministry. In particular they have available on the site an issue from their *Newfrontiers* magazine of December 2004–February 2005 which discusses their position.[42] It relies on Grudem's work on male headship and states that women are not to be found in 'governmental leadership' in New Frontiers churches. It supports the use by women of distinctive gifts which do not challenge overall male headship. This is highlighted as an argument over against the culture of twenty-first-century British (western) society, and, the movement believes, is to be commended for that. Yet there are also arguments that even this movement has seen an expansion in the roles of women over the last few years, so that women can participate in eldership teams and facilitate cell groups even if they are still not in what are regarded as 'headship' positions.[43]

In contrast to this, the Ichthus Christian Fellowship, founded by Roger and Faith Forster, took a strong stand from its beginnings on the appropriateness of women exercising the whole range of spiritual gifts. They stress the use of gifts for the work of evangelization. In an article published in 1987, Faith and Roger Forster describe the use of a range of gifts by women, in Scripture and early church history, thus demonstrating the theological perspective from which they begin their thinking about leadership and ministry generally, as well as with specific reference to women's ministry.[44] The introduction to them as writers in the book which contains this article is unequivocal: 'Faith and Roger Forster are founders and leaders of the Ichthus Fellowship, South London. Both have an extensive ministry in teaching, training, counselling, church planting and evangelism, all of which are hallmarks of Ichthus. They have taken a lead in involving women in Church leadership and speak extensively on the subject.'[45]

The contrast between these two again shows the basic tension between a biblical theology of gifting which often opens up ministry for women and other interpretations of the Bible which impose restrictions.

Conclusion

Theologies of leadership, ministry and ordination are made up of a number of strands, including those examined in the first half of this chapter. The priority given to particular strands varies with the Christian tradition being examined. When it comes to discussions about women's ministry, these elements of Christian belief have been examined afresh. However, they have been re-examined not simply for themselves, but through the lens of beliefs about women and men more broadly. When women's ministry is discussed, the focus is often more on women than on ministry.

The factors I have highlighted, even in the latter half of the chapter, do not represent the whole of the debate. In any one denomination or tradition's discussion about women's ministry, many arguments are deployed. In particular, disputes about biblical texts have usually appeared somewhere in all denominations' debates. Social factors will have been implicit in most discussions, even to the New Frontiers movement's insistence that it is proper to stand out against certain social trends.

It must be remembered that the ministries of women in British Free Churches cover a huge range of activities, from facilitating small groups to music ministry, from maintenance of buildings to participation in worship, from teaching and preaching to pastoral work and prayer. Women are part of the ministry of the whole people of God. However, this chapter has examined the point at which there have been debates about the restrictions on women's roles in ministry ('thus far but no further'). From the survey in this chapter, in British Free Churches, the elements of a theology of ministry which seem most to have *enabled* women in a full engagement with ministerial roles are those to do with gifting, followed by call (though a woman's testimony to her call from God is rarely enough on its own). For some traditions, demonstrating appropriate learning is also a factor, though it might also be regarded as part of an understanding of someone's proven gifts.

Those factors which have made ministry least accessible, which have *disabled* women seeking to minister in ways previously reserved to men, have been particular interpretations of the Bible and the restrictions on women assumed in the social milieu within which the church debates happened especially in the first sixty or so years of the twentieth century. There is a meshing of these two in some debates, but not in others. In some, opposition to what are seen as more 'liberal' interpretations of the Bible go hand in hand with suspicion of 'liberal' social attitudes, including a greater freedom for women to operate in society beyond the sphere of home and family. That combination, within Free Churches, remains the most restrictive theological environment for women to operate in ministry by holding authority and taking part in the governance of the

Church. On the other hand, those churches which mirrored society's expectations of women earlier in the twentieth century but accepted more varied interpretations of Scripture tended also to move at the pace of society as women's roles have been reshaped.

But in the end these theological debates are not confined to the area of leadership, ministry and ordination. They are much more wide-ranging than that. The roots of the many arguments about women's ministry can be traced to bigger theological debates about who and what human beings are before God. These roots are in beliefs about how men and women should relate to each other; how they are made and have developed and how that relates to God's purposes. They are linked to beliefs about Christ and about the Church. (How and whom does Christ save? How is Christ represented in the world today? How is the Church to be the body of Christ? How should the Church be ordered?) But the theological disputes are also similar to the debates of many other academic disciplines about sex and gender, even though the theological arguments have a particular perspective in relating those issues to God-talk. That is where the role of feminist theology has been so important in questioning and reshaping the whole theological agenda.

Notes

1. See John N. Collins, *Deacons and the Church: Making Connections between Old and New* (Harrisburg, Pennsylvania: Gracewing, Morehouse Publishing, 2002).

2. *Baptism, Eucharist and Ministry* (Geneva: World Council of Churches, 1982). This was not new theology! *Baptism, Eucharist and Ministry* simply shows a relatively recent broad ecumenical recognition of the key place of this doctrine.

3. E.g. *Commitment to Mission and Unity: Report of the Informal Conversations between the Methodist Church and the Church of England* (London: Church House Publishing and Methodist Publishing House, 1996). This report cited ten obstacles to unity, of which six are to do with specialized ministries, pp. 8–15.

4. For instance, in Max Thurian (ed.), *Churches Respond to BEM*, vol. 1 (Geneva: WCC, 1986), Baptist Union of Great Britain and Ireland, p. 72; Church of Scotland, p. 94; United Reformed Church, p. 107 and in *Churches Respond to BEM*, vol. 2 (Geneva: WCC, 1986), Presbyterian Church of Wales, pp. 171–2 – to take just a few examples of many.

5. See discussion in David Peel, *Reforming Theology* (London: United Reformed Church, 2002), pp. 239–40; also Janet Wootton, 'The Priesthood of All Believers – Is This What You Want?', *Feminist Theology* 1 (Sept. 1992), pp. 72–9.

6. There is a liturgical 'summary' of this in services of welcome or commissioning: 'Do you believe that you are called by God to serve as a Lay Worker in this Circuit?', *The Methodist Worship Book* (Peterborough: Methodist Publishing House, 1999), p. 338, with equivalent question for pastoral visitors,

THE GROUNDS OF DISPUTE

p. 346, and for workers with children and young people, p. 349.

7. I come to this discussion from the personal experience of being told categorically by a school friend that I couldn't have a call to preach since God didn't call women to preach. I have heard many similar stories since.

8. Janet Everts Powers, 'Recovering a Woman's Head with Prophetic Authority: a Pentecostal Interpretation of 1 Cor. 11:3–16', *Journal of Pentecostal Theology* 10.1 (2001), p. 36. See later in the chapter for disputes about women's ministry in Pentecostal traditions.

9. 'The URC, therefore, is heir to a tradition in which scholarship is affirmed and a learned ministry is expected', Peel, *Reforming Theology*, p. 208.

10. See Powers, 'Recovering a Woman's Head', for discussion of these different methods of interpretation.

11. The New Frontiers group of churches explicitly use Ephesians 4 as their key model of church leadership, http://www.newfrontiers.xtn.org/our-mission/training1/module_index (accessed 2/06/06).

12. There were, of course, class assumptions in these expectations. Working-class women were always the exceptions to the rule that expected women not to work, proving that the rule was very much a creation of a wealthy elite, particularly in the Victorian era.

13. Some exceptions to this link with 'the sacraments' would be ordination to diaconal ministry in the Methodist Church and the ordination of elders in the URC. The latter are also seen as remaining 'lay'.

14. Interviews in the early 1980s with five black pastors included material on their attitudes to family life: three of the male pastors have very clear views about women being primarily involved in the family, or about male headship. Anita Jackson, *Catching Both Sides of the Wind: Conversations with Five Black Pastors* (London: British Council of Churches, 1985). This could be replicated in many other traditions. More recently, personal experiences of attitudes clearly influenced by social expectations around women and the family were recounted in papers given at the conference 'Women and Ordination in the Christian Churches: International Perspectives', sponsored by the Lincoln Theological Institute, July 2006: Miranda Threlfall-Holmes, 'Ordination and the Theology of Work: Perspectives from Young Ordained Women in the Church of England'; Helen Cameron and Gillian Jackson, 'One Ministry, Separate Spheres: Ordained Women and Senior Leadership in the Salvation Army'.

15. Margaret Fell, *Women's speaking justified, proved and allowed of by the scriptures*, first published 1666 (Amherst, Mass.: New England Yearly Meeting of Friends, 1980); Catherine Booth, *Female Teaching*, 1859, discussed in Roy Hattersley, *Blood and Fire: William and Catherine Booth and Their Salvation Army* (London: Little, Brown and Company, 1999), pp. 107–11.

16. http://www.quaker.org.uk/templates/internal.asp?nodeid=89729 (accessed 12/01/06).

17. 'We have a problem. When two officers marry, by some strange mistake in our organisation, the woman doesn't count' (William Booth, 1888).

18. Research with women in senior leadership in the Salvation Army confirms that married women officers still often expect to be in a supportive role in relation to their husbands, and certainly that congregations expected it of them. Reported in Cameron and Jackson, 'One Ministry, Separate Spheres'.

19. Elaine Kaye, Janet Lees and Kirsty Thorpe, *Daughters of Dissent* (London: United Reformed Church, 2004).

20. Kaye, Lees and Thorpe, *Daughters*, pp. 55–9.

21. Ruth M. B. Gouldbourne, 'Reinventing the Wheel: Women and Ministry in English Baptist Life' (Oxford: Whitley Publications, 1997), pp. 26–7.

22. Gouldbourne, 'Reinventing the Wheel', p. 27.

23. Gouldbourne, 'Reinventing the Wheel', p. 29.

24. Deed of Union, in each year's edition of *Constitutional Practice and Discipline of the Methodist Church*, vol. 2 (Peterborough: Methodist Publishing House). See clause 4.

25. 1974 was the year in which women were eventually ordained into the Methodist ministry as it was then constituted, though the language of the document acknowledges that shift only by an asterisked note that 'the masculine includes the feminine throughout'! 'Ordination', in *Statements of the Methodist Church on Faith and Order, 1933–1983* (London: Methodist Publishing House, 1984), p. 135.

26. The journey towards women's ordination in Methodism is narrated in detail alongside analysis of the debates in the Church of England and Roman Catholic Church in Jacqueline Field-Bibb, *Women Towards Priesthood: Ministerial Politics and Feminist Praxis* (Cambridge: Cambridge University Press, 1991). Pauline Webb's story, elsewhere in this volume, also explores the journey.

27. 'Women and the Ministry, 1933', in *Statements 1933–1983*, p. 117.

28. 'The Status of Deaconesses and the Admission of Women to the Ministry, 1961', in *Statements 1933–1983*.

29. *An Anglican–Methodist Covenant* (London: Methodist Publishing House and Church House Publishing, 2001), paragraph 161.

30. *In the Spirit of the Covenant: Interim Report (2005) of the Joint Implementation Commission under the Covenant between the Methodist Church of Great Britain and the Church of England* (Peterborough: Methodist Publishing House, 2005), pp. 103 and 109–10.

31. *In the Spirit of the Covenant*, p. 110.

32. Harvey Cox, *Fire From Heaven: The Rise of Pentecostal Spirituality and the Reshaping of Religion in the Twenty-first Century* (London: Cassell, 1996), p. 121.

33. Diana Chapman, 'The Rise and Demise of Women's Ministry in the Origins and Early Years of Pentecostalism in Britain', *Journal of Pentecostal Theology* 12.2 (2004), pp. 217–46.

34. Chapman, 'The Rise and Demise of Women's Ministry', pp. 231–2.

35. Elaine Foster, 'Women and the Inverted Pyramid of the Black Churches in Britain', in *Refusing Holy Orders: Women and Fundamentalism in Britain*, ed. Gita Sahgal and Nira Yuval-Davis (London: Virago Press, 1992), p. 48. See also Joe Aldred (ed.), *Sisters with Power* (London: Continuum, 2000), for examples of black women's involvement in many ministries.

36. John Piper and Wayne Grudem (eds), *Recovering Biblical Manhood and Womanhood: A Response to Evangelical Feminism* (Wheaton, Illinois: Crossway Books, 1991).

37. Powers, 'Recovering a Woman's Head', pp. 18–20.

38. 'The basis of distinctively Pentecostal belief is the "baptism in the Holy

Spirit as evidenced by tongues" and the purpose of this experience is to empower the believer for ministry . . . So what is at stake for Pentecostals in the discussion of 1 Cor. 11.3–16 and the issue of whether or not women can hold authoritative ministry positions is whether or not they will continue to champion this distinctive doctrine of ministry.' Powers, 'Recovering a Woman's Head', p. 36.

39. Fran Porter, *Changing Women, Changing Worlds: Evangelical Women in Church, Community and Politics* (Belfast: The Blackstaff Press, 2002).

40. Acknowledged by Piper and Grudem, *Recovering Biblical Manhood and Womanhood*, p. xiv.

41. Porter, *Changing Women, Changing Worlds*, pp. 127–8.

42. http://www.newfrontiers.xtn.org/magazine/volume2issue9 (accessed 02/06/2006). The whole issue is available to read online.

43. Val Abbott, 'Cutting the Gordian Knot: Marriage and Women's Ministry in the Anglican and House Church Movement', paper given at conference, 'Women and Ordination in the Christian Churches: International Perspectives', July 2006.

44. Faith and Roger Forster, 'Women's Spiritual Gifts in the Church', in Kathy Keay (ed.), *Men, Women and God* (Basingstoke: Marshall Pickering, 1987), pp. 48–59.

45. Keay, *Men, Women and God*, p. 47.

2. Women's Ministry – a Developing Story

KIRSTY THORPE

Were it possible to ask every woman now exercising Free Church ministry in Britain when they considered women's ministry in the Church to have started, no doubt their answers would be highly personal. Some would date the story from the twentieth century, during which period many denominations began ordaining women as ministers. Others might go back to women's lay ministry of preaching and social campaigning in the nineteenth century. A number might trace a line of women leaders back to the New or even the Old Testament, claiming for this witness the term 'women's ministry'. At whatever point one regards the story of women's ministry as having begun, few people would disagree that women have always figured among those who have tried to serve God. As a result of the influence of Christian feminism over the last half-century, the stories of women in the Church are now becoming better known, and being claimed as a powerful inheritance by some within the contemporary Church.

Those women who have entered ordained ministry, or its equivalent, in the Free Churches of England and Wales over recent generations have normally gone through a candidating process alongside men. This has been designed to show God's calling on their lives to the satisfaction of others in the Church, using the language and processes of a particular tradition. By establishing their vocation in this way, these women have consciously or unconsciously been placing themselves in line with earlier generations of women. The fact that women's ordination is a relatively recent phenomenon does not mean there had been no women exercising ministry or leadership in the Church until the twentieth century.

Since the start of the Church, in fact, women have fulfilled their God-given calling by putting their gifts to practical use, long before the existence of any formal process of selection that included them. During the nineteen centuries before ordination was possible for women, indeed, there was little formal recognition for the minority of them who exercised some form of leadership in the Church. Because of the problems they had in finding institutional space within which to develop their ministry, many of them remained outside the official structures or on the margins of them. As and when questions or challenges arose about the validity of their unofficial ministry, these women could do little more than point to the fruits of their work, in the hope that these demonstrated that their calling arose from responding to God as opposed to the promptings of their own ego.

Occasionally during this long period, women leaders received public recognition within and beyond the Church, but more often knowledge of them remained limited to one tradition, historical period or geographical area. At certain points, women's ministry was almost totally confined to private, domestic settings. Whatever their achievements, women in the Church have rarely had their stories fully recorded or reliably handed on to future generations. This silence about women's ministry is a supreme irony considering the way that Matthew's Gospel records Jesus himself declaring, after an unnamed woman had anointed him: 'wherever the good news is proclaimed in the whole world, what she has done will be told in remembrance of her' (Matt. 26.13).[1] Far from remembering the ministry of women, the Church has largely forgotten their service, so creating a challenge for those contemporary Christians who want to show that women's ministry is a phenomenon with a long history.

However, Free Church history represents something of a special case in this regard. Since Free Church polity allows a greater degree of institutional freedom to the local congregation than exists in other parts of the Church, this has had advantages for the development of women's ministry. Where local groups have been able to recognize individuals possessing leadership gifts, without necessarily expecting them to undergo selection or training in any formal way, a few women have found a way to serve over the centuries. Within Free Church traditions, which stress the work of the Holy Spirit, the occasional presence of women carrying a strong sense of God's call to preach and teach has been more difficult to silence and overlook.

What follows is an attempt to trace a line of women in church leadership, stretching from women of the Bible to contemporary women ministers in the Free Churches of Britain. At the same time the different models of ministry by which these women were operating will be considered. The hope is to allow some of this diverse and fascinating story to be viewed through the lenses of gender and church tradition, so its inspiration can be claimed afresh by women and men within denominations and churches in England and Wales today.

Revisiting the Bible

The Bible, as the foundational document of the Christian faith, is the obvious starting place for anyone trying to trace the succession of women's leadership. Until the nineteenth century, however, it was almost always seen as a collection of writings by an all-male authorship, predominantly centred on the way men related to a god who was usually described in male terms. This began to change slowly when the generation of early nineteenth-century women who had been part of the anti-slavery campaign in Europe and North America turned their attention to women's rights. Some of these pioneer feminists were solely interested in voting rights for women. Others saw that issue as part of a wider agenda encompassing women's rights in education, employment, and all parts of society including the Church, where for the first time talk of women's ordination would soon begin.

One of those advocating such a broader list of concerns was the American author Elizabeth Cady Stanton, who produced *The Woman's Bible* between 1895 and 1898. As the wife of a prominent abolitionist, she had observed during the anti-slavery campaign that male ministers were some of the loudest defenders of male privilege. Her pioneering book drew on the insights of the new higher criticism of the Bible, then popular in liberal circles, to argue for a revised understanding of women in the text. This attempt to reinterpret biblical references to women in a positive way, so raising rather than lowering the self-esteem of contemporary women, proved controversial. It did, however, lay the foundation for the development of feminist interpretations of the Bible in the second half of the twentieth century.

Over the last fifty years, the movement which has been termed 'second wave feminism' has given birth to Christian feminism, and a group of reformist scholars has taken forward the work begun by Stanton. Writers such as Phyllis Trible, Rosemary Radford Ruether and Elisabeth Schüssler Fiorenza have searched the Bible for examples of women's stories both positive and negative, from which to construct a fresh theology for women in today's Church. Although mainstream biblical interpretation does not go all the way with this approach yet, there is now wider acceptance for readings of both Old and New Testament texts which acknowledge the contribution and presence of women. At the same time as this reformist approach has had some influence, contemporary radical feminist theologians such as Mary Daly have chosen to reject the Bible, and indeed Christianity, altogether, as irredeemably patriarchal, in preference for creating a new community beyond the Church.

Women in the Old Testament

There is no escaping the fact that the societies reflected in the Hebrew scriptures were deeply patriarchal. While the Ten Commandments contain the requirement to 'honour your father and mother', they set a wife alongside a house or ox as a neighbour's possession which it is sinful to covet (Deut. 5.16, 21). Women were legally the property of men and they figured among the spoils of war to be distributed after victory. In two instances, daughters were offered up to the mob, which had come howling for sex with male guests (Gen. 19.4–8; Judg. 19.22–4). In the second instance, the guest's concubine was sent out instead, and raped to death. Despite this, Hebrew society did consider sexual relations within the context of marriage as 'good' and never interpreted the stories of Genesis 2 and 3 as justifying negativity towards women, unlike the Church later on. One scholar has written: 'The Old Testament is a collection of writings by males from a society dominated by males.'[2] However, there are stories of women in strong leadership roles, though these are generally secondary to men, as well as rare references to the feminine aspects of God. These must be held in counterbalance to the negative stories about women as victims which are also to be found. Many scholars now see the mere fact that women figure at all in the Old Testament as highly significant, despite their lesser roles, taking into account the male-dominated nature of the societies out of which these texts came over almost a millennium.

One woman leader of the Old Testament is the prophetess and military leader Deborah who figures among the judges. The text introduces her with no suggestion of surprise that a woman should have held a position of authority involving the teaching and leading of men, although such women were rare. At a time when the scattered tribes of Israel needed arousing and unifying for their struggle against the Canaanites, Deborah is portrayed as someone called by God to inspire others, predominantly men. A magnificent poem from the twelfth century BC called 'The Song of Deborah' is one of the oldest examples of Hebrew literature in existence. It is easy to see how Deborah's example could have encouraged women in the Church, centuries later, to explore their own call to prophetic leadership. Significantly, it seems that it was only at the time of pre-monarchic, charismatic leadership of the judges that a woman could so naturally assume a leadership position. The reign of the only queen of Israel, Athaliah, is narrated with very little sympathy (2 Kgs 11.1–16).

Much later, the officials of King Josiah consult another woman prophet, again with no comment on her gender. The act is described as consulting the LORD, and Huldah speaks directly in God's name: the phrase, 'The LORD says' appears twice in her prophecy (2 Kgs 23.14–20). The king acts unquestioningly on her words.

For some women, leadership becomes possible because they are close to powerful men and so acquire a platform from which to command attention. This could be said of Miriam, sister of Moses and Aaron, also described as a prophetess, whose song of triumph is found in the Exodus account of flight from Egypt. The song of Hannah, on which Mary's song, known to us as the Magnificat, is based, is remembered because of her relationship to the last of the judges, the reluctant king-maker, Samuel.

Several women in the Old Testament stand out as models of faithfulness in responding to God. In 1 Kings the prophet Elijah is sent to stay with a widow in Zarephath, near Sidon, who is close to death from starvation. Because she follows his instructions her jar of meal and jug of oil continue to be replenished, and the prophet also saves her young son from death. Equally praiseworthy and courageous are the Hebrew midwives Shiphrah and Puah, whose clever avoidance of the king of Egypt's orders to kill all male children means the future of their race is safeguarded. It seems that on occasion God requires simple obedience in following instructions while at other times God's servants must use their own resourcefulness to advance God's purposes.

Feminist biblical interpreters draw parallels between Ruth and Esther, whose stories operate cross-culturally as well as challenging gender stereotypes.[3] The story of Ruth is set at the time of the judges, though probably written down much later. This Moabite woman, whose husband was a Hebrew, remains with her mother-in-law Naomi when both are widowed, and accompanies her back to Bethlehem. There she marries Boaz, a kinsman of her late husband, and so according to Matthew's Gospel acquires a place in the genealogy both of David and of Jesus himself. Despite being a foreigner, Ruth wins approval in Israel because of her kindness and affection for Naomi, which crosses racial boundaries.

Esther, a member of King Ahasuerus' harem in Persia during a time of exile, rises to be queen. At first she hides her Hebrew heritage but as a result of her clever dealings she succeeds in winning religious freedom for her race and vengeance for them over their enemies. Some would see Ruth and Esther as dubious models for later women's ministry because they could be said to have relied on feminine wiles to advance their cause. Others might argue that both are to be admired for their wit and wisdom in deploying skilfully the limited influence they had, thus achieving valuable ends. In both cases, too, there is an interaction between concerns of gender and ethnicity. Does Ruth betray her native culture by assimilating to her chosen one, or cleverly use the rules of her new culture to preserve her life? What does it mean for Esther to admit her Jewish roots, and for the Jews to have one of their own people in such a powerful position in a foreign court?

These ancient scriptures contain a variety of lessons for women seeking to follow God in the contemporary Church. They show examples of women who come to the fore because suitable men are absent, or who rise to public recognition because of their close relationships with strong, male leaders. Such women are capable of offering powerful, prophetic, charismatic leadership in words that call people to faithful following of God's way. The Old Testament also gives us models of women who display prayerful obedience or resourceful independence by their actions. As a result God's interests are defended and God's purposes promoted. The ministry of priesthood may have been completely closed to women according to Jewish law but the Old Testament shows that the ministry of living by and proclaiming God's word has been open to individual women who have had the strength of mind and faith to claim it.

Jesus and women

The Gospel accounts of the life and teaching of Jesus offer a range of positive models for women in ministry and provide an interesting contrast with evidence from other sources that show first-century Palestinian Judaism was increasingly unenlightened in its treatment of women by comparison with earlier generations.[4] Viewed against this backdrop, the way in which the Gospels portray Jesus as relating positively to women is even more significant. In considering these interactions it is helpful to consider the contacts he has with women in his inner circle as well as the Gospel accounts of his response to the women he meets on single occasions during his ministry.

It has taken the insights of feminism to bring to public attention new theological thinking about the refreshing and unpatronizing way in which Jesus treated women, as seen in the Gospel accounts. The author Dorothy L. Sayers declared over half a century ago that Jesus never nagged, flattered, coaxed or patronized women, and that none of his actions, sermons or parables could be said to gain their force from female perversity.[5] One wonders how many men, lay or ordained, contemporary or historical, could claim a similarly progressive outlook. More recently, the American writer Leonard Swidler has asserted that Jesus was a feminist, although opinion is divided as to whether or not this label is helpful.[6] Even so, feminist readings of the Gospels have prompted reassessment of the role of the female figures found there and have helped to raise their profile as models for the ministry of women in the contemporary Church.

One of the most significant women in the Gospels is Mary the mother of Jesus, who in past centuries has often been portrayed as a model of purity and quiet subservience, obediently agreeing to God's purposes. 'Then gentle Mary meekly bowed her head', says a nineteenth-century

Basque carol ('The Angel Gabriel'), adding that such humility made her a 'highly favoured lady'. Whereas Mark's Gospel does not show Mary as being prominent among Jesus' followers, Luke's Gospel portrays her in a strong light as someone who sees from the first moment of her pregnancy what this birth will mean for the world. In this account, Mary is the first to hear and accept God's will about Jesus at the time of the Annunciation. Those wishing to dispel the doormat image of Mary point to the Magnificat, the radical hymn to God's revolutionary love that is placed on her lips at the start of Luke's Gospel. It is interesting that the liturgical use of the Magnificat has moved out from its habitual recitation at Evensong to a recognition of its radical message in new prayers and hymns, from Fred Kaan's 'Magnificat Now' to 'Heaven shall not wait', from the Iona Community.

They may also make reference to the wedding at Cana, in John's gospel, where Mary's maternal intervention once the wine ran out at the feast could be interpreted as pushing Jesus towards the actions that would start his public ministry. John's gospel also depicts Mary at the foot of the cross during the crucifixion, describing how Jesus asks 'the disciple whom he loved' to take her into his home after Jesus' death.

Centuries of church tradition still influence us when we try to look back and assess the significance of Jesus' relationship with his mother. It can be hard to put aside idealized male visions of femininity as seen in the cult of the Virgin Mary or the way Mary has been depicted in religious art over the centuries. Returning to the Mary found in Scripture, however, means encountering a woman with a voice of her own and a deep faith to bring to her model of discipleship and service. It is intriguing to consider the various meanings which her name can convey. Mary, or Miriam in its Hebrew form, can mean one who is corpulent – at a time when fatness and beauty were equated – or one who is a rebel. The Church has always tended to promote the attractions of Mary as person of beauty but has rarely portrayed her in a radical, rebellious light.

Another key female figure among those whom the Gospels show around Jesus is Mary of Magdala. Despite later traditions that suggest she had been a prostitute, and parts of the Church which have associated her name with help for so-called 'fallen women', there is nothing in the text to back this interpretation. All we are told is that seven demons had gone out of her, with no indication as to whether this should be taken to mean some form of physical or spiritual sickness that kept recurring or a very complex condition from which she was healed on one occasion. Whichever of these understandings is chosen, the significant message is the way the Gospels portray her as an important disciple and follower of Jesus. She is not only present at his death but, following an early visit to the empty tomb on the first Easter morning, Mary of Magdala receives a commission to go and tell his male followers that Jesus has risen from the dead. It is easy to overlook how remarkable it would have been in first-century Jewish culture for anyone to choose a woman as a witness. In that society the testimony of women was not even allowed in court but Jesus does not seem to have had any problem in using women to tell the remarkable news of his resurrection.

The directness with which the sisters Mary and Martha talk to Jesus in Luke 10.38-42 and John 11.17-44 suggests that a real and unselfconscious relationship existed between this male teacher, traditionally presumed to be unmarried, and the two, confident single women. In the Lukan version of the narrative, when Jesus affirms Mary's choice as the better one, he appears to be sanctioning the role of women as disciples, for that was the technical meaning of 'sitting at the feet' of someone. Interpretations of the story which stress the value of practical service over and above theological preparation for evangelism, or vice versa, often overlook thereby the significance of the way Jesus was prepared to discuss religion with Mary at a time when Jewish women were not allowed to study the Torah.

Also important among the women close to Jesus are those who support his ministry financially, referred to in chapter 8 of Luke's Gospel at the end of a section on the ministry of Jesus in Galilee. Mary of Magdala, Joanna the wife of Herod's steward Chuza and Susanna are mentioned by name, along with many others who provide for Jesus and his disciples 'out of their resources'. This brief passage of Scripture is important both for confirming that women were among those who followed Jesus in his itinerant ministry and for its message that they provided for the material needs of the whole group. This might not sound remarkable until one realizes that in the Palestinian society of Jesus' day women did not have property rights, so for a woman to have private means would presumably have been quite unusual.

As well as the women with whom the Gospels show Jesus being in close and regular contact during his ministry, there are also those he meets during his travels, whose exchanges with him are recorded with varying degrees of detail. The Syrophoenician mother of a sick daughter, mentioned in Mark's Gospel, argues her case articulately in a discussion with Jesus. As a gentile from a Hellenistic culture, leave alone as a woman, she would not be expected to engage with Jesus or to recognize his power to heal her child. She sees who Jesus is more clearly than the disciples, however, and receives from him her daughter's healing as a reward for her assertiveness. The Samaritan woman at the well, who figures in John's gospel, also faces similar multiple obstacles to being taken seriously in theological debate with a Jewish teacher such as Jesus. Not only is she female but also a Samaritan and someone whose personal morals are suspect. All these issues are overcome when Jesus asks her for a drink and chooses to use the ensuing multi-level conversation to share with her the revelation that he is the Messiah. This message is so powerful that the woman immediately takes the good news back to her village, and preaches it to them with startling results, which lead to Jesus spending several days in that Samaritan community. Because Jesus has broken through the limitations of history, culture, religion and gender the Samaritan woman is empowered to do the same.

As well as the Gospel portrayal of the way Jesus related to women there are also indications of his attitude towards them in the female characters and imagery of his storytelling and teaching ministry. Characters such as the persistent widow in the parable from Luke's Gospel, who continually demands her rights until the judge gives her justice, seem to suggest Jesus is advocating the courage of this determined, intelligent woman. Equally, his parable of a woman in search of a lost coin praises the female character for her diligent search, as a comparison with God who searches for those who are lost.

From this brief summary of the interactions of Jesus with women it is clear that he acted neither to put women down, nor to place them on a pedestal above and beyond other people. Instead, the Gospels portray him as relating to women naturally and unselfconsciously, accepting them as full individuals in the process. We have stories of women whom Jesus respected and healed, of those who found a voice through him, and of those who left home to follow him.

This latter group, many people would now argue, should be seen as disciples just like their male companions on the road who made up the great number of those following Jesus. According to the Gospels, a disciple's role consists of preaching, healing the sick and exorcising demons, of feeding the hungry and of service. The Gospel evidence is that Jesus was pleased to include women in this pattern of discipleship, having encouraged them to share the good news, healed some of them from sickness, benefited from their provision of food and experienced their skill in serving the care needs of others. If discipleship could be said to be the great adventure in which Mary of Magdala, Joanna, Susanna and the rest of the women were engaged, then the lifetime of Jesus was truly a highpoint for women's ministry.

Women in the earliest Christian communities

Much evidence about the ministry of women in the early Church comes from the Acts of the apostles, and the letters in the New Testament. These scriptures use a new term for followers of Jesus, namely 'apostles', meaning those who have been sent out on a mission. Paul believed that apostles must have seen the risen Jesus and been commissioned to ministry by him.

WOMEN'S MINISTRY – A DEVELOPING STORY

Until Pentecost the symbolism of twelve male apostles representing the twelve tribes of Israel seems to have been paramount. After the coming of the Holy Spirit to the group of women and men in an upper room in Jerusalem, the need to keep an inner circle of twelve male apostles appears to have diminished, and the term 'apostle' began to be applied more widely. The New Testament evidence shows that the leadership of the early Church was not limited to men, even if women apostles might have travelled less as missionaries. As well as the male apostles who took the Christian message from Jerusalem to Judaea and Samaria, and then to such important empire cities as Corinth, Ephesus, Antioch and Rome itself, there were also missionary couples where one partner was a woman. What is striking, also, is how many of the converts who responded to the gospel were women, and influential women at that.

Acts mentions the four daughters of Philip, the Hellenist leader, all of whom prophesy. The couple Prisca and Aquila appear several times in the New Testament as former members of the church in Rome and colleagues of Paul in Corinth and Ephesus. In Ephesus they both take the missionary Apollos aside to instruct him in some finer points of Christian teaching. Dorcas, a disciple in Joppa with a varied ministry, is also introduced in Acts, the only person in Scripture said to have been raised to life by an apostle. Lydia, a businesswoman, is Paul's first convert in Europe, being baptized along with her household and so beginning the church in Philippi.

The possible numerical significance of women in the early Church is suggested by the letter to the Romans, where women comprise one third of the fellow workers singled out for closing messages by Paul. Phoebe is commended as 'our sister', as a deacon of the church in Cenchrae and as a benefactor of Paul and others. Her ministry is now seen as having probably included the whole Christian community in Cenchrae, rather than being limited to other women, as was the later work of deaconesses.

Paul's greeting to Junia and Andronicus has caused lengthy disagreement over the centuries as, from the thirteenth century onwards, Junia's name was translated in a male form, and used to bolster arguments that the Church's official ministry was always all-male. Feminist interpreters point out there is no evidence of a male name 'Junias' at this time, but plenty of examples of the female name Junia. They see Junia as having been the minister of an early diaspora church, a woman of great importance and one half of a missionary couple, whom Paul himself acknowledges to have predated him in their faith.

Elisabeth Schüssler Fiorenza has written of women's early ministry: 'The few references which survived in the New Testament records are like the tip of an iceberg indicating what we have lost. Yet at the same time they show how great the influence of women was in the early Christian movement.'[7]

Women's status in the Church changed significantly between the first and the second centuries. By the later period, women's leadership survived only on the Gnostic edges of the early Church, and the main roles for women in the mainstream Christian community were marriage and martyrdom. This is a familiar pattern which has been replayed throughout church history. In times of change, when the authority of the Holy Spirit has been recognized, women's leadership has flourished. As the ferment has died down, however, and the authority of spiritual gifts has been replaced by that of the Church as an institution, the role of women has once again been restricted and downplayed.

Although women were gradually excluded from the leadership roles they had exercised in the first years of missionary expansion, other opportunities for ministry arose, based not on teaching but on service and prayer. Evidence exists for an order of widows, which survived until the latter part of the fourth century, admission to which was conducted by the bishop. The *Didascalia*, third-century Christian documents found in Northern Syria, speak of an order of women who serve other women, since men cannot minister to women living in pagan homes. The fourth-century *Apostolic Constitutions*, written for the church in Antioch, refer to deaconesses who minister to their fellow women, as well as guarding the women's door at the church building, and keeping discipline during worship.

Deaconesses were effectively forbidden in the Western church during the sixth century. This ministry survived for several centuries more in the Eastern Church, where members of the order were needed to assist at immersion baptisms, as well as caring for the sick and needy.

Another path for women in the early centuries of the Church was that of a consecrated virgin, whose vocation of asceticism and prayer emerges first among the Desert Mothers of the Egyptian desert. By the fourth century a pattern of solitary living was being replaced by the establishment of male and female religious communities, spreading from the Middle East to the Mediterranean and beyond.

It is noticeable that these later examples of women's service within the early Church all demanded celibacy, and thereby a woman's choice not to express her sexuality. Meanwhile, the Church was developing its teaching on sexuality and gender, referring back as it did so to the figure of Eve, the first woman of the Hebrew creation story. The fourth-century theologian Augustine of Hippo advocated the doctrine of original sin, which stressed procreation as the chief reason for sexual intercourse. Feminist theologian Rosemary Radford Ruether comments that Augustine thus reduced the female to the role of a 'baby-making machine'.[8] By depersonalizing sexual relations, she says, Augustine allowed the Church Fathers three basic ways of defining women in the Church: as whores, as wives or as virgins. Only in the last role could a woman aspire to a fully redeemed life, according to this approach, while a married woman in post-first-century Christianity would find herself with less status than her equivalent in later Roman society enjoyed.

Sometimes the vocation of celibacy brought power with it, as exemplified in the story of the Church in Britain by Abbess Hilda of Whitby. She was born about 613, the daughter of Edwin the Northumbrian king, and devoted herself to her faith from the age of 13. The religious house she founded became a prime centre for northern England, visited by clerics and kings, who came seeking Hilda's advice. It was here that the famous Synod of Whitby met, ostensibly to agree one date for the observance of Easter, but in reality to resolve whether the church would follow Roman teaching as the southern half of England did or go with the less ritualistic, less authoritarian Celtic-derived northern church. Hilda herself seems to have kept silent, and Roman influence won the day. Even so her example shows that the religious life could offer capable and gifted women a path to learning and leadership within the Church though they were excluded from priesthood.

The Middle Ages

The period between the end of antiquity and the flowering of the Renaissance has sometimes been overlooked by those searching for examples of women's ministry in the history of the Church. At the level of popular piety this was a time when a rich cult of Mary evolved, based on the Church's teaching about the mother of Jesus as the ultimate model of spiritual womanhood. Religious art, music and literature extolled both Mary and the female saints, indirectly emphasizing the distance between their lives and the experiences of contemporary women.

Women of high social standing at this time were uniquely able to use their influence to advance the cause of religion, and one such figure was Margaret of Scotland. This figure of piety was a niece of Edward the Confessor, who married Malcolm, King of Scotland, between 1067 and 1070 and expressed her faith by encouraging church building and the preservation of sacred relics. During her reign, religious practices in Scotland were considered by a synod, which enacted several reforms. Through her connections, the Benedictine monastic order was introduced to Scotland from the continent, and the foundations of what would become Dunfermline Abbey were laid. She was canonized a century and a half after her death in 1093.

Between 1200 and 1500 there was a period of great social and intellectual unrest, which saw waves of witchcraft allegations against large numbers of women in Britain and continental Europe as well as the emergence of some striking female religious figures. Incredibly enough, two of these were Englishwomen, who were contemporaries and met one another.

Margery Kempe, who lived from around 1373 to some date after 1439, was the first writer of an autobiography in English. At around 40 years old, after almost twenty years as a wife and the bearing of fourteen children, she consulted the anchorite Dame Julian of Norwich for spiritual advice about the visions of Christ she was receiving. She had already broken off marital relations with her husband to live a solitary life, in response to what she believed was God's will, but after her conversations with the nun her actions became more dramatic. The woman from Norfolk began a series of pilgrimages on foot to the Holy Land, Italy, Portugal, Norway and Danzig. For six years during this period she nursed her bedridden husband until his death, once more basing her actions on what she said Christ had told her to do. In an age when many women were being accused of witchcraft or heresy, Margery was fortunate to escape with nothing worse than being taken to answer for her theological views before the Archbishop of York, who saw no sin in her.

The religious journey undertaken by Julian was an interior one, conducted from her cell attached to the side of a church in Norwich. Born in 1342, and living until sometime before 1423, Julian wrote her book *Revelations of Divine Love* to recount a series of visions she had received at the age of 30, lying on what she believed to be her deathbed. These visions, complete with her interpretations of them, form a spiritual treatise which is the first of its kind to have been written in English.

Both women write in striking language about God, Margery Kempe referring to her marriage to Christ and Julian speaking of 'Christ our Mother' and 'the Motherhood of God'. What their lives illustrate, despite the contrasts of their experiences, is the way that medieval women could find freedom of religious expression by withdrawing from the world and claiming time for prayerful reflection. Official church structures gave very little organizational space to women in the fourteenth and fifteenth centuries, but there has never been a formal selection process for the role of a Christian mystic, and that allowed some women the opportunity to explore their ministry in remarkable ways.

The Reformation legacy

As this brief survey has shown, the teaching roles and leadership profile that women held within some of the early Christian communities in the first century did not last. Once the Church developed socially, culturally and structurally, women's involvement was sidelined. What was left for women was personal piety and pastoral care, usually offered to other women or those on the margins. Women's religious houses were cloistered, and their freedom curtailed. It was not until the sixteenth century Reformation that women again began to find opportunities for public leadership in the Church.

It would be misleading to assume that the Reformation was of immediate benefit to women's ministry, however. Constance Coltman, the first woman ordained to ministry in the Congregational Union of England and Wales, described it as having been a 'two-edged sword'.[9] In the short term it deprived women of the opportunities for education and exercise of their gifts previously available through religious communities. Protestantism threatened to confine women to marriage, childbearing and domesticity once again. By rejecting the Marian devotion the Reformers also inadvertently contributed to a climate where women's overall status was lowered. Combined with these factors was an intense concentration on the letter of Scripture, leaving no room for critical interpretation of passages that seemed hostile to women's leadership.

Despite these issues, Protestantism's emphasis on individual liberty in Christ could be of help to women's ministry, as events slowly revealed. The existence of women activists on the radical fringes of the Reformation, among sectarian groups such as the Anabaptists, was evidence that the new theology could embolden a wide range of people to witness to their faith. In 1550, Joan of Kent became the most famous of the Anabaptist martyrs, being burnt at Smithfield. She was generally regarded as a theologian of some distinction, well capable of debating the finer points of the incarnation with learned scholars.

The freedom to die for one's faith is a dubious privilege, if held in isolation from other liberties. It would take the seismic social and religious upheavals of the seventeenth century to open up the possibilities for women's preaching and teaching ministry in somewhat less dangerous ways. In what may be the earliest reference to a woman preacher in Britain, the writings of Arthur Lake, who was Bishop of Bath and Wells from 1616 to 1625, mention penances imposed on those in Wells attending conventicles (early house churches) where women preached. The first direct evidence of women preachers arose about twenty years later among Baptists in Holland, and in 1641 a Brownist (early Congregationalist) journal referred to 'our she fellow-labourers', who 'preach both in their families and elsewhere'.[10] At the General Baptist Church in Bell Alley, London, a Mrs Attaway and several other women were regular preachers in the 1640s. In 1641, with political and religious friction about to boil over into civil war, the Independent preacher Katherine Chidley published a defence of religious independency.[11]

The conflict with King Charles I produced limitless opportunities for new, unlicensed preachers among the Parliamentarians, especially within groups on the radical fringe of the Civil War, who were also more open to receive women's ministry at this time of upheaval and religious ferment.

Not all the Puritans were equally enamoured of women in this role. A 1653 document, during Cromwell's Protectorate, refers unflatteringly to 'feminine tub preachers' among Baptists and Brownist congregations in London and in the provinces.

Meanwhile the Society of Friends, established by George Fox from 1647 onwards, taught that the Inner Light which alone allows true interpretation of the Scriptures can be held by women just as well as by men. In 1650 Fox's followers acquired the nickname of 'Quakers', and their message began to be spread far and wide by fearless bands of female preachers. Pioneers such as Elizabeth Hooton and Margaret Fell were influential in spreading Quakerism at home, while Mary Fisher, a servant girl from Selby, became a missionary first to New England and then to the Turkish Sultan. For their pains, nearly all these early Quaker women suffered severe physical trials including public whippings. After Fox's death in 1691, the first fervour which had given rise to women's leadership diminished, and the public and itinerant ministry of women reduced with it.

The restoration of the monarchy ushered in a quarter-century of persecution for those clergy and congregations who refused to use the Book of Common Prayer when this became subject to legislation in 1662. Dissenting groups continued to meet, often in private houses where the hosts might be female householders. One such was the 'brave widow' Elizabeth Petit, who according to 1680 conventicle records then housed a Nonconformist congregation in Cambridge and in 1669 had sheltered the 'only important congregation of Nonconformists that Cambridge then possessed'.[12]

An evangelical century

The rise of Methodism in the eighteenth century brought another flowering of women's preaching and public leadership, although John Wesley himself displayed some ambivalence about the desirability of women in the pulpit. Several women activists within the new movement felt called not just to pastoral care or private teaching but the leading of public worship and, encountering opposition, sought Wesley's advice. He advised them to continue, as their calling along with their lay itinerant male colleagues and the entire work of Methodism was an 'extraordinary' work of God.[13]

During the Evangelical Revival women were also inspired to explore their religious gifts in other ways. Ann Griffiths, who lived from 1776 to 1805, experienced conversion at a Methodist revival meeting in Pendref Chapel, Llanfyllin, Wales, in 1796. She went on to compose seventy of the most memorable hymns ever produced in the Welsh language, powerful expressions of personal spirituality which were probably not intended for congregational singing. After her death her maid, who had memorized these hymns during their long walks to chapel, dictated them so they would survive.

Other women exercised influence by their economic resources, notably Selina, Countess of Huntingdon, whose 'Countess of Huntingdon's Connexion' is the only denomination founded by a woman to be in existence today. Her widowhood in 1746 left her in possession of considerable means. She championed the ministry of George Whitefield and his Calvinistic Methodist connexion, building 'tabernacles' for him and his preachers and establishing a college for ministers at Trefeca, near Brecon.

Mission at home and abroad

The early nineteenth century saw a closing down of opportunities for women's preaching within Wesleyan Methodism, though it would survive throughout the other branches of that part of the Church for several more generations. Primitive Methodists and Bible Christians in particular held on to the original pattern of Methodist itinerancy, including women preachers, and conducted their affairs in ways which gave a greater voice to the laity. Since women have always tended to predominate in church gatherings, there may well have been a link between women's degree of involvement in church affairs, and their presence in the pulpits.

At the same time as openings for ministry were closing down at home, the century saw the opening up of new vocations for women in the expanding mission fields of South America, Africa and Asia. Escaping the limitations imposed by marriage and childbearing, or polite yet impoverished spinsterhood, an increasing number of middle-class, single Victorian women offered themselves as missionaries. Most concentrated their work in the field on issues such as women's health and education, and the translation of the Bible into other languages, keen to channel their energies into the combination of evangelism and imperial expansion which characterized the missionary movement.

The Salvation Army was a nineteenth-century religious movement with a worldwide impact, which had begun within Methodism. It was famous for its women officers, or 'Hallelujah Lassies' as they were known, and its 'Mother' in the person of Catherine Booth. This formidable theological thinker had married the Methodist minister William Booth at the age of 26, and thereafter shared in his evangelistic work first in London, and then outwards to all points of the compass. Despite her husband's initial opposition she established and maintained a powerful, continuous preaching ministry, as well as bringing up four children, although suffering serious ill health. The Salvation Army always welcomed the service of women from the start, and Evangeline Cora Booth, one of Catherine Booth's daughters, was elected General of the Salvation Army USA in 1934. Perhaps this policy regarding women officers was partly due to a recognition of their special suitability for the humanitarian work the Army undertook in the roughest parts of communities, places where a woman's presence would be seen as less threatening than that of her male colleagues.

This period also saw the emergence of women campaigners for social reform whose views were informed and inspired by their Christian faith. Prominent among these was Elizabeth Fry, a Quaker, best remembered for her work in reforming the prison system. She began visiting women prisoners and their children in Newgate prison, where she was appalled by the conditions she encountered. A House of Commons committee invited her to give evidence on the state of women's prisons in 1818. In the same year she also began caring for women about to be deported to the colonies. Her other concerns included a training school for nurses, district visiting societies to work with the poor, libraries for coastguards and care for homeless women and children.

Early feminists gave support to social issues such as the advance of female education, the temperance campaign, the anti-slavery movement, the call for women's suffrage and the campaign against the Contagious Diseases Act, which was being misused to hamper women's freedom outside the home. There was considerable overlap between the women who espoused these causes and those who established women's missionary societies to promote the expansion of Christianity around the world. All of these campaigns, both religious and secular, invariably involved the setting up of committees, raising of funds and holding of meetings. Thus they provided ideal opportunities for women to hone their organizational and public-speaking skills within all-women settings. It was then a short step for them to start accepting invitations to address mixed gatherings on these issues, or on religious themes, possibly within church buildings.

There was no surprise in the fact that this progression advanced most quickly through the Free Churches, where leadership and the right to teach were recognized at local level, and not necessarily dependent on formal theological qualification so much as on the evident calling of an individual by the Holy Spirit. By the late nineteenth century, some local Baptist and Congregational churches were starting to ask why women could not become their ministers, rather than remaining as lay leaders or unofficial deaconesses. The question led to the actual emergence of ordained women in these two traditions in the early twentieth century, with a resulting challenge to other Free Churches with ordained leadership to explain why they were not following suit.

Other factors influencing the advance of women's ministry during this period were developments in the United States. Women's preaching blossomed there in the nineteenth century, generally among lay women whose ministry crossed denominational boundaries and was not confined to one local setting. For women in the Quakers, Freewill Baptists, Free Methodists and Holiness movements, the call of the Holy Spirit overrode the need for official, institutional selection and approval for their public ministry. The American preacher Phoebe Palmer, known as the 'Mother of the Holiness Movement', created a sensation when she visited Leeds, Sheffield, Manchester and Birmingham on a tour in 1859.[14] Women's ordination officially began in the United States, when Antoinette Brown was the first woman to have her ordination recognized by a denomination, becoming minister of the Congregational Church in South Butler, New York, in 1853. However, her ministry lasted less than a year before she resigned due to the gulf between her liberal theology and the traditional views of some in her congregation.

Another way in which North America pioneered women's ministry was the nineteenth-century emergence of black women preachers. Amanda Smith, a former slave and revivalist Methodist, travelled throughout the post-Civil War United States preaching, and also evangelized in England, India and Africa for fourteen years. Although not a feminist she met with opposition when, in 1870, she attended the African Methodist Episcopal Church general conference in Nashville, where women were not allowed as delegates. For Amanda Smith, being cited as an unusual addition to those leading a meeting in a list of white speakers was no bad thing, for it validated her ministry both in the eyes of white people and within the black community. Most nineteenth-century black denominations would not license women to preach though, and the African Methodist Episcopal Zion Church alone ordained them, from 1895 onwards.[15]

The roots of modern ministry

It is tempting, but unhelpful, to romanticize the early history of women's ordination in the twentieth century. The early pioneers had to be remarkable characters in order to succeed at all, yet they were always in a minority, and usually confined to poor pastorates in challenging places where a male minister would not have gone. Constance Coltman alone from the first generation of inter-war Congregational women in ordained ministry managed the challenging balancing act of combining ministry with marriage and motherhood. She did so partly because of her private means and the fact she was sharing one stipend with her ordained husband. Interestingly, their ordination took place the day before their marriage, which may have been significant since in this era women were expected to relinquish paid employment on their marriage had wartime conditions not prevailed.

There is also a need to avoid reading back into the early twentieth century a degree of theological debate and understanding about women's ordination that is not evident from contemporary accounts. By contrast with the doctrinal arguments generated by the Church of England's late-twentieth-century exploration of women's ordination, there seems to have been remarkably little discussion in the Free Churches some eighty years earlier about the theological basis for women's ministry. Rather, advocates of this proposition based their arguments on the changing status of women in society as a whole, while opponents relied on referring back to the centuries-old traditions of the Church, selectively chosen, and their own views as to what polite, decent women should or should not do.

In 1924, seven years after her own ordination, Constance Coltman wrote: 'The torch of women' ministry even among the Free Churches has often burned very low, but never without kindling another flame to take its place.'[16] She was not to know how fragile the basis of women's ordination would prove to be among the Free Churches, or of the low ebb to which it would sink at times in the later twentieth century, but her confidence in the passing on of the flame has been vindicated.

Notes

1. *In Memory of Her: A Feminist Theological Reconstruction of Christian Origins* (New York: Crossroad, 1983) is an early work by the Christian feminist writer Elisabeth Schüssler Fiorenza.

2. Phyllis Bird, 'Images of Women in the Old Testament', in Rosemary Radford Ruether (ed.), *Religion and Sexism* (New York: Simon & Schuster, 1974), p. 41.

3. See e.g. Athalya Brenner (ed.), *Ruth and Esther: A Feminist Companion to the Bible* (Sheffield: Sheffield Academic Press, 1999).

4. Elizabeth M. Tetlow, *Women and Ministry in the New Testament* (New York: Paulist Press, 1980), p. 23.

5. Dorothy L. Sayers, *Unpopular Opinions* (London: Gollancz, 1946), p. 122.

6. Leonard Swidler, 'Jesus was a Feminist', *Catholic World* 212 (January 1971), pp. 177–83.

7. Elisabeth Schüssler Fiorenza, 'Women in the Early Christian Movement', in Carol P. Christ and Judith Plaskow (eds), *Womanspirit Rising* (San Francisco: Harper & Row, 1979), p. 92.

8. Rosemary Radford Ruether, 'Virginal Feminism in the Fathers of the Church', in Rosemary Radford Ruether (ed.), *Religion and Sexism*, p. 162.

9. Constance Coltman, 'Post Reformation: The Free Churches', in Maude Royden (ed.), *The Church and Woman* (London: James Clarke & Co., 1924), p. 80.

10. *The Brownists Conventicle*, 1641, quoted in Coltman, 'Post Reformation', p. 95.

11. Katherine Chidley, *The Justification of the Independent Churches of Christ. Being an answer to Mr. Edwards his booke, which hee hath written against the government of Christs Church, and toleration of Christs publicke worship; briefly declaring that the congregations of the Saints ought not to have dependence in government upon any other* (London, 1641).

12. Courtney S. Kenny, 'A Forgotten Cambridge Meeting-House', *Transactions of the Congregational Historical Society* 4 (1909–10), p. 223.

13. Letter of John Wesley to Mary Bosanquet, 1771, quoted in Jacqueline Field-Bibb, *Women towards Priesthood: Ministerial Politics and Feminist Praxis* (Cambridge: Cambridge University Press, 1991), p. 11.

14. Ruth A. Tucker and Walter Liefeld, *Daughters of the Church: Women and Ministry from New Testament Times to the Present* (Grand Rapids, Michigan: Academie Books, 1987), p. 263.

15. Bettye Collier Thomas, *Daughters of Thunder: Black Women Preachers and their Sermons 1850–1979* (San Francisco: Jossey-Bass, 1998), p. 19.

16. Coltman, 'Post Reformation', p. 112.

3. Worship and Preaching

JOHN DRANE AND
OLIVE M. FLEMING DRANE

Women in worship and preaching may appear to be a relatively uncontentious subject – and fifty years ago, it would have been. It might also have turned out to be one of the shortest chapters of the entire book. Though the picture is very uneven, women's participation in church leadership is generally less controversial today than it once was – but now preaching and worship are both hotly contested categories. What exactly is 'worship'? Historically, it was assumed to be the same thing as a church service, but today it is not uncommon for 'a time of worship' to consist of the singing of choruses or modern (never ancient) hymns. Identical questions are being raised in relation to preaching: is 'preaching' the same thing as a sermon – and if not, what is it? The personal stories in this book raise these questions. Pauline Webb wonders whether her ministry within the apparently secular world of radio constituted preaching, while Kate Cotterill's account of her encounter with 'Danny' and 'Tracey' provokes a similar question (see p. 129). Our own experience in ministry regularly highlights the same issues. When Olive ministers as a clown – whether in informal settings of storytelling, or more prescribed contexts such as Eucharistic celebrations – how does that connect with what John was taught about either worship or preaching in his rather more traditional theological education?[1] This is more than just a theoretical question for the two of us, not only in relational terms as we work at ministry alongside one another, but also in missional terms, for it is beyond dispute that Olive's creative, visual, tactile style of celebrating and sharing the gospel speaks far more powerfully to the unchurched masses of Britain than the more 'normal' format of Sunday services, especially within the Free Church tradition with its inherited emphasis on the educational (if not intellectual) nature of faith, and the accompanying suspicion of anything artistic and intuitional. Moreover, empirical research is suggesting that growing numbers of people now give up on their churches, not as a result of jettisoning their faith, but because they want it to be more authentic and can find no connection between that aspiration and the sort of things that they experience in worship and hear in sermons.[2]

There is a whole book in here, not just a single chapter![3] Talk about women, preaching and worship brings into focus some of the major challenges facing all churches today, especially the Free Churches. In order to put it in context, we have adopted a largely historical approach to unpacking these issues, beginning with the New Testament, followed by an all too brief overview of some significant issues in the ensuing centuries, before considering the part played by women preachers in the emergence of the Free Church tradition. Finally, we identify some important questions that these churches will need to address if they are to survive far into the twenty-first century, illustrated by reference to our own experience in shared ministry. In this process, we have interwoven themes from many different sources, some of which will no doubt overlap with other chapters in this book. We have, however, deliberately limited the discussion here to *preaching* and *worship*, so that even if we do cover similar ground to other chapters we might do it in a more focused way, by excluding institutional arguments about topics such as women's ordination or participation in church life more generally.[4] In the event, it turns out that we have said very little about worship as such, though in doing so we are merely reflecting the tendency of the Free Church tradition to regard sermons as the central aspect of 'worship', with other liturgical elements being regularly described as 'the preliminaries' in a service of worship. No wonder that Fleur Houston asks not only 'What does one do in an act of worship?' but more importantly, 'What does an act of worship do?' There are many questions to be asked about what constitutes 'an act of worship' that would be relevant here, but would take us far beyond our main subject.

One of the curiosities of British theological education is that, though the churches regard preaching as supremely important, homiletics virtually never features in the formal training of ministers. An exhaustive search has come up with only two British theological colleges that appear to offer a fully accredited course in either the study or the practice of preaching, and both of these are at postgraduate level rather than being part of initial theological education.[5] This is in sharp contrast to American seminaries, where it would be impossible to obtain the MDiv degree (the basic clergy qualification) without undertaking the formal study of homiletics. As a result, even full-time ministers rarely pause to reflect on what they might be doing as preachers, still less why they might be doing it the way they do. One widely accepted view among Free Churches is that Christian preaching was rooted in the post-exilic Jewish synagogues, as typified by the example of Ezra who stood on a raised platform reading and expounding the scriptures 'while the people remained in their places' as passive hearers (Neh. 8.1–8). This, of course, represents a very narrow view of the life of ancient synagogues, but it has had a far-reaching effect on the format of both preaching and worship in many Free Church circles.[6] Other scholarship has not only highlighted the diversity within synagogue life,[7] but has also suggested that perhaps this was not the major influence in the life of the early Church. Several studies have instead proposed a formative connection between the first Christians and the traditions of Graeco-Roman rhetoric, suggesting that this style of public speaking was actually the original model for Christian preaching.[8] There can be no question that this tradition deeply influenced the likes of Augustine of Hippo (354–430), and came to be the dominant form of scholastic preaching in the Middle Ages. It is still one of the most widely adopted models for preaching, with its emphasis on analysis, themes, point-making, and so on. Its usefulness in past generations cannot be denied. But the one thing we can say for certain is that it was not the most original form of Christian preaching.

It is actually anachronistic to apply the term 'preaching' to any activity described in the Bible. The Greek verb most often translated as 'preaching' (*kērussō*) referred to the announcing of a message on behalf of someone else (usually a sovereign or other significant person). To identify a biblical model, therefore, it makes most sense to ask: 'How is God's will made known and communicated?' Three themes emerge that can inform our subsequent discussion here:

- Throughout the Bible, God's voice is communicated through a variety of media: poems, prophetic oracles, songs, dance, drama, stories, along with dreams and other personal experiences. While the exposition of Scripture is not excluded, it is by no means the primary medium for the divine message. On the contrary, the messenger's own personal spirituality is the main channel through which God's will for the community is both revealed and communicated. This was as true for the apostle Paul, whose Damascus road experience was the touchstone of all else that he wrote and thought,[9] as it had been for all the Hebrew prophets before him.[10]
- Somewhat surprisingly, the New Testament contains only one narrative account of what might be regarded as a regular meeting of the church, namely the story of Paul's final visit with the church in Troas (Acts 20.6–12),[11] during which the unfortunate Eutychus dozed off and fell from the window. Because we read Scripture through our own experience, we tend to conjure up a scene in which Paul spoke in boring monologue style for an exceedingly long time. A careful reading of the text, however, tells a different story. For one thing, the terminology used to describe Eutychus could as easily be applied

to a toddler as to a teenager or young adult (which would explain how he fitted on the window sill in the first place, as well as shedding light on why he might have been asleep). More significant still is the way Luke describes the speaking: Paul, he records, engaged in a dialogue with them until midnight (Gk *dielegeto* = NRSV 'holding a discussion'), after which they 'continued to converse' until dawn (NRSV = Gk *homilēsas*, the word from which 'homiletics' is derived). In other words, in a typical church gathering the apostolic preaching was interactive, first in a semi-structured way (dialogue), then more informally (conversation). This matches what is implied elsewhere about the nature of worship as an interactive experience of the whole community,[12] and has important consequences for definitions of preaching in relation to the contributions that women have historically made to the life of the Church.

- The third indisputable characteristic of New Testament preaching is its kerygmatic nature. C. H. Dodd (1884–1973), himself a Free Church minister, drew attention to this more than seventy years ago. His somewhat artificial distinction between what he regarded as *kerygma* ('preaching') and *didache* ('teaching') never found wide acceptance.[13] But his insistence that the heart of apostolic preaching was to be found in the declaration of God's actions in Christ, culminating in the resurrection and gift of the Spirit, and accompanied by an invitation to others to the spiritual journey of Christian discipleship, was well-founded.

By these definitions of preaching, women were actually the very first preachers of all, for despite differences of detail each of the four Gospels insists that the risen Christ himself commissioned women to communicate the good news of the resurrection.[14] Olive has a distinct childhood memory of being part of a church where women were officially silenced, and wondering how that made sense in light of these passages. What she did not know at the time was that the women's communication of the resurrection message followed the biblical pattern just outlined: it was kerygmatic (they declared the truth of what God was accomplishing), experiential (incorporating a report of their own encounters with the risen Christ), and interactive (shared with the other disciples, to become a topic of further conversation). Nor was she aware that this realization had encouraged Hippolytus of Rome (170–235) to bestow on Mary Magdalene the title of '*apostolorum apostola*', or that Robert de Sorbon (1201–74), priest and founder of the famous Sorbonne college in Paris, had defended the Beguines, a group of religious women, by reminding their critics that Mary Magdalene was the first preacher of the resurrection.[15] These were lone voices, though, for women's contribution as preachers had been marginalized centuries before that. The New

Testament itself gives out mixed messages on the subject, with prohibitions on women's speaking alongside clear evidence of their doing just that – and, in one instance, both permission and prohibition appear in the very same context.[16] Since most gatherings of the early Church took place in the relative privacy of homes, it would be surprising if there had been a universally applicable rule of silence on anyone who was part of the family and its wider networks, whether women or men, children or servants – an assumption that finds further support in some catacomb inscriptions that depict women praying, prophesying, and preaching, as well as apparently celebrating the Eucharist.[17] The real change came when Christianity emerged from the relatively obscure world of private devotion to become part of the civic life of the Roman empire. In this patriarchal context, the masculinization of the Church was inevitable. The Council of Laodicea (352) banned women from leading churches, and the Council of Carthage (398) subsequently prohibited them from preaching – though the very fact that these topics had to be discussed at all (and the acrimony which it provoked) is itself indicative of the likelihood that from the beginning women had engaged in these roles.

The practices of the medieval Church are of little direct relevance for any discussion of the experiences of today's Free Churches – with one significant exception. For this was when preaching was first given a clear definition, by Alain of Lille (1125–1203), who understood it to be 'an open and public instruction in faith and behaviour, whose purpose is the forming of men; it derives from the path of reason and from the fountainhead of the "authorities" [Scripture]'.[18] This understanding merely reflected the prevailing pattern of preaching, influenced by Aristotelian rhetorical art, but its codification in this way influenced all subsequent definitions of preaching in a way that impinged directly on the ministry of women. It marginalized the homily, a more discursive and homely style of speaking, as being less than acceptable, but more significantly it ensured that 'proper preaching' could only be practised by an intellectual elite who were familiar with the Greek and Roman classics. This had the further consequence of creating a gulf between educated clerical culture and the ruder understandings of popular culture. With no access to education, women would never be a part of this cultural elite, and could therefore never be preachers. Even in those days, some were prepared to bend the rules a little, and Henry of Ghent (c.1290) distinguished between teaching that was 'ex officio' (and prohibited for women) and private teaching that was 'ex beneficio' (and allowed, with appropriate controls by ecclesiastical authorities). He also accepted 'prophesying' as being allowable for women because (unlike 'preaching') it was not regarded as a rational process, and therefore did not challenge the prevailing opinion that women were by definition intellectually inferior to men. As we shall see below, these distinctions had consequences in some unlikely places, not least in the formation of John Wesley's opinions on women preachers, and continue to be influential in some circles even today. Perversely, none of them noticed that Paul identified 'prophecy' as the most desirable charism of all (1 Cor. 14.3)![19]

It has been observed that very little happened at the Reformation, except that the altar was upended to become a pulpit.[20] Though the logic of belief in the priesthood of all believers implied a more egalitarian form of church, it was still only men who gained access to the inner sanctum of preaching. Calvin recognized that those New Testament passages prohibiting women from speaking were contextually determined, but neatly avoided addressing the matter by arguing that the citizens of sixteenth-century Geneva would be as easily scandalized as their counterparts in first-century Corinth by women who crossed conventional cultural boundaries.[21] Luther, meanwhile, was a thoroughly unreformed misogynist on this issue, describing women as having 'lots of filth and little wisdom' and 'created for no other purpose than to serve men'.[22] In any case, to gain state approval the Reformed churches had to support the patriarchal and hierarchical attitudes of the day. In the process, church itself was defined as 'Word preached, sacraments administered, and discipline applied', something that (like the Roman understanding that the Reformation claimed to displace) still required a professional caste of clergy. Since most of the pre-Reformation priestly functions had been done away with in relation to worship, the sermon came to be all-important. Alain of Lille's ecclesiology might have been rejected, but his definition of a sermon was not only welcomed, but redefined in an even more narrowly intellectual way than had previously been the case. No longer able to wear the priestly garb of the past which (at least in theory) was said to be a reflection of the divine sphere, Protestant clergy eagerly adopted academic gowns as their preferred attire, thereby drawing attention to their own intellectual prowess and implying that anyone who was not entitled to wear such garb could never be a real preacher. The construction of large towering pulpits with their thinly disguised phallic imagery only served to reinforce the domineering masculine nature of preaching.

This was the sort of preaching that provoked Samuel Johnson's (1709–84) oft-quoted comment that 'a woman's preaching is like a dog's walking on his hinder legs. It is not done well; but you are surprised to find it done at all.'[23] Some groups had already questioned whether it needed to be done by either men or women. Separatists such as the Amish, Mennonites, Quakers, Moravians and Baptists had no concern for the approval of the state, and followed through the logic of reformed theology by emphasizing the believer's personal experience of divine grace as the basic qualification for a preacher, rather than the educational attainments (or, for that matter, ordination) of a select few. By the mid-seventeenth century, the renowned 'tub preacher' Mrs Attaway was preaching weekly at the General (or Arminian) Baptist Church in Bell Alley, London, to crowds that were large enough to attract the widespread disapproval of both civic and church authorities.[24] The General Baptists are credited with articulating the notion of an 'inner light of Christ' that was subsequently elaborated by George Fox (1624–91) and the Quakers, and it was among them that women preachers initially found most acceptance. Fox insisted that since the 'inner light' was intrinsic to being human, and not conditional upon either position or gender, then any individual – male or female – must have the potential of being a preacher, since this skill depended only on a person's spiritual attentiveness. This challenged the notion that special training in biblical interpretation might be necessary, because conventional understandings of the Scriptures could be set aside under the influence of the direct guidance of the Spirit – a view that surfaced again at the beginning of the twentieth century with the rise of the Holiness and Pentecostal movements. A refusal to acknowledge the sacraments likewise ensured that Quakers were able to side-step the assumptions or expectations of other groups with regard to questions about the proper conduct of worship: Quaker worship simply defined itself in relation to the God-given intuitions of the worshippers. Contrary to the claims of their opponents, such apparent openness to the Spirit did not lead to a free-for-all, as certain individuals came to be recognized as possessing talents for preaching, and they became in effect official spokespersons for the movement. They included women, the most notable being Fox's colleague Margaret Fell (1614–1702), who wrote a pamphlet entitled *Women's speaking justified* (1666) explaining why women should be allowed to speak in church. Predictably, this right was not universally appreciated, and Elizabeth Hooten (1600–72), one of the earliest Quaker converts, was imprisoned four times in England for such speaking, and later fell foul of the authorities in Boston when she went to the American colonies as a missionary.[25] One of the reasons adduced for denying women the right to preach was that they were 'bold impudent housewives, without all womanly modesty'[26] – or worse, that they were mentally unbalanced, if not dangerous witches. It is certainly the case that the activities of some self-styled prophetesses did nothing to enhance the cause of women's preaching – and even the generally tolerant Quakers ended up rejecting groups such as the Shakers, Philadelphians, and Millenarians, all of which grew from within the Society of Friends, and all of them led by women.

By the eighteenth century, a major source of debate among the various Nonconformist groupings was the tension between the perceived need for order and discipline (which tended to exclude women) and belief in direct inspiration by the Spirit (which tended to include them). Early

Methodism provides the most extensive evidence of this because of the very many documents which survive from the ministry of John Wesley. It is widely agreed that Wesley himself was deeply influenced in his thinking on the subject of women and preaching by his mother Susannah, who emerged as the *de facto* pastor of her husband's Church of England parish in Epworth during his extended absences at the parliament in London. She was not formally recognized, of course, but whereas the curate who was officially left in charge of affairs could attract only a handful of people to his services, hundreds turned out for the regular devotions that Susannah ostensibly held for the benefit only of her own family. This pattern of informal meetings became the model for the Societies and class meetings that Wesley established to complement the more formal aspects of church life, thereby attempting to unite the institutionalism of groups like the Presbyterians and the spontaneous spirituality of the Quakers. Right from the start, Wesley evidently had no problem with women taking a leading role in his Societies, and he was often criticized because of the prominence he allowed to women. William Bowman was typical, insisting that 'A Third Mark of Imposture propagated by these mad Devotionalists is their teaching, that it is lawful and expedient for mere laymen, for women . . . to minister in the Church of Christ, to preach . . . and to offer up the prayers of the congregation in the public assemblies.'[27] Wesley initially sought to avoid unnecessary conflict with Anglicanism, and claimed that such activities were not really 'preaching', nor (because of their informal nature) did women's leadership of such groups constitute the exercise of authority over men, because in the context of what was in effect an extended family 'You do not act as a superior, but an equal; and it is an act of friendship and brotherly [*sic*!] love.'[28] There is a remarkable similarity between this and the nostrums of Henry of Ghent which we have already noticed, and such arguments are still used by those who wish to preserve a patriarchal hierarchy within their church structures while not appearing to deny the logic of their own theology of freedom and equality.

Wesley was unable to hide behind this subterfuge for long, and once the role of lay preaching was formally recognized it was inevitable that the question of women preachers would return. He was still resistant, though it could be argued that in the social circumstances of his day, the pragmatic approach advocated by Wesley was a wise one, for by insisting that the women in his Societies were operating as prophets and evangelists, and not pastors or priests, he avoided traditional arguments about authority and formal accreditation. Women, he claimed, engaged in prayer, testimony, and exhortation, but were not preachers because the speaking ministries in which they engaged did not technically correspond to the proper definition of a sermon – another distinction with its origins in the medieval Church. A crucial difference between the 'exhorters' and the 'preachers' was that the latter began with a biblical text that was expounded, whereas the former grounded their messages in their own personal experience.

But just as no-one is a leader unless others follow them, so with preaching: no-one is a preacher unless others listen. The fact that women were being listened to – often by large numbers of people – highlighted the nonsensical distinctions that were being made between different forms of public speaking, and when in the early 1760s Sarah Crosby (1729–1804) wondered if she was transgressing by addressing large and eager crowds in Derby, Wesley effectively said that she was doing no wrong, just so long as she never called it 'preaching'. In a later letter, he advised that 'you may properly enough intermix short exhortations with prayer; but keep as far from what is called preaching as you can: therefore never take a text; never speak in a continued discourse without some break, about four or five minutes'.[29] Wesley did eventually accept that women's speaking could be real 'preaching', and at the Manchester Conference of 1787 Sarah Mallet (1764–1846) was formally recognized as a preacher. It was, however, a short-lived victory and within a decade of Wesley's death women's preaching was restricted, and then banned, which is where matters rested in British Methodism until the third decade of the twentieth century.

Meanwhile, the influence of Wesleyan theology was developing in new ways within what came to be the Holiness Movement, with its roots in the Second Great Awakening in early nineteenth-century America – so-called because of obvious similarities to the (first) Great Awakening of the 1720s–40s.[30] George Whitefield (1714–70, a leader in the first Awakening) had denounced preaching that was 'in the manner of a prepared essay rather than a living speech' as being 'a deficiency in faith', a view shared by others at the time, and one that began to open the door to the possibility that uneducated women might have something to say.[31] A century later, the evangelist Charles Finney (1792–1875) regularly invited women to speak at his many revivalist meetings,[32] and justified the practice by insisting not only that the work of Christ reversed the consequences of the Fall, but that those who were truly sanctified by the Spirit were free from all sin – including, crucially, any inferiority that women might be supposed to have inherited as a consequence of the primeval actions of Eve. By the middle of the nineteenth century, denominations influenced by these revivalist movements were giving official sanction to women preachers, one of whom (Phoebe Palmer, 1807–74) published a book entitled *The Promise of the Father,* in which she defended women as preachers, while describing what they did as 'talking to' or 'addressing' congregations rather than 'preaching', because she regarded that word as irredeemably connected to the arid intellectualism and personal pomposity of male preachers.[33] When she visited Britain, she was defended in the face of her critics by another woman whose influence was to be, if anything, even more extensive: Catherine Booth (1829–90), who, though originally unsure whether women could be preachers, was won over by the Holiness message that since sin was no longer a present reality in the life of the believer, women could never be regarded as second-class Christians on account of the actions of Eve. When the mission she co-founded with her husband William was formally constituted as the Salvation Army, she ensured that women were recognized from the outset as equal with men in all respects, including preaching.

By the beginning of the twentieth century, women preachers were highly visible in groups influenced by the Holiness Movement, represented in Britain by the Calvary Holiness Church and the Church of the Nazarene, but most especially in the many independent Holiness missions that sprang up spontaneously among working people in industrial centres such as Glasgow and Liverpool. The precise relationship between these movements and the rise of Pentecostalism is the subject of much discussion, but there can be no doubt that all the key players in the events of Azusa Street, Los Angeles, in 1906 (widely regarded as the origins of modern Pentecostalism) had previous connections with Holiness preachers.[34] One of the much-vaunted hallmarks of the early Pentecostal movement was that the experience of the Spirit created a level playing-field in which the only qualification for ministry was a person's own direct experience of God. True to this promise, one major Pentecostal denomination was founded by a woman – the flamboyant Aimee Semple MacPherson (1890–1944), whose Angelus Temple near downtown Los Angeles is still packed every Sunday, and from where in 1922 she preached what is claimed to be the first ever sermon to be broadcast (on radio). At the time of her death, 67 per cent of all the ordained clergy in her International Church of the Foursquare Gospel were women, though the number has consistently diminished ever since. While Pentecostal women are naturally concerned about this,[35] by the end of the twentieth century more than 50 per cent of all the women who had ever been ordained in any church anywhere in the world were Pentecostal.[36] It was only with the rise of the charismatic movement that questions about women preachers began to be asked, under the influence of individuals from fundamentalist evangelical churches who brought their own hermeneutical baggage with them.

So far, we have restricted this discussion to a consideration of the role of women as preachers in more or less formal situations within the life of the churches. But if we adopt a slightly wider perspective, there is a good deal more that can be said in relation to the part played by women preachers in the wider Free Church tradition. For example, if instead of focusing on the formal recognition of women's contributions as preachers, we reflect on the biblical pattern of communicating God's will, it is arguable that preachers are not the only ones to have done this, and may not be the most important either. For many congregants, the major source of their understanding of God has come not through sermons, but through hymns – often to the dismay of theological purists, who dislike what they regard as the over-simplification of the message. In the Victorian and Edwardian eras especially, many women found an unexpected way into the hearts and minds of Christian people by becoming hymn-writers. In the Free Churches in particular, this could become an especially influential role, as the singing of hymns compensated for the absence of visual and tactile symbols of the divine, and offered some possibility of interaction with other worshippers in churches that had rejected the natural responsiveness of traditional ancient liturgies. In many Free Churches today, the place of singing has been elevated to even greater liturgical importance, with the widespread adoption of an extended 'time of worship' that consists of nothing but singing, largely under the influence of the charismatic movement though not restricted to such congregations. While this often tends towards a dumbing-down of 'worship', with the singing of individualistic banalities rather than the praise of God, at its best such worship can be the liturgical equivalent of a traditional choral Eucharist. Even today, many women are still 'preaching' to chauvinistic congregations through the words of their songs.

Women have also made significant contributions in terms of outreach ministries to other women. Throughout the twentieth century, Free Churches in particular had a tradition of vibrant mid-week meetings for women who were ostensibly 'unchurched', but for whom such meetings actually were their church – and again, women played a significant part as preachers in such contexts. Women also had a huge influence in the Protestant missionary movement, often accomplishing much more than men ever did, and exercising ministries of all kinds, whether officially approved or not. There have been many attempts to understand why women were allowed to do overseas what they were forbidden to do at home. Sometimes it was just a matter of 'out of sight, out of mind'. But tolerance of their activities may also have been underwritten by imperialism and patriarchy, for in a world where non-white people were regularly regarded as not fully human it could seem perfectly natural that other second-class humans should minister to them. Such thinking certainly operated in Britain, where the teaching of the young in Sunday schools was mostly regarded as women's work. Being a child was also regarded as a less than fully human state, as evidenced by the way in which children were not fully included in the household of God until attaining 'years of discretion' – at which stage only men would teach them. Even in these days of supposed equality, women still find themselves on the margins and a much higher proportion of women than men end up working with congregations in poor circumstances. A key to understanding some of this undoubtedly lies in the way in which singleness was also regarded as the ideal for women who were involved in Christian work.[37] Male fear of female sexuality is definitely a sub-text here – and is not just yesterday's problem, for it surfaces in one way or another in more than one of the personal stories recounted elsewhere in this book.

Much more could be said on all these subjects. In conclusion, though, we identify several key questions that have emerged which are of some importance for the future practice of the Free Churches. One obvious question is how to acknowledge the value of rigorous theological study while also affirming the faith experiences of those who have not had access to such education. A huge amount of harm has been inflicted on gifted women, who have not only been baffled by the highly intellectualized nature of much preaching, but have also been taught to believe that their own understandings of God are so simplistic that even talented communicators of the gospel can feel obliged to insist that, 'I'm not really a preacher, of course'. It is also the case, however, that women with theological education can find themselves put down by male clergy who pride themselves in their own ignorance by disdaining any form of intellectual endeavour. The two of us frequently find ourselves faced with both these reactions, especially when we minister among the Free Churches.[38] As we write, we have on our desks an invitation to lead weekend workshops on mission issues from just such a church, with the hope that John will do 'serious' sessions on the changing nature of our culture in relation to gospel issues, and for Olive to run sessions on storytelling. In our case, there is no empirical reason at all why churches should pigeonhole us in that way, as we both have postgraduate degrees in theology and both teach regularly in a graduate school in California as well as in degree courses in the UK. There are therefore no prizes for guessing the real agenda! At the same time, though, the likely outcome is equally transparent and predictable. For when we go we will both share equally in the 'serious' sessions (as also in the Sunday worship), and John will likely join the storytelling workshop as a participant along with everyone else. On past experience, the further outcome will almost certainly be that this sort of partnership will be well received and may just encourage that congregation to move beyond what is still the medieval distinction between a 'real' sermon and a more homely 'story'. Paradoxically, churches that think this way also tend to be the sort of people who display bumper stickers asking, 'What would Jesus do?' If they thought about it, the answer to that might also surprise them! Many churches seem to end up with this kind of thinking not because they are card-carrying chauvinists, but rather because they don't actually think at all about what they do and how they do it.

Beyond traditional chauvinist arguments, some would argue that there is an intrinsic difference between the ways in which men and women function and communicate, and of course we all have different strengths and weaknesses and function best in one form rather than another. But ultimately it is the culture that makes these distinctions and imposes them on us, not our innate humanity or gender. These cultural expectations can be spiritually damaging to both women and men, but are also deeply rooted in the way we now do theology, indeed in what we think theology actually is.

In addition to such pragmatic concerns, we also need to take account of the way that both the form and function of preaching is being closely scrutinized today, and at least one well-informed study has claimed that it is both unbiblical and unnecessary.[39] This question is especially pressing in the Free Church context because of the way that preaching is claimed to be central to worship. If the sermon is to be the main dish, it needs to offer spiritual nourishment. Jarena Lee (b. 1783) was the daughter of freed slaves, and an officially endorsed itinerant preacher within the American Methodist Episcopal Church. Her autobiography eloquently expresses the question that women preachers have struggled with through the ages. Referring to Mary Magdalene as the first preacher of the resurrection, she observed that 'some will say that Mary did not expound the Scripture, therefore, she did not preach, in the proper sense of the term. To this I reply, it may be that the term "preach", in those primitive times, did not mean exactly what it is now made to mean; perhaps it was a great deal more simple then, than it is now – if it were not, the unlearned fishermen could not have preached the gospel at all, as they had no learning.'[40]

We have both argued elsewhere that storytelling (especially as personal faith story) is a particularly appropriate medium for communication of the gospel in a postmodern culture,[41] but style is just as important as content. Eunjoo Mary Kim gets to the heart of things when she points out that 'if the preacher uses prescriptive, propositional, imperative, authoritarian, and judgmental language, which has traditionally been categorized as male language, the congregation is tamed to acknowledge the hierarchy between the pulpit and the pews and thereby becomes passive believers', whereas 'if the preacher uses descriptive, imaginative, poetic, inviting, and inspiring language, which has traditionally been categorized as feminine language, the congregation becomes active believers, autonomous in nurturing their faith and understands the church as an egalitarian community'.[42] This correlates very well with the account of Acts 20.6–12 and also resonates with our own experience. Reference has already been made to Olive's ministry through clowning,[43] and part of the genius of a clown sermon is that it recasts preaching in an entirely different genre, and in the process creates a space in which people no longer feel bound by their traditional expectations and assumptions.

Further, by focusing on the element of witness and personal testimony – though in connection with the historic tradition, especially through its emphasis on the centrality of the cross as divine marginalization and identity with redemptive suffering – it has an authenticity that points to a God who is not found in clever answers, but in the ambiguity and complexity of life as we all experience it.[44]

We cannot leave this without saying something about the nature of the Church, and of theology and theological education. Free Church ecclesiology has always prioritized 'the priesthood of all believers', whether or not that actual phrase is used. A recurring feature of this story is the way that women have found relatively easy acceptance at times of spiritual renewal, but the ensuing institutionalization of the very structures that set them free has then conspired to marginalize them. In the context of the Free Churches, the social processes of rationalization have also tended to create an aspiration to be indistinguishable from other, more ancient and established, forms of church. More often than most are prepared to admit, Free Church clergy can operate in an even more hierarchical mode than their colleagues in the wider catholic tradition, albeit being held to account by congregations in ways that frequently undermine their ability to accomplish much at all.[45] In fact, the congregational ecclesiology that in theory ought to have created spaces for women as preachers and leaders of worship often turns out to be the major blockage, for many (perhaps most) local congregations are still resistant to regarding the preaching of women as the real thing. Ultimately, the experience of women as preachers is unlikely to be changed until the way that we do theology is also reimagined – doing theology in the strictest sense of the word, that is, namely asking how we can know God. Is theology a deductive or an inductive process? Do we begin from theories and abstract ideas, or with human experience? Is it a philosophical system, or a matter of praxis-reflection?

The frequently made distinction between expounding Scripture and telling a story is in fact purely arbitrary and artificial. Forty years ago, majority-world Christians were discovering that their own stories were inextricably bound up with how they read the Bible. Western Christians had, of course, done the same thing for centuries, but because of their love affair with Cartesian rationalism they managed to convince themselves that they were 'objective' (a good thing) and untarnished with 'subjectivity' (a bad thing). It has taken us a long time to appreciate that there is no such thing as a presuppositionless exegesis, and that to espouse such a thing can produce a very emaciated version of the gospel that might feed the intellect, but does little to nourish the soul. The hermeneutical cycle now so beloved of practical theologians has at its heart the integration of personal experience with wider historical and biblical awareness. In sorting out matters of personal identity and meaning, most people intuitively start with their own experiences of life, and then ask questions of the wider tradition. Most clergy, on the other hand, are still trained to start with the tradition and then to apply it to the circumstances of real life. Even then, it tends to be other people's lives, rather than their own experience of God. There is a serious discontinuity here that goes to the heart of the subject we have been considering, and which contributes to the widely held notion that theological education tends to stifle the life of the Spirit.

Consideration of women as preachers, then, raises some profound questions about the nature of Christianity in the twenty-first century. In the context of the Free Churches, and taking account of recent developments in the wider context of the world Church and ecumenical relationships, it also brings back to haunt us the observation first made by Paul Tillich almost sixty years ago: 'The Protestant era is finished, after nearly all the historical conditions upon which it rested have been taken away from it.'[46] If 'Free Churches' is substituted for 'Protestant', could that be the biggest question of all?

Notes

1. On clowning as ministry, see Olive M. Fleming Drane, *Clowns, Storytellers, Disciples* (Oxford: BRF, 2002).

2. Cf. Alan Jamieson, *A Churchless Faith* (London: SPCK, 2002). For a personal story, see Andrew Strom, *The 'Out-of-Church' Christians*, at http://homepages.ihug.co.nz/~revival/oo–Out-Of-Church.html

3. Many books have of course been written that impinge on this subject. Those we have found most useful include the following: Barbara J. MacHaffie, *Her Story: Women in Christian Tradition*, 2nd edn (Minneapolis: Fortress, 2006); Eunjoo Mary Kim, *Women Preaching: Theology and Practice through the Ages* (Cleveland, Ohio: Pilgrim Press, 2004); Paul W. Chilcote, *She Offered them Christ* (Nashville: Abingdon, 1993); Linda L. Belleville, *Women Leaders and the Church* (Grand Rapids: Baker, 2000); Dan Doriani, *Women and Ministry* (Wheaton: Crossway, 2003); Anne Jensen, *God's Self-confident Daughters: Early Christianity and the Liberation of Women* (Louisville: Westminster John Knox Press, 1996); Lynn Japinga, *Feminism and Christianity: An Essential Guide* (Nashville: Abingdon, 1999); and not least, David Scholer's collection of *Selected Articles on Hermeneutics and Women in Ministry in the New Testament* (Pasadena, CA: Fuller Seminary, 2005) published as a reader for his course NS 561, 'Women, the Bible, and the Church'.

4. Though it is worth noting that ordination itself is becoming another contested subject in many Free Churches, partly as a result of the shortage of full-time ministers; but its relevance is also being questioned in relation to core underlying theological values of freedom and equality. The Baptist Union of Victoria (Australia) has described it as 'the catholic fly in the Baptist ointment',

and abandoned it as a formality (while still recognizing the importance of full-time ministry). The New Church streams in the UK (arguably the most successful Free Churches today) also generally sit lightly to notions of ordination in a formal sense. Though this is not the place to explore the topic, discussion of it raises similar issues to those identified here with respect to preaching, as the inherited sense of the word implies a status that is quite different from biblical norms or expectations.

5. We may have missed something, and if we have, readers will no doubt be quick to tell us. The courses we have identified are Master's degrees at International Christian College in Glasgow (http://www.icc.ac.uk/courses_desc. php?course_id=26) and Spurgeon's College in London (http://www.spurgeons. ac.uk/site/pages/ui_courses_masters.aspx).

6. R. P. Martin offers a classic account of worship along these lines, with his claim that it consisted of 'praise . . . prayers . . . instruction', *Worship in the Early Church* (London: Marshall, Morgan & Scott, 1964), pp. 24–7. Other classic treatments of the topic from the same generation took a similar line: cf. C. F. D. Moule, *Worship in the New Testament* (London: SCM Press, 1961); G. Delling, *Worship in the New Testament* (London: Darton, Longman & Todd, 1962); Oscar Cullmann, *Early Christian Worship* (London: SCM Press, 1953) – all of them offering detailed accounts of worship 'services' with a confidence that is not justified by the evidence. For a more nuanced account, see Paul F. Bradshaw, *The Search for the Origins of Christian Worship* (New York: Oxford University Press, 1992).

7. Ancient synagogues evolved in the post-exilic period out of the need to create community centres for the preservation and celebration of traditional Hebrew culture as Jewish people moved away from their traditional homelands, and the sort of biblical exposition frequently identified as the main activity of the synagogues was in fact only one aspect of their operations. Cf. Isaac Levy, *The Synagogue: Its History and Function* (London: Vallentine, Mitchell & Co, 1963); Azriel Eisenberg, *The Synagogue through the Ages* (New York: Bloch, 1974).

8. See, for example, Burton L. Mack, *Rhetoric and the New Testament* (Minneapolis: Fortress, 1990); Duane A. Litfin, *St Paul's Theology of Proclamation: 1 Corinthians 1–4 and Greco-Roman Rhetoric* (New York: Cambridge University Press, 1994); Carl Joachim Classen, *Rhetorical Criticism of the New Testament* (Tübingen: Mohr Siebeck, 2000).

9. For a spirited presentation of this opinion see Seyoon Kim, *The Origin of Paul's Gospel* (Grand Rapids: Eerdmans, 1983) and, more recently, *Paul and the New Perspective: Second Thoughts on the Origins of Paul's Gospel* (Grand Rapids: Eerdmans, 2002).

10. The emphasis on personal divine encounter is so widespread in the Hebrew prophets that this claim scarcely needs any justification. But see, among many others, Amos 1.1; 7.1–9; Isaiah 6.1–13; Jeremiah 1.1–19; Ezekiel 1.1—3.11.

11. There are of course many other references to church life in the New Testament, but all of them are correcting aberrations of one sort or another rather than describing a typical gathering.

12. Cf. Acts 1.43–7; 1 Corinthians 14.26–33.

13. C. H. Dodd, *The Apostolic Preaching and its Developments* (London: Hodder & Stoughton, 1936).

14. Matthew 28.1–10; Mark 16.1–8; Luke 23.55—24.10; John 20.11–18.

15. R. W. Southern, *Western Society and the Church in the Middle Ages* (New York: Viking, 1970), p. 309; Marygrace Peters, 'The Beguines: Feminine Piety Derailed', *Spirituality Today* 43 (1991), pp. 36–52 (available at http://www.spiritualitytoday.org/spir2day/91431peters.html).

16. Contrast 1 Corinthians 11.5, where women are encouraged to 'prophesy', with 1 Corinthians 14.33b–35, where they are forbidden to speak in any capacity.

17. Cf. Karen Jo Torjesen, 'The Early Christian *Orans*: An Artistic Representation of Women's Liturgical Prayer and Prophecy', in Beverly Mayne Kienzle and Pamela J. Walker (eds), *Women Preachers and Prophets through Two Millennia of Christianity* (Berkeley: University of California Press, 1998), pp. 42–56.

18. Cf. Richard Lischer, *Theories of Preaching: Selected Readings in the Homiletical Tradition* (Durham, NC: Labyrinth Press, 1987), p. 10.

19. David M. Scholer, 'Women in Ministry', *The Covenant Companion* 1 January 1984, p. 13.

20. Gordon Donaldson, *The Faith of the Scots* (London: Batsford, 1990), p. 65.

21. On Calvin's egalitarian tendencies, see Jane Dempsey Douglass, *Women, Freedom, and Calvin* (Philadelphia: Westminster Press, 1985).

22. See Ann Loades (ed.), *Feminist Theology: A Reader* (London: SPCK, 1990), p. 123.

23. James Boswell, *Life of Dr Samuel Johnson*, vol. 1 (entry for 31 July 1763).

24. Richard L. Greaves, 'The Role of Women in Early English Nonconformity', *Church History* 52.3 (1983), pp. 299–311.

25. Chilcote, *She Offered them Christ*, p. 14; MacHaffie, *Her Story*, pp. 141–5.

26. John Vickers, *The Schismatick Sifted*, quoted in Julia O'Faolain and Laurel Martines (eds), *Not in God's Image: Women in History from the Greeks to the Victorians* (New York: Harper & Row, 1973), p. 264.

27. William Bowman, *The Imposture of Methodism Display'd* (London: Joseph Lord, 1740), p. 27.

28. John Wesley, *The Letters of the Rev. John Wesley, A.M.*, ed. John Telford (London: Epworth Press, 1931), vol. 2, p. 233.

29. Letter of 18 March 1769: *The Letters of the Rev. John Wesley, A.M.*, ed. Telford, vol. 5, p. 130.

30. For a detailed account of the activities of women in this movement, along with biographical information on the leading individuals, see Susie C. Stanley, *Holy Boldness: Women Preachers' Autobiographies and the Sanctified Self* (Knoxville: University of Tennessee Press, 2002).

31. Harry Stout, *The New England Soul: Preaching and Religious Culture in Colonial New England* (New York: Oxford University Press, 1986), p. 192.

32. Kim, *Women Preaching*, pp. 88–99.

33. MacHaffie, *Her Story*, p. 199.

34. For a recent accessible account, see Cecil M. Robeck, *The Azusa Street Mission and Revival: The Birth of the Global Pentecostal Movement* (Nashville: Thomas Nelson, 2006). Also Harvey Cox, *Fire from Heaven: The Rise of Pentecostal Spirituality and the Reshaping of Religion in the Twenty-first Century* (London: Cassell, 1996).

35. Cf. Sheri R. Benvenuti, 'Pentecostal Women in Ministry: Where Do We

Go From Here?', *Cyber Journal for Pentecostal-Charismatic Research* 1 (January 1997), accessed at http://www.pctii.org/cyberj/cyber1.html

36. Rosemary Skinner Keller and Rosemary Radford Ruether (eds), *In Our Own Voices: Four Centuries of American Women's Religious Writing* (San Francisco: HarperSanFrancisco, 1995).

37. Cf. Philip B. Wilson, *Being Single: Insights for Tomorrow's Church* (London: Darton, Longman & Todd, 2005).

38. In our experience, Anglicans and Roman Catholics seem much less likely to react like this – though whether that relates to the nature of the different traditions, or is more a reflection of the sort of church that chooses to engage with us, is not easy to decide.

39. David C. Norrington, *To Preach or Not to Preach: The Church's Urgent Question* (Carlisle: Paternoster, 1996).

40. Jarena Lee, *Religious Experience and Journal of Mrs Jarena Lee, giving an account of her call to Preach the Gospel* (Philadelphia: Printed and published for the Author, 1849), p. 36. Can be accessed at http://digilib.nypl.org/dynaweb/digs/wwm9716/@Generic_BookView

41. John Drane, *The McDonaldization of the Church* (London: Darton, Longman & Todd, 2000); Fleming Drane, *Clowns, Storytellers, Disciples*.

42. Kim, *Women Preaching*, p. 75.

43. For the record, she does not always minister in this guise, though it has become one of her more distinctive images.

44. Cf. Fleming Drane, *Clowns, Storytellers, Disciples*, pp. 110–45.

45. Significantly, the only group that seems to have navigated that particular minefield with some success (at least as far as women are concerned) is one that from the outset has had a hierarchical structure, namely the Salvation Army. This parallels the Anglican experience, in which women have made significantly greater progress in a shorter space of time than in any of the major Free Church denominations. This must be saying something about an ecclesiology that generally prefers committee-based decision-making over against the inspired leadership of visionary individuals.

46. Paul Tillich, *The Protestant Era* (Chicago: University of Chicago Press, 1948), p. 286.

4. Are there Traditional Women's Ministries?

CHAM KAUR-MANN

Introduction

Are there traditional women's ministries? This question at first glance appears obvious, benign and clear-cut, until further qualifications are sought. Which group of 'women' are the subjects? Whose tradition is in question? What context is being considered? Women theologians all over the world continue to wrestle with these themes. Indeed, the question that at first appears straightforward is actually multilayered and complex. Where does this notion of traditional 'women's ministries' come from? Who determines the suitability and applicability of this label to women's ministries? This is a Eurocentric question, with Eurocentric overtones, yet the answers are not as easy to come by as initially anticipated. Ann Clifford writes:

> Women theologians in sub-Saharan Africa and Asia almost always take note in their theologies of the long-term effects of European colonial exploitation on their countries, not only to reflect to their constituencies what they already know first hand, but also to expand the consciousness of First World persons who may read their works. The effects of colonialism are pervasive, coloring everything, including how the Bible was originally presented.[1]

First of all, let me take you on a personal journey, my journey. The journey will take you through the continents of India and Africa, pausing in Europe and America. I will give consideration to the perspectives, lives and stories of the women from these lands and from there raise some questions. Why have western notions about 'women' prevailed and why are these notions considered to be normative for *all* women? How has the colonial legacy impacted women within their context and influenced subsequent behaviour? On this journey it will become evident

Are there traditional women's ministries?

Depends on who you are

Any received social, cultural, historical and religious experiences inevitably impinge and influence the perspective and action of any individual. The collective experiences from my personal journey as a British Indian, Sikh convert to Christ have similarly influenced my outlook, interpretation and assimilation of life's drama. Let me explain . . .

I was born in Birmingham and raised within a working-class immigrant Sikh family. While growing up, life was centred on worship and service at the local gurdwara (Sikh place of worship).

Memories flood back of incense-filled rooms, of scriptures read out faithfully from the Granth Sahib (Holy Book), of hospitality and food available in abundance, of women and men active in a multiplicity of roles around the gurdwara. Within this context, stories were shared with the younger generation, informing us about our rich heritage. The accounts were inspiring and yet deeply challenging at the same time, particularly with regard to the role of women within Sikhism.

Perhaps as you take off your shoes, and dare to sit where I sit, and try to understand the influence of my context, then you may begin to appreciate the difficulty I face in responding to the question of traditional 'women's ministries'.

Where it all began

Sikhism was established by Guru Nanak in the fifteenth century in India, in a continent full of inequalities and discrimination at many levels. The status of women, particularly, had been degraded through the enforcement of the caste system, through notions of impurity associated with menstruation and childbirth and the denial of rights to education and inheritance. Women were not permitted to participate in the social, economic, political or cultural arenas. The life of a woman was relegated to childbearing, housework and serving men. Female infanticide and sati (where females were expected to throw themselves on the funeral pyres of their dead husbands) were both encouraged.

Against such a backdrop of oppression and discrimination, the Sikh Gurus sought to address the inequalities and discrepancies in the status and relationship between men and women and to also challenge the inequities of the caste system. Guru Nanak writes:

> From the woman is our birth, in the woman's womb are we shaped;
> To the woman we are engaged, to the woman we are wedded;
> The woman is our friend and from woman is the family;
> Through the woman are the bonds of the world;
> Why call woman evil who gives birth to the leaders of the world?
> From the woman is the woman, without woman there is none.[2]

The birth of the Khalsa signalled a new era for women, as they joined men in the act of baptism, and embraced the 'five Ks', the ubiquitous code of conduct pertinent to all disciples.[3] The Sikh Gurus further promoted and endorsed the role and status of women by introducing practical steps towards equalizing the roles between men and women. First, women were invited to join the congregation (Sangat). Second, they were permitted to lead the congregation and to take part in the continuous recitation of the holy scriptures (Akand Path). Third, women were permitted to lead worship (Kirtan). Fourth, women were invited to share the common meal in the institution of the common kitchen (Langar). Fifth, women were permitted to serve as a priest (Granthi), to preach and teach, and to participate fully in the religious, social, military, political and cultural activities in society.[4]

The steps taken by the Gurus to advocate and promote the equality of women through Sikhism served to transform many aspects of traditional Indian life for women. As women began to contribute to the religious, social and political arenas of life, their equality with men became more obvious. Within the annals of Sikh history there are many examples of Sikh women who rose up to be sources of inspiration, heroines who demonstrated bravery, self-sacrifice, serving as warriors, missionaries, soldiers and leaders of battalions.[5]

Admittedly, the teachings within Sikhism were five hundred years ahead of their time. True equality as envisioned by the Gurus has never been fully realized. However, the memories of women actively and freely participating in the life and various ministries of the gurdwara, alongside men, remain with me, as they continue to serve in their faith.

Having grown up within a specific religious and cultural setting, having heard the stories of the brave heroines in daily life, having witnessed the participation of Sikh women of all ages in various ministries and responsibilities within the gurdwara, imagine my confusion! As a recent convert and young follower of Jesus, I entered the doors of the church expecting to see my fellow women freely engaging in the many diverse ministries, regardless of gender, caste, colour or class. However, my expectations were quickly dashed. Instead, I was greeted by a white male at the door, the worship was led by a white male, the notices were given by a white male, Scripture was read by a white male, the message was given by . . . yes, you've guessed it, a white male! The women . . . well, I spotted some in the back, making the tea and coffee . . . and active in largely auxiliary roles. Was I caught up in a time warp? What was going on? I felt like an 'observer' in a Victorian drama. Where was the evidence of the liberating message I received in my encounter with Jesus? The Jesus I knew and served was an encourager to everyone, calling all to fulfil their purpose and destiny in the Kingdom. Where was he? Had I made a bad choice? Was my conversion a mistake? Should I abandon my faith? No.

I had to constantly recall my journey of faith in order to maintain my focus. It all began when I was introduced to Jesus as a child at the local Christian youth club. I became fascinated with this god-man, incredulous that he wanted to be a part of my life and the lives of others. Jesus became a reality for me as I read the miracle stories and then witnessed the presence of his transformative power in people's lives. After many years of soul-searching, and dealing with the sense of fear, shame and dishonour my actions would bring on my family, I finally made my decision to follow Jesus. The cost of commitment was painful. I gave up everything that was significant to me, namely my family, my friends and my community, in order to follow Jesus and to serve him alone. The decision to convert from Sikhism to Christ was not to be taken lightly. Having made my choice I would have to live with the consequences of my decision. Imagine my consternation as I later discovered the discrimination towards women in the Church, a clear contradiction of the biblical accounts of Jesus' interaction with women, and the role of women in the early Church. What was taking place here? Had I joined an 'all white' misogynist sect?

The years have been kind to me. I have learnt much and experienced first-hand how the contours of sexism, racism and colonialism can and have 'coloured' people's perceptions to such a degree that biblical passages and interpretation become distorted.

So, are there traditional women's ministries?

Depends on where you are from

African and African-American women

In West Africa women were accepted as religious leaders. Women held roles as priestesses and cult leaders, in addition to the responsibilities of being daughters, wives and mothers influencing and affecting the community life. The significance of the levels of influence exerted by these women is not to be underestimated:

> The importance of West African women to production and markets was reflected in the religious life, and the religious life exalted the roles of women in a way that Europeans, particularly the English, would find unthinkable.[6]

African societies should therefore not be interpreted through Eurocentric traditions or social constructs.

> The promulgation of Western patrilineal and patriarchal ideologies by missionaries as well as the introduction of colonial education concretized the subordination of women by imposing replicated Western patterns of sexism.[7]

The arrival of colonialism inevitably altered the religious life of the Africans, including the role of women, through the forced entry into slavery and the patriarchal racist values of the white slave owners. Consequently, the religiosity which emerged later from among American-born African women was tinged by the influence of colonial powers, although the strength of the African religions remained.

When examining the contribution of African women to the Church, attention must be given to the context from which they have emerged and recognition must be ascribed to the significant roles and responsibilities they carried within their indigenous contexts. The colonizers, however, ignored the spirituality of the African people. However, for Africans the spiritual realm was not to be divided or compartmentalized from the rest of life. Mbiti comments:

> there is no formal distinction between the sacred and the secular, between the religious and the non-religious, between the spiritual and the material areas of life. Wherever the African is, there is his religion: he carries it to the fields where he is sowing seeds or harvesting a new crop; he takes it with him to the beer party or to attend a funeral ceremony . . .[8]

Within African religions many representations existed of the divine, perceived through the symbolic forms of animals, mountains and other aspects of nature. Worship involved embracing ancestral spirits and tribal members. The use of the oral tradition was effectively applied in connecting Africans to a Supreme Being. Life with all its permutations was to be celebrated and enjoyed with verve and vigour. Within this context women were included and were fully participant in a multiplicity of roles such as priest, diviner, healer, prophet and sage. In many tribes women were as prominent as their male counterparts in conducting the religious affairs of the community.[9]

ARE THERE TRADITIONAL WOMEN'S MINISTRIES?

At the beginning of the eighteenth century, during the course of the Great Awakening, the newly formed missionary societies sent missionaries to the colonies for the specific purpose of preaching Christianity to the slaves. Slave owners permitted missionaries to preach to the slaves, particularly on the subject of personal salvation and guilt. The intention of the slave owners was to instil fear and docility into the slaves. However, the prayer meetings, the sermons, the songs and the spirituals provided hope and refuge to the enslaved men and women. The slaves captured the story of Moses' exodus from slavery, they heard about Jesus, the advocate for the poor and downcast. The slaves initiated countercultural approaches to the Bible.[10] Townsend Gilkes comments:

> Whatever the Euro-American religious forms appropriated by the slaves, the content of these forms was not appropriated without extensive critical reflection on the source – their oppressors.[11]

For example, the call for Moses to 'go and tell old Pharaoh, to let my people go' would have identified Pharaoh as the slave master, and Moses as the freedom fighter. Similarly, ideas about women's subordination were rejected and African constructs of a woman's place in the religious life of the community were embraced.

> As slaves, Africans arrived with a religious perspective that did not exclude women from [cult] service. Indeed, African religious systems, regardless of how patriarchal they were, exalted both the male and the female in their various collective expressions of the holy (cult). There was a tradition of religious independence as well as leadership among African women.[12]

During the slave era, networks of mutual support developed among slave women, within which religious life was expressed. The biographies of slave women and missionary accounts identify references to women leading, preaching and directing worship.

Davis, Dill and White[13] recognize that slavery and the countercultural community of slaves produced a distinctive and oppositional model of womanhood which exuded a spirit of independence, strength and determination, insisting on the right to sexual equality, unlike the female role model determined by Euro-American patriarchy. This model reflected a culture of independence, tenacity, insistence on sexual equality and strength. Remarkably: 'Black women emerged as worship leaders, preachers, catechizers, exhorters, prayer warriors, singers, teachers, and story tellers – all authoritative agents of the black religious tradition.'[14]

In the nineteenth century, a few white preachers from the northern states, while committed to sharing the gospel of Jesus Christ, began expressing commitment to the abolition of slavery. Black men such as Frederick Douglass (1817–95) and W. E. B. Dubois (1868–1963) were also involved in the abolition movement, speaking out against the injustices against the black community. Similarly, black women were also active participants in both women's rights and the movement for the abolition of slavery. Among these some of the more popularly known include Maria W. Stewart (1803–79), Harriet Tubman (1823–1913) and Sojourner Truth (1797–1883). Stewart attended the Boston African Baptist Church. As an orator she spoke strongly on the subject of slavery, calling for its abolition by violent means if necessary. Harriet Tubman came to be known as 'Black Moses', because of the nineteen trips she made to the South leading over three hundred slaves to freedom, between 1850 and 1857. She accomplished this mission via what eventually became known as the 'Underground Railroad', which comprised a series of routes and safe houses between the slave-owning South and Canada. Sojourner Truth was born as a slave in New York and later became a member of the African Methodist Zion Church. She was known for her personal struggle for freedom from slavery and her advocacy of women's rights. She did much to raise the awareness of the struggles facing black women in the areas of race and identity.[15] Her calling is noteworthy: her name changed from Isabella Baumfree when on a road God called her to *sojourn* over the land and (because she asked for a last name), to preach the truth regarding slavery.[16]

> Though she never learned to read or write, Sojourner Truth became a legendary figure in the annals of American feminism, an icon for contemporary feminists, and the link for black women to their activist foremothers.[17]

> Truth counters the idea that so-called 'traditional' female roles apply to all women. Her speech famously entitled 'Ar'n't I a woman?' clearly elucidates how colour and status determine the expectations surrounding female roles. Speaking with a combined Dutch and Southern American accent she declared:

> Nobody eber helps me into carriages, or ober mud puddles, or gibs ma any best place! And a'n't I a woman? Look at my arm! I have ploughed, and planted, and gathered into barns, and no man could head me! And a'n't I a woman? I have borne thirteen chiler, and seen 'em mos' all sold off to slavery, and when I cried out with my mother's grief, none but Jesus heard me! And a'n't I a woman? ... Den dat little man in black dar, he say women can't have as much rights as men, 'cause Christ wan't a woman! Whar did your Christ come from? Whar did your Christ come from? From God and a woman! Man had nothin' to do wid Him![18]

> Once abolished, slavery was simply replaced by other forms of exploitation for African-American women. Women's 'traditional' roles

continued as they worked in the fields and as domestic servants, abused by white masters and mistresses, exploited and poorly paid. Townes recognizes that the black women began to embrace a spirituality in which they uniquely defined themselves, that stood in contrast to the position of most white women.[19] The image of 'true womanhood' held by society perceived white women as weak, delicate, deferential towards their husbands and easily impressionable. By contrast for black women, this concept was alien. So instead, as women embraced the person and message of Jesus, they defined and recognized themselves as 'ministers' within their homes, and as evangelists and prophets serving in the wider community. Townes observes:

> This was possible through their intense evangelical spiritual drive to live a higher and better life and their concern to shape families and a society that reflected Christian morals and precepts. Black women took the images of Phoebe, Priscilla and Mary as co-workers with Paul and translated them into their own work. Their stress was on their ultimate allegiance to God and not to men.[20]

From as early as 1830, black women speakers challenged and overruled the biblical arguments demanding silence among women as public speakers. Cheryl Townsend Gilkes quotes Paula Giddings to the effect that:

> 'the moral urgency of their being black and female . . . suffused black women with a tenacious feminism', and, further, that black women, 'bypassed the barrier of religious thought that circumscribed even radical white activists until the late 1830's.'[21]

One noteworthy orator, Maria W. Stewart, insisted on exercising her right to speak publicly:

> What if I am a woman? . . . Did (God) not raise up Deborah to be a mother and a judge in Israel? Did not Queen Esther save the lives of the Jews? And Mary Magdalene first declare the resurrection of Christ from the dead?[22]

Stewart further rejected what she considered to be an abuse of the Pauline scriptures. Instead, like many others before her, Stewart gave prominence to the words and actions of Jesus, which were used to counter the biblical arguments proposed. In addition, Stewart strengthened her appeal by turning to the examples of women from other world religions who served as cult leaders and even deities.[23]

Such black women did not permit western notions of womanhood to stifle notions of self-belief or activity. Many white western women were enslaved by the cult of 'true womanhood'. They were deprived of freedom in different ways to their black female counterparts, who were presented in the public eye as 'brood cows' and 'work oxen'[24] of the world, while they (white women) were being presented as weak, fragile and helpless.

Subsequently, African-American women have a long legacy of active involvement and participation in their churches. However, the combined influence of Eurocentric church structures, often imposed by those who brought the gospel to the plantation and urban areas, has led to a paradox of the under-representation of women in the ordained ministry within some black churches. While the role of 'ordained' preacher and pastor is considered the domain of the black male in some black churches strongly influenced by colonial paradigms, this has not been the case in others. However, the voices and stories of black women have been formidable, and as Gilkes comments:

> The religious experience of black women, in spite of their strong commitment to their churches, has offered a persistent challenge to the European model of church order and to the technologies and biblical interpretations which defend oppression and exploitation. In the process of maintaining that challenge, black church women have asserted their spiritual independence and have explored alternative models of power and authority.[25]

So, are there traditional women's ministries?

Depends on what you look for

As we have already seen, context and community determine even what we consider worthy of note in the Bible. Earlier, I declared my credentials as a Christian British Asian woman, and as I consider the question of traditional 'women's ministries' from a biblical perspective, once again I see diversity of expression.

Biblical evidence: Jesus' response

The Bible was composed in the East, within the context of patriarchal cultures. The woman's role was confined to the spheres of the home, to childbearing and rearing and serving the needs of the extended family. Marriages were arranged and dowries were exchanged. Women assumed subservient roles, while attending to the wishes of the father, the husband or the male of the household.

The Gospel accounts, however, describe Jesus' counter-cultural response and behaviour within the public and private arenas of his time:

> Now as they went on their way, he entered a certain village, where a woman named Martha welcomed him into her home. She had a sister

ARE THERE TRADITIONAL WOMEN'S MINISTRIES?

named Mary, who sat at the Lord's feet and listened to what he was saying. But Martha was distracted by her many tasks; so she came to him and asked, 'Lord, do you not care that my sister has left me to do all the work by myself? Tell her then to help me.' But the Lord answered her, 'Martha, Martha, you are worried and distracted by many things; there is need of only one thing. Mary has chosen the better part, which will not be taken away from her.'[26]

The interplay of dialogue between Jesus and the two sisters, Mary and Martha, reflects a radical attitude and behaviour which was contrary to the norms and expectations of the day. In the biblical text, we read that Martha is distracted by the concerns of serving and meeting the needs of her guests. Meanwhile, Mary sits at the feet of Jesus, in the attitude and disposition of the disciple. Such a posture was normally reserved for male followers of a rabbi. The Gospels uniformly depict Jesus' willingness to associate with women, even to the 'radical' extent of including them among the group who supported his mission. On his journeys, Jesus displays acceptance and encouragement towards women to assume roles and responsibilities which were contrary to the expectations of the day: 'Mary has chosen what is better.'[27] Accepting such a 'radical' departure from societal tradition poses few questions to the culturally Sikh convert. Indeed, Jesus' behaviour makes perfect sense! That women should be elevated from the confines of the kitchen to serve at the feet of the Master is consistent with my perception of Jesus' actions and teaching and his promotion of women to the status of disciple (in other words equal to men).

Passages often used as evidence in debate, to limit and prohibit women from serving within the Church in a public capacity (namely, preaching, praying, reading Scripture), are generally based on contentious passages such as 1 Corinthians 14.33–5 and 1 Timothy 2.8–15. The various contours of the debate are familiar and have been touched upon elsewhere.

Clearly, women did serve in a multiplicity of ministries as evidenced in the biblical text. Women served as prophets in the Old Testament, namely Miriam, Deborah and Huldah, and in the New Testament we have the examples of Philip's four daughters and Anna. These prophets exercised their roles with conviction and an expectation that the messages given would be received and heard by the community. Women also served as house church leaders. In Romans 16, Paul appreciatively acknowledges a large number of women who exercised the valuable gift of hospitality. Luke, the author of the Acts of the Apostles, refers to women such as the Gentile convert Lydia. She provides her home as a venue for a house church in Philippi. Priscilla (Prisca) is another example who together with her husband Aquila was a co-worker with Paul (Rom. 16.3). Priscilla was also renowned for her gift of teaching.[28]

While many in Eurocentric traditions contend that God does not endorse women to exercise leadership, Asian,[29] and particularly culturally Sikh women, would look to the many 'obvious' examples of women who were approved by God in the Bible. Miriam's leadership gift is exercised as she performs the prophetic dance for the women (Exod. 2.1–10; 15.20), with a further endorsement in Micah 6.4. In Judges 4.4, Deborah is raised as a leader, a prophet and judge over her commander Barak and the people of Israel. In Romans 16.2 Paul commends Phoebe as a leader, a fellow worker and a deacon (servant) to be received and helped by the Roman believers.[30] The biblical evidence is extensive in promoting and endorsing the ministry of women even within the patriarchal culture of the East.

Women in the early Church

Historical evidence exists to indicate that women taught, preached, led and exercised spiritual gifts in the Christian communities of the first century and beyond. For example, the gift of pastor was essential in the early Church. In a largely segregated community, propriety required that women made home visits to fellow women. As pastors, women attended to the sick, prepared people for baptism, encouraged and taught others. Within the first three centuries of the Church, women elders existed until the role was disbanded by the Council of Laodicea in 363 AD.[31]

A considered reading of the New Testament reveals the liberative nature of the message expressed through the person and mission of Jesus. Women's lives were transformed in the first century AD. They were free to serve God as full participating members within the local church. Such women worked alongside men together with people who previously would have been considered outcasts and marginalized. With such a plethora of evidence supporting women's ministries, it is frustrating to witness the continued oppositional behaviour exhibited by men and women alike, against those women who pursue the call of God on their lives.

Many recognize a disparity between how Jesus related to the women in the Gospels and how women are treated within the Church today. Carr and other feminists advocate the application of a hermeneutic of suspicion, concluding that a misinterpretation has occurred at the core of Christianity regarding the roles of women within the Church. She insists that the Gospels portray Jesus as one who gathered around himself a community of men and women, from diverse backgrounds and experiences, to work together in mission.

Western paradigms have shaped the western Church and consequently western expectations of women's roles. Later incursions have predetermined what we now consider to be traditional women's ministries, yet these owe more to the public/private divides of Roman imperial culture. Clifford concludes:

> the patriarchal patterns of civil society overcame the discipleship of equals that Jesus had instituted. The spirits were tested and cognitive dissonance emerged between Jesus' behavior and gender roles defined by society. The churches chose to conform to the status quo as it became Romanized. This is particularly true after the Roman emperor Constantine converted to Christianity early in the fourth century and the church then underwent a transformation from a persecuted sect to a state religion ... With the shift to state religion ... the church began to model itself on Imperial Roman authority with its hierarchy, a paradigm adopted by the church along with the subordination of women.[32]

Hunt further comments on the different expressions used to convey and punctuate the inequality which existed between men and women within the Church in the West:

> Everything from church architecture to the structures of decision-making, from the designs of the bishops' headgear to papal authority, was construed in a top-down way with virtually no horizontal lines. Implicit in this culture and often explicit in its teachings, was the radical inequality of men and women, of clergy and lay people.[33]

Conclusion

Throughout the course of this chapter, I have considered the question, 'Are there traditional women's ministries?' I have responded in three different trajectories. It will depend on who you are. And I have declared that my view is influenced by my British Indian culturally Sikh Christian roots. I have established that the response to this question will also depend on where you come from and I have demonstrated, through using the rubric of African and African-American women's paradigms, that geography and experience influence the outcomes of what are considered to be 'traditional' women's ministries. I have also approached the question by reflecting on some biblical themes and early church history revealing that what one sees in these areas is also influenced by the contours of a person's race, culture, gender and class. Wherever western colonial paradigms persist, Eurocentric conventions regarding the cult of true womanhood are pervasive. Such paradigms determine what it means to be acceptably female and what it means to be in an acceptable ministry. However, where other cultural paradigms have predominated, traditional women's ministries have been very differently configured.

Notes

1. Anne M. Clifford, *Introducing Feminist Theology* (Maryknoll, New York: Orbis Books, 2004), p. 82.
2. From *Sri Guru Granth Sahib Ji*.
3. The 'five Ks' were adopted and applied by both men and women: Kesh (uncut hair), Kara (steel bangle), Kanga (comb), Kacch (shorts), Kirpan (sword). Guru Gobind Singh sanctioned women to wear the kirpan/sword, clearly perceiving women as activists engaging with the world as fearless warriors, which many did later become. After baptism, all male Sikhs were given the designation of the surname 'Singh' meaning lion, and all female Sikhs were given the surname 'Kaur' meaning princess, to further designate equality particularly in challenging the caste system. The surname remains unchanged for Sikh women, even when they marry, thereby giving women an identity in their own right.
4. http://en.wikipedia.org/wiki/Women_in_Sikhism
5. http://www.sikhs.org/women_h.htm
6. Cheryl Townsend Gilkes, *If It Wasn't for the Women: Black Women's Experience and Womanist Culture in Church and Community* (Maryknoll, NY: Orbis Books, 2001), p. 95.
7. Pamela J. Olubunmi Smith, 'Feminism in Cross-Cultural Perspective: Women in Africa', *Transformation: An International Dialogue on Evangelical Social Ethics* 6.2 (1989), p. 13.
8. John S. Mbiti, *African Religions and Philosophy* (Oxford: Heinemann, 1989), p. 2.
9. Clifford, *Introducing Feminist Theology*, p. 156.
10. Clifford, *Introducing Feminist Theology*, p. 156.
11. Gilkes, *If It Wasn't for the Women*, p. 97.
12. Gilkes, *If It Wasn't for the Women*, p. 97.
13. Gilkes, *If It Wasn't for the Women*, p. 100. Angela Davis, Bonnie Thornton Dill and Deborah Gray White all recognize the model of womanhood which emerges out of an oppositional culture. (Further reading: Angela Davis, *Women, Race and Class* (New York: Random House, 1981); Bonnie Thornton Dill, 'The Dialectics of Black Womanhood: Toward a New Model of American Femininity', *Sign: Journal of Women in Culture and Society* 4 (Spring 1979), pp. 543–55; Deborah Gray White, *Ar'n't I a Woman? Female Slaves in the Plantation South* (New York: Norton, 1985), p. 227.
14. Gilkes, *If It Wasn't for the Women*, p. 102.
15. Clifford, *Introducing Feminist Theology*, p. 157.
16. Wade Hudson and Valerie Wilson Wesley (eds), *The Afro-Bets Book of Black Heroes From A–Z: An Introduction to Important Black Achievers for Young Readers* (Orange, NJ: Just Us Books, 1988), p. 40.
17. Beverly Guy-Sheftall (ed.), *Words of Fire: An Anthology of African-American Thought* (New York: The New Press, 1995), p. 35.

ARE THERE TRADITIONAL WOMEN'S MINISTRIES?

18. Sojourner Truth, 'Woman's Rights', in Guy-Sheftall, *Words of Fire*, p. 36.

19. Emily M. Townes, 'Black Women From Slavery to Womanist Liberation', in *In Our Own Voices: Four Centuries of American Women's Religious Writing*, ed. Rosemary Radford Ruether and Rosemary Skinner Keller (San Francisco: HarperCollins, 1995), p. 159 in Clifford, *Introducing Feminist Theology*, p. 82.

20. Townes, 'Black Women From Slavery to Womanist Liberation', in Clifford, *Introducing Feminist Theology*, p. 88.

21. Paula Giddings, *When and Where I Enter: The Impact of Black Women on Race and Sex in America*, (New York: William Morrow, 1984), p. 52, in Gilkes, *If It Wasn't for the Women*, p. 109.

22. Giddings, *When and Where I Enter*, p. 52 in Gilkes, *If It Wasn't for the Women*, p. 110.

23. Giddings, *When and Where I Enter*, p. 53 in Gilkes, *If It Wasn't for the Women*, p. 110.

24. Clifford, *Introducing Feminist Theology*, p. 159.

25. Gilkes, *If It Wasn't for the Women*, p. 117.

26. Luke 10.38–42.

27. Luke 10.42.

28. Faith and Roger Forster, 'Women's Spiritual Gifts in the Church', in Kathy Keay (ed.), *Men, Women and God* (Basingstoke: Marshall Pickering, 1987), p. 51.

29. The term 'Asian' is used to describe people from Asia or a region of Asia. However, the use of the term varies according to each country. I have chosen to combine the use of the term 'Asian' as defined within the US census (predominantly people of East Asia or Southeast Asian – more specifically people with an ancestry that is Malaysian, Indonesian, Japanese, Korean, Filipino, Taiwanese, Chinese, Asian-Indian, Thai, Laotian, Pakistani, Vietnamese) and as defined within the UK context (predominantly people of South Asian origin, namely Indians, Bangladeshis, Pakistanis, Sri Lankans). http://en.wikipedia.org/wiki/Asian

30. Faith and Roger Forster, 'Women's Spiritual Gifts in the Church', pp. 54f.

31. Faith and Roger Forster, 'Women's Spiritual Gifts in the Church', p. 56.

32. Clifford, *Introducing Feminist Theology*, p. 135.

33. Mary Hunt, 'We Women are Church: Roman Catholic Women Shaping Ministries and Theologies', in *The Non-Ordination of Women and the Politics of Power*, ed. Elisabeth Schüssler Fiorenza and Hermann Häring (London: SCM Press), p. 104, in Clifford, *Introducing Feminist Theology*, p. 135.

5. Women's Leadership in the Church and Feminist Theology

JANET WOOTTON

Given the long history of women's leadership in the Christian faith in its many forms, it is quite extraordinary that the tradition is subject to such frequent bouts of amnesia. Not only the tradition of women's leadership, but the theologies and liturgies that develop when women exercise leadership alone or alongside men suffer from this.

Each generation feels like pioneers. Perhaps until the present generation (although that may simply be the foreshortening of a current perspective, where hindsight may tell a different story), we have no sense of stepping into a long line of foremothers, taking our place as the inheritors of ways of being, ways of thinking, that are passed on to us, to be changed and tuned and honed and handed on into the future. This is not only true in the Church. In music, the visual arts, the sciences, business, in almost every sphere of life, the unbroken line consists of men. Women are occasional interlopers, and their contribution, no matter how great, is made by extraordinary individuals, who buy into male categories, attitudes and methods. Where social change has made it possible for a generation to make a greater impact, succeeding generations have rolled over their achievements with a great cloak of silence.

Part of the work of feminist theology over the last forty years has been to piece the story together, and reclaim the long, though broken, tradition of women's religious leadership in all its diversity, and to see what patterns of praxis, theology and action might come out of it as it emerges. The next steps have been to build on the tradition, to develop a kaleidoscope of new language, concepts, ways of speaking, acting and being, and step out into our new variegated world.

Much of the feminist theology during this period, and before, has been conducted in the context of a white, middle-class Christian tradition. Feminist theology has been justly critiqued and challenged from non-western perspectives by womanism, mujerista theology and others largely within the Christian tradition. There has also been some tentative reaching out to feminists in other patriarchal religions. A wider context has been the rediscovery of non-patriarchal and pre-patriarchal cultures, for example in the goddess movement, and a still wider context, that of human rights, social concerns and environmental issues. So feminist theology has found its place among a great variety of liberation theologies and creation-centred theologies, and wider disciplines.

But it still feels precarious. Who is to say that our optimism, insofar as we feel it, is not as evanescent as that of the 1920s in the heady days following the first ordinations and women's suffrage, or the seventeenth century when radical Protestant groups were inspired by women preachers and house church leaders, or, for that matter, the days when Jesus broke the barriers and talked theology with a Samaritan woman, and gave the evangel of his resurrection to the woman he loved, to carry into the world? Who is to say that the next generation will not be apathetic, or hostile, or that the so-called 'war on terror' will not bring about a suffocating conformity or backlash, and our story will not be forgotten again, with all its buzz and excitement and scholarship and inspiration, to be painstakingly and frustratingly recovered in another thirty or forty years' time?

This chapter will look at the work of feminist theology in recovering the story or stories of women's leadership, theologically, rather than historically, since that is the task of another chapter. It will go on to explore paradigms of church and leadership, issues of language, thought and action, and, finally, to see where the relatively conservative story of women's leadership in the Free Churches interacts with developments in feminist theology and in ways of being Church in the twenty-first century.

Uncovering the tradition

Elisabeth Schüssler Fiorenza writes that feminist theologians and scholars in religion

> must resist the temptation to be motherless daughters who are proud to be 'firsts' among wo/men and to have sprung from the heads of the fathers. To prove our intellectual brilliance and religious faithfulness by demonstrating our 'fit' with malestream theories and theologies means to disqualify other feminist work, deprives us of our roots, and diminishes our power for change.[1]

Being a pioneer is a temptation. It carries with it the pride of being among the first, the kudos of having suffered and prevailed in a male-dominated world, and the excitement of a clean slate, a new start. To search for and celebrate our roots is harder, since they both nourish and confine us. We are not rootless, but earthed in our mothers' strong stock. One of the consequences of this discovery is to honour our femaleness. We struggle from womb as well as springing from head. The trick that we have so often played on ourselves is that we start by despising our mothers, our sisters, womankind in general and (though we try to be free of it) the female in ourselves. Our own struggle to be heard contributes to the silencing of women.

This is not new. The institutions of the Church have again and again put women 'back in their place' following periods of greater freedom. In fact, the pattern can be discerned in the patriarchal religion of the Hebrew Scriptures, in the suppression of female deity and women's stories, and in the way the Epistles of the early Church tended to institutionalize the place of women, turning their backs on the astonishing freedom with which Jesus encountered women as well as men. These points are already argued strongly by writers of the nineteenth and early twentieth centuries, including Maude Royden in *The Church and Woman*[2] and Catherine Booth in her pamphlet, *Female Ministry; or, Woman's Right to Preach the Gospel*.[3]

This pattern has been repeated through the two millennia of the Christian story, but, notably for our purposes, particularly in the case of the women in the Free Churches. Maude Royden writes, 'What they [women] thought and felt and suffered is chronicled only – if at all – in the writings of satirists, moralists, or of a rare occasional defender.'[4] A couple of generations earlier, Zechariah Taft was forced to publish his reply to Dr Knight's 'Strictures on Women Preaching' as a tract. Dr Knight's article had appeared in the *Methodist Magazine*, which declined to publish Taft's response.[5] Taft later published *Biographical Sketches of the Lives and Public Ministries of Various Holy Women* in two volumes, in an explicit attempt to overcome the failure of other biographers to include women preachers and leaders, 'as though they had never existed; or if any account of their exemplary piety is preserved, their public labours are either suppressed, or passed over in silence'.[6]

A preliminary task of feminist theology, then, has been simply to rediscover and retell these stories, throughout the whole length of the record. So we have celebrated our foremothers in scholarship, in liturgy and in song, lifting them from the shadows cast over them by more prominent male characters, by anonymity in the text, or even by the acrimony of centuries of vilification. Eve becomes our first mother, not the prototype of weak, sinful woman. As she reclaims her name, which means 'Life', her consort, Adam, is reduced to normal size. 'Adam', which means 'Earthling', is no more prototype of Man than Eve is of Woman. The words for 'man' and 'woman' are found hiding later in Genesis 2.23. There is no 'man' until there is 'woman'. Long years of tradition have conflated 'Adam' with 'Man' and 'Eve' with 'Woman', with weakness, temptation and sin.

We have wrestled with the multiple oppression of Hagar (Gen. 16), as a woman, a slave and a foreigner, oppressed by Sarah, who in other circumstances is herself a subject to be reclaimed from the shadow of her husband and son. Women are both oppressors and oppressed and we participate in many layers of victimization. Here again we hear the challenge of black and Asian theology – Hagar challenges not only Abraham but Sarah too.

Jesus drew women as well as men into his circle of disciples. Feminist theology has looked beyond the twelve chosen men, to revel in the stories of the women who encountered Jesus: women whose ritual uncleanness, symbolic sinfulness (the adulteress and prostitute were powerful biblical symbols of apostasy, and condemned under the familiar double standard which exonerated the men involved), subservient positions, and ethnicity were as breathtakingly irrelevant as their gender, as Jesus welcomed them into the new humanity as co-heirs to the subversive reign of God.[7]

The narrative task moves beyond Scripture, to light upon women in the earliest churches, through the medium of the Gnostic texts, for example, and women who formed communities in the European Middle Ages, escaping from the norms of marriage and motherhood to some form of independent living. From the traditions which led to the Free Churches in Britain come such splendours as the Quaker women's writing collected by Mary Garman and others in *Hidden in Plain Sight*.[8] The foreword by Rosemary Radford Ruether describes this as 'the emergence, not only of the first feminists, but also of the first feminist theology', and goes on to say that, 'It was in seventeenth-century England that there was enough disruption of the systems of hegemonic cultural control by the dominant society that sub-cultures could emerge, such as the Society of Friends, that could not only organize dissenting movements, but also produce and preserve their writings for the future.'[9]

Often, women's concerns found expression in great crusades such as temperance, the campaign against slavery, and social reform to counter the evils they saw in society. A wonderful book of mini-biographies of women ministers in the 1920s demonstrates the breadth of their interests. Revd Winifred Kiek was actively involved in the National Council of Women, the Women's Non-Party Association and the Women's Christian Temperance Union in Australia; Revd Grace Mewhort worked among the very poor in Edinburgh and tried to ameliorate social conditions: 'To this end she allied herself with Women's Suffrage and the Trade Union and Labour Movements'; Revd Ada Tonkin worked hard for the establishment of a 'Women's Division' in the local police force, and took charge of the new Division once it was formed in 1929. Maude Royden wrote a tremendously stirring preface to the book, in which she proclaims that 'women are asking now, not for improvement of status, but for absolute equality'.[10]

In the USA, Judith L. Weidman roots black women's preaching in the mid-week women's prayer service: 'It was here that one recognized the same rhythmic, tonal quality of the preacher . . . Sometimes the women were illiterate, but they were wise and their witness was sure . . . A typical, traditional prayer meeting could be the setting for female "preaching".' [11] She comments on morning prayer meetings in Washington DC led by Mrs Nannie Burroughs, a Baptist woman educator: 'I remember hearing the feet of many women who responded to her powerful messages by walking to the early morning prayer meetings in protest of the treatment of blacks and women in the capital of our country.'[12]

In accounts such as these, what is being uncovered is not simply women's stories, but early feminism, in that women have reflected on their stories, and critiqued and challenged the norms of their cultures. Rosemary Radford Ruether pinpoints the cyclic nature of this, in that she recognizes specific social conditions that must prevail. The tendency of religious institutions to erase women from the narrative is part of a wider social phenomenon. During times of relative freedom, perhaps seen by some as relative chaos, women's voices emerge, only to be re-submerged when society becomes more controlled and controlling.

Women's movements and the Church

What is evident is that the freedom of women to operate within the Church is bound up with wider societal attitudes and freedoms. Mark Chaves documents the relationship between heightened interest in women's leadership in the churches and women's movements in society at large.[13] I am avoiding using the term 'secular' at this point to describe what may be perceived as such by the churches, though it creates an unhelpful dualism between the Churches and the wider social milieu.

Chaves gives figures for the USA, which show how churches have responded to social changes. There were two types of change. First, churches' official policy changed. During first-wave feminism, Congregational, Baptist and Unitarian churches began to accept that women could be ordained, though, in fact, few were (though more than we might think, as evidenced by the short biographies mentioned above). Chaves notes that 'the pioneering place that these denominations occupy in the story of women's ordination is attributable more to their decentralized organizational structure than to any broad progressive spirit permeating the denomination'.[14] Response to the second wave was stronger: 'Indeed, more denominations began to ordain women during the 1970s than during any other decade in the past 140 years. No fewer than seven of the largest denominations in the United States began to ordain women during the 1970s.'[15] The pattern is similar in England and Wales, except that the discussion in the Church of England overshadowed the changes that might have otherwise been possible and prominent in the 1970s. In that decade, the United Reformed Church was formed from denominations that had had a policy of ordaining women for some decades, and the Methodist Church changed its policy so that women could be ordained as presbyters. This meant that the three largest Free Churches had a policy and practice of ordaining women.

On the other hand, decisions of churches against leadership by, or ordination of, women also cluster around these two periods of social change. Chaves suggests that this is because the churches on both sides of the argument have *perceived* the issue as secular, the pressure for change coming from outside the Church, and have responded in different ways. Where the decision was to ordain women, the focus of the argument moved from charismatic calling to human rights. No longer was this a matter of a few extraordinarily gifted women, as in early Methodism, for example, but rather an engagement with the role and place of women in the human race. Chaves argues that: 'a denomination's formal policy permitting female clergy should be understood in large part as a symbolic marker signalling orientation to, support of, and co-operation with a broader norm for gender equality. Similarly, a denomination's formal policy against female clergy should be understood as a symbol of resistance to this norm of formal gender equality.'[16]

The exception to this was the churches most influenced by the Holiness Movement in Britain and the USA. Chaves agrees with writers such as Susan Kwilecki that here the focus is not on the equality of women as a human right, but rather on a recognition of charismatic gifting. Kwilecki interviewed 53 Pentecostal clergywomen in the USA, both black and white, many of whom were involved in sacrificial forms of leadership in challenging circumstances. Their rationale for being in leadership was the sense of a special and individual call by God, and the gifting of the Holy Spirit.[17] This very specifically did not challenge general patriarchal assumptions, such as, 'ideas that wives should obey husbands; that a woman's first obligations are her husband and children; that men are more suited than women for leadership in society; that God is more masculine than feminine; and that in the church, women should not exercise authority over men'.[18]

This was true, during first-wave feminism, of the Salvation Army, which was founded by a husband and wife team and famously had full equality between women and men built in to its foundation documents. Knowing this, I can remember being puzzled to learn that, until recently, married female officers could not outrank their husbands, and that a wife took on the rank of her husband, without having to undertake the necessary training and qualifications, though the reverse was not true. This has now been swept away, with each officer holding rank in his or her own right, but it persisted well into the twentieth century.

Despite the openness of every rank to both sexes, and the tremendous work done in leadership by women, the Salvation Army actually had a very complex relationship with the feminism of the nineteenth and twentieth centuries. The complexity lies in the definition of womanhood, not just as a role but existentially within society. The urbanization and industrialization of the nineteenth century brought about a dichotomy between the public and private spheres. The public sphere, which was always masculine, moved further and further from the home, both in its location and in its expectations. Industrial urban life was brutal at every level of society, and the home, the female private sphere, took on the characteristics of gentleness, even innocence, which made it a haven from the 'world'. Where possible, women were withdrawn into the home, and, by a pernicious interweaving of domestic and assumed female attributes, became the bearers of gentleness and innocence for society at large – 'the angel in the house'. Of course, this was not the case for the majority of women, who still had to work in factories, down mines and on the streets. Thus the ideal of the angel in the house was doubly pernicious. It enslaved those who aspired to it, and excluded those for whom it was an impossible dream.

Further, this moral injunction on women arose out of a particular theology of sin and self-sacrifice, which was itself disempowering. Andrew Mark Eason, in a study on gender and equality in the early Salvation Army, writes of this complex situation, 'The equation of sin with selfishness in Salvationist circles was prone to affect women adversely, because this theological construct failed to account for the types of vices that they were likely to experience in their lives . . . Self-assertion and self-confidence were the qualities that Salvationist women needed to cultivate if they were to enter and remain within the public arena.'[19] Therefore women tended to operate in highly sacrificial areas of work (cellar, garret and gutter work) or with women and children, while men tended to take prominent positions of leadership.

A great cry of frustration sometimes arises from this double bind for women. I find it heartbreaking to read the words of Elizabeth Hurrel, an early Methodist preacher, recorded in Zechariah Taft's biography: 'I am going to die . . . I am entering the eternal world, but all is dark before me: neither sun, moon, nor stars appear. O that I had my time to live again. I would not bury my talent as I have done.'[20] I share the sentiment of Mrs C. R. Batten in her 1955 presidential address to the National Free Church Women's Council, where she exclaims, 'There is nothing now in these days to prevent a woman from achieving her goal in the scholastic world, most professions are well open to her, and where she does brilliantly, but in the Churches the ordination of a woman, and the calling of a woman to a Church is rarely done . . . How dare we close this most vital door . . .? Why must the people, because of their personal feeling, keep closed this avenue of service to the Kingdom?'[21] I expressed it myself in my sermon at the service held at Westminster Abbey, under the auspices of Women in Theology, to launch the World Council of Churches Ecumenical Decade – Churches in Solidarity with Women: 'We've even taken the glorious message that thunders from the pages of scripture . . . and we have maimed and tortured and twisted it . . . and with the wreckage we have reassembled the barriers that Christ died to destroy. How dare we? How dare any human being stand before God and say "him you may choose, but her, God, you may not choose"?'[22]

Such denial of the equality of women, and therefore stifling of their calling and gifts, is immensely subtle and complex. The situation was further complicated in England and Wales by the overwhelmingly prominent position of the Church of England, and the non-established Anglican Church in Wales. These two members of the Anglican Communion ordained women deacons and women priests at different times, in a kind of counterpoint. As has been noted elsewhere, as far as the general population was concerned, a view exacerbated by the media, the question of women's ordination arose only in connection with priesthood in the Church of England. The first women to be ordained following the decision of the General Synod of 1992 were widely regarded as the first ordained women in the UK. On the other hand, the influx of women to the priesthood in the Church of England and the Church in Wales did increase the number of ordained women and women in leadership of churches in these countries dramatically. This was the point in England, which churches in the USA reached in the 1970s, when it became 'normal' to find a woman in charge of a church, or presiding at a wedding or funeral.

The time lag meant that a good deal of work had been done, based on the American situation, on the theology of women's leadership, and its impact on ecclesiology and other disciplines, while the churches in England and Wales were still in limbo, unable to move forwards because of the situation of the Church of England, and, so far as the Free Churches were concerned, still living in an age when women in ministry were unusual. Patricia Wilson-Kastner, an American Episcopal priest who visited England in 1981, comments with perspicacious humour on the situation at the time. She noted that people responded to her, as a woman priest, with some astonishment that she was 'normal': 'For them, an intense fear of the unknown "woman priest" clashed with any acceptance of me as a human being who is a priest.'[23] She recognized both the ignorance and the reality behind their fear. Their ignorance arose from not having experienced women in ministry, and from a distorted view of what had happened following the ordination of women in the Episcopal Church in the USA. The reality was ironically recognized and stated more clearly by the opponents of women's ordination, that, 'The change which feminism portends in the church is massive and radical.'[24]

The ecumenical situation was raised by some of her interlocutors as an objection to the change. Wilson-Kastner recognizes as does Jean Mayland in her contribution to this book, the Church of England's bias, in ecumenical vision, towards the Roman Catholic and Orthodox Churches. She says of the women working for ordination in the Church of England, 'These women keep the church honest about ecumenism, which must extend to Protestant Christianity as well as to Orthodox and Roman Catholic.'[25]

My own experience during those years, as an ordained minister, was that I was often regarded as a peculiarity – 'Oh, I didn't know you were allowed to do that . . .' Post-1992, people said, 'Oh you're one of these new women priests, are you?' After more than a decade of ministry, I think I found that more enraging than the former attitude, because it meant that women, whom I had supported and campaigned for, were complicit in the same silencing and denial of my ministry as had been experienced by women through time.

This means that the period of adjustment to women's ministry has been foreshortened in Britain, which in turn has given rise to something of a mismatch between the impact of women's leadership in the churches and the development of feminist theology. For instance, at the height of the campaign for ordination in the Church of England, a community of Christian women started to meet in London, known as the St Hilda Community. Not wishing to act illegally, the community, which was largely made up of Anglicans, invited Ann Peart, whose story appears in this volume, to preside at Communion. I also did this, but only once. Later, Suzanne Fageol, an Anglican who had been ordained in the USA, did courageously preside at 'illegal' Eucharists.

My own experience of doing this was a two-fold challenge. The community was already experimenting with alternative liturgies, and an alternative ecclesiology. It was an example of what Rosemary Radford Ruether was already calling 'Women-Church'.[26] The liturgy used words, actions and images in new and creative ways. Some of this is documented in Janet Morley's *Celebrating Women*.[27] I was coming from a church tradition which took for granted some things that were being claimed as new discoveries by the community: mainly, the ministry of women, and a view of the Church as a covenanted congregation which gave each member equal responsibility in ordering its life. I felt rather offended that these were being claimed as discoveries. On the other hand, I had never experienced inclusive language in worship, nor thought of God in

WOMEN'S LEADERSHIP AND FEMINIST THEOLOGY

the feminine gender, nor encountered liturgical actions which related to creative imagery. The first two burst on my mind like a new tide coming in, and I wrote my first hymn, 'Dear Mother God' based on the song of Moses in Deuteronomy 32 and the vision at the end of Isaiah 40. The last had no direct relation to my experience of worship, since congregational worship is deliberately stripped of most liturgical actions. I have come to that enriching experience much later. The discussion and development that was becoming mainstream in the USA was still experimental and marginal in Britain.

This was in the early 1980s. The vote to ordain women in the Church of England was still ten years away (though we did not know that at the time). But the restraining and liberating effect of waiting for the vote, which for all we knew might never come, was felt across the Free Churches by those to whom women's ministry mattered.

Challenging worshipping traditions

The St Hilda Community expressed its challenge to the patriarchal nature of the Church largely in worship. This was a major part of the wider enterprise of feminist theology in the Church. As we created new liturgies and wrote new words for worship, we retold our foremothers' stories, connected with the feminine divine and celebrated the wholeness of life. Encouraged by the World Council of Churches Ecumenical Decade – Churches in Solidarity with Women (1988–98), Women in Theology collaborated with the publisher Stainer & Bell to produce the hymnal *Reflecting Praise* at the mid-point of the decade in 1993.[28] In 1995, Hannah Ward and Jennifer Wild brought together liturgical resources around a variety of life-experiences in *Human Rites*,[29] and reflected on the process in their book, *Guard the Chaos*.[30]

While use of this kind of material can still cause a quite disproportionate outrage, it is becoming part of the fabric of worship in some situations. Recently, Uta Blohm conducted a survey of women ministers and rabbis[31] and found that it was often in pastoral or liturgical situations that the need for alternative or inclusive responses arose. She quotes a Methodist woman minister who had responded in situations where no existing liturgy existed: 'I've developed rituals for miscarriages, and a ritual that we've used also for a couple of women who were dying of cancer. We actually had transitional rituals really moving on and looking to the future. . . . I based that on something that I'd been doing with women who were going through the menopause . . .'[32] The interviewees discussed the relationship between their own gender and their responses. In some instances, they did feel that their own experience of childbirth, for example, made it possible for them to respond to women who had undergone miscarriage or still-birth. But in general, they felt part of wider changes in ecclesiology and liturgy in a more inclusive age, and they pointed to creative male pastors and liturgists who were doing the same kind of thing.

What emerges in this and other similar surveys is a serious and sincere search for truly inclusive theology in worship; not just inclusive language, 'brothers and sisters', but a deeper sense of what worship says about God and the world. One of Blohm's respondents speaks indignantly about *The Methodist Worship Book* published in 1999:[33]

> When the Methodist church was rewriting its prayer book we had some services sent out to try. The baptism service included the blessing of the water and it had the phrase 'through the waters of the womb in pain and in joy the child is delivered'. I just thought that was lovely and I talked to women I visited about how the baptism of the baby was one way of saying thank you to God for what they had come through and that this part of the liturgy honoured the role of women – that they did carry the baby and that they did bring it forth in pain. When the prayer book was published that piece had been omitted. It had just been wiped out by the complaints of the church; people didn't want this. They obliterated all references to women bar one, the word mother appears in one service in the book. They took out this lovely piece of the liturgy so I've put it back in my service and that's probably the only kind of forthright thing I've done in order to be able to say to women, 'This is a rite of passage: you've come through something difficult and painful and we'll acknowledge it in the service.'[34]

Letty Russell challenges liturgists to re-image the sacramental life of the Church in this kind of way. For example, traditional forms of infant baptism do not flow from an inclusive theology. The centrality of Trinitarian language emphasizes a masculine image of God. And the theology of original sin tends to demean the mystery of procreation and birth: 'The new life the baby receives as God's child conveys the message that the life of salvation comes through the males who administer and control the rite, not through the mother's gift of life.'[35] Russell also calls for a re-traditioning of Eucharistic liturgy, with a change in its focus on the sacrificial victim.

Here, again, the Free Church experience should have a distinct contribution to make, having already dissented from Catholic and Anglican liturgies.[36] In some traditions, the sacraments as liturgical acts have disappeared. Both the Salvation Army and the Society of Friends regard the births and deaths, the meals and feasts of ordinary life as sacramental, and see no reason to create separate rituals. The practice of believers' baptism in Baptist and some Pentecostal Churches uncouples the theology of dying to sin and rising in Christ to new life from the beginning of natural life in childbirth, though the language of both infant dedication and adult baptism still tend to exclusivity in language and theology, and the opportunity is not taken to celebrate birth-giving as a gift of God. And the practice of Congregationally ordered churches, among others, of taking communion seated in the pew, and eating and drinking in unison was introduced to make the link between communion and shared meals slightly less tenuous, though tiny glasses of de-alcoholized wine and miniature squares of white bread are scarcely even tokens of the feast!

What the variety of Free Church worship does is at least to loosen some of the chain links which bind liturgical tradition to patriarchal theology, and make it possible to re-image and re-tradition, though the opportunity has hardly been grasped in this context. Indeed, some of the stoutest resistance to freer forms of language and worship come from the Evangelical Free Churches.

Finding authentic language and practice in worship is no academic exercise, but takes place daily and weekly in real pastoral settings. Martha Long Ice, like Blohm, has conducted a survey of women clergy, and finds that,

> For the informants wrestling with the 'language question,' there are no exceptions to the rule that they are utterly serious about arriving at effective words for sharing their deepest and fullest experiences as women, in faith, with God. This is no frivolous pastime; nor is it, as language, their most important concern in ministry. It is painful for them to observe people judging the issue as a petty partisan pursuit or a merely administrative matter.[37]

The seriousness of the question is demonstrated for Ice by the fact of the struggle itself:

> It is when they address God ceremonially on behalf of the congregation that they and others are apt to feel most groping and linguistically bereft. The tortuous struggle for meaningful words to express the present full experience of God shows how nontrivial the issue is. If the whole of our language lacks fitting words for a major area of consciousness, something new, indeed, is happening and the words *will* come, but it may be a long time before today's tinkering settles into an unself-conscious vernacular for this problematic area of expression.
>
> Still, there remains a yearning for just the right terms to address and describe God in ways that are authentic for both women and men of faith.[38]

While women clergy live the struggle in churches where they meet the pastoral and liturgical challenges day by day, greater creativity is often possible outside the traditional church context. Serving women clergy may not, in fact, be best placed to create inclusive liturgies in their own congregations. Their pastoral concern for the congregation and, sometimes, insecurity in their role, makes it difficult to instigate change. Parachurch organizations such as Christian Survivors of Sexual Abuse, or worship at conferences, in homes or on special occasions, can give space for radical forms of worship and the re-imaging of ritual and symbol. The Iona Community[39] has led the way in exploring new ritual and language. I have also documented some small portion in the journal *Worship Live* over ten or more years of publication,[40] and described some of the theology of inclusive forms of worship in *Introducing a Practical Feminist Theology of Worship*.[41]

Exploration of new forms of worship is a participation in the heart of feminist theology for practising Christians. If I believe that I am made in the image of God, it must be possible to sing praise to God in the feminine gender. And we have sung long enough about Abraham and Moses, Peter and Andrew, without mentioning Sarah or Miriam or the women who walked with Jesus. Neither can gender-inclusive language divorce itself from other inclusivities, or from the vision of a new world where none is repressed and all can thrive. Challenging worship must eventually challenge the structures of the Church itself. And women leaders who challenge and are challenged by worship must eventually find themselves asking what kind of leadership they are called to and exercise, and what kind of Church they want to be part of.

What kind of leadership?

When I received my call to the ministry at thirteen years old, I had never heard a woman preach, or known a woman minister of a church. It didn't occur to me, in my naivety, that it was something to which a girl could not aspire. Indeed, I was soon told about Elsie Chamberlain, who had been my mother's minister and had married my parents, though I did not meet her for some years. My model of ministry was built on those male ministers I had known, and my pattern of preaching on them, and on my father, who was a lay preacher. Nothing that I saw or heard, from women or men, challenged or changed my view that I was called to be a minister, not a woman minister, and that I would be entering into the calling that I had seen exercised, as it happened, by men. Once I was ordained, I eschewed any notion of my gender affecting my ministry. I had no notion of what there was in being female that might shape my ministry. All my education and training had followed patriarchal patterns and norms, and, insofar as I had chosen an academic and pro-

WOMEN'S LEADERSHIP AND FEMINIST THEOLOGY

fessional career path, I felt as though I had cheerfully turned away from femaleness at every crossroads.

So I readily became co-opted into male patterns of ministry. I completely empathize with those whose stories, told in this book, include periods of being 'one of the boys', and playing power games in all-male fraternals or local, and later national, church gatherings. Alongside this went the suppression of femaleness, my own and – perhaps more tragically – that of others. I did not promote women's leadership in my churches, nor did I even see what changes might come about if women were empowered to serve and lead in a fully equal, fully human community. By allowing themselves to be thus co-opted, women ministers, in their small numbers, could be said to have actually bolstered the status quo of patriarchy in the Free Churches. Certainly, the impetus of feminist theology in Britain has come from Roman Catholic women and Anglican women.

Paula Nesbitt recognizes this in the American context:

> A historical comparison of feminist theology generated from denominations that have ordained women and from Roman Catholic women systematically excluded from ordination serves to illustrate the difference that the potential for co-option can make. By the early 1980s, many Roman Catholic women conceptually had moved beyond working for a gender-inclusive ordination process toward transforming the nature of priesthood, questioning the need for ordination at all, and the need for church as it is now institutionally configured.[42]

Such radical questioning, like challenging worship traditions, is very hard from inside the power structures of a denomination. Clergywomen are, to some extent, least likely to rock the boat in which they are wrestling their way towards the bridge in order to take a hand at the controls. If a denomination has spent several generations working towards women's ordination, or if a woman has spent half her life working towards the fulfilment of her vocation, it is unlikely that the big questions of leadership and ecclesiology will be asked.

But many are asking those questions. Elisabeth Schüssler Fiorenza, for example:

> [Many Catholic feminists] ask, What will ordination do to wo/men and for them in their struggles for liberation? Is ordination into kyriarchal structures good for wo/men if it incorporates them into violent and abusive hierarchical situations of domination?[43]

Schüssler Fiorenza challenges feminist Christian leaders to bring about real changes in patterns of leadership: 'committed to a ministry in the discipleship of equals'. She goes on, 'Such feminist ministers will continue to nurture individuals and to empower communities for realizing justice and love as the heartbeat of any religious institution.'[44] Religious institutions include the academy, which she sees as continuing to demand that women adopt 'the language and discourse of those clerical and academic communities that have silenced them, have excluded them as the 'other' of the Divine . . .'[45]

Rosemary Radford Ruether throws down the same challenge:

> We begin to see that the securing of women's ordination through liberal assumptions contains the seeds of its own contradiction . . . The shaping of the form and symbols of ministry by patriarchal culture, to the exclusion of women, is not seen as making the historic form of ministry itself problematic. Women win inclusion in this same ministry, without asking whether ministry itself needs to be redefined.[46]

In particular, women 'adopt the same garb, the same titles . . . the same clerical modes of functioning in a hierarchically structured church. They too stand in the phallically designed pulpit and bring down the "seminal" word upon the passive body of the laity.'[47]

What is the alternative? Well, perhaps from a Free Church point of view, the challenge needs restating. Surely the various struggles which gave rise to many of the Free Churches were precisely battles with old forms of hierarchy. When I have described the functioning of a Congregational church to feminist or to non-church friends, there has always been a positive response. 'Well, if that was what the Church was like, I would be happy to be part of it.' The common perception of the Church is that of a heavily top-down hierarchy, in which the laity is completely disempowered. And that is not a fair description of many Free Churches. Radford Ruether herself recognizes that, 'These kinds of change are possible only in denominations of relatively free polity where local churches do not face constant intervention and coercion from hierarchical authority.' But she goes on,

> even in such churches there are many other constraints that keep the Church tied to its role as validator of patriarchy. Conservative laity use both lay voting power and financial contributions to block the efforts of ministers with feminist consciousness from changing language or social commitments.[48]

Her comments about the pulpit, the 'seminal' word and the passive or conservative laity are still relevant. Many Free Churches function in an entirely clergy-led way, with little or no liturgical or ecclesiological place for lay people.

Churches that value a highly educated ministry naturally create a hierarchy of theological understanding. The minister preaches and teaches, and the people listen and learn. Whether the minister is a theologically educated woman or man does not necessarily change this paradigm.

On the other hand, as we have seen, a paradigm of ministerial 'service' is not necessarily beneficial to women or to the Church either. Just as this worked against the full equality of women with men in Salvation Army leadership of the nineteenth century, so it tends to work against the establishment of an equal community of leadership in our own time. Schüssler Fiorenza calls this language 'theological double-speak', and argues that, 'Since the theology of service has different implications for men and women, black and white, ordained and nonordained, powerful and powerless, the understanding of ministry as service has quite different implications for socially subordinated groups.'[49] As more and more women enter the ministry, in fact the ministry itself undergoes institutional change. Our own experience, as well as studies in the field, show what Melanie May describes as the erosion of women's leadership: ' "liberal" denominations are restructuring ministry in ways that marginalize women, e.g., more part-time positions, more partially or non-stipendiary positions, more ordination tracks to institute a new hierarchy of specialized ministries, more retired male ministers and priests used as an alternative labour supply'.[50]

What kind of Church?

Both Rosemary Radford Ruether and Elisabeth Schüssler Fiorenza sought early on to define new ways of being Church, which took account of feminist ecclesiology and feminist views of leadership. Radford Ruether talks of 'Women-Church' and Schüssler Fiorenza of the 'ekklēsia of women'. In either case, the concept is broader than a community of women alone, and stretches to the kind of community which would be created by the full inclusion of women's perspective. In both cases, the concept interweaves theology, symbol, liturgy, common life and praxis, in patterns which undermine what, for example, Jacqueline Field-Bibb recognizes as existing in the frozen 'tradition' which bolsters patriarchal hierarchies. She defines 'institutionalization' as 'the process whereby new imagination, initiatives and ideas are formalized into belief systems and structures by their androcentrically orientated adherents'. She goes on to say that, 'As these structures formalize, symbols evolve, and become "frozen" and form "tradition", which is subsequently appealed to to fend off change. Such symbols are used to justify androcentric hierarchies which have been dominant in societies, including Christian ones. Hence the tendency to see authority in terms of maleness.'[51]

The combination of symbol and praxis is not new, but is often perceived as novel and dangerous because the status quo does not reveal its own complexity. This is an example of the failure of dominant cultures to recognize their inculturation of gospel and church, and their tendency to see their own view as simple, correct and normative.

Both Radford Ruether and Schüssler Fiorenza, then, describe the new communities in holistic terms. Schüssler Fiorenza describes a new style of leadership:

> As more and more Christian wo/men, for instance, become schooled in a feminist liberation theological perspective they will be committed to a ministry in the discipleship of equals. Such feminist ministers will continue to nurture individuals and to empower communities for realizing justice and love as the heartbeat of any religious institution. In liturgy and ritual, in bible study and shelters for the homeless, in preaching and pastoral counseling, in day care centers and town meetings, feminist ministers proclaim and enact the 'good news' that wo/men, the weak, and the marginal are 'beloved' in the eyes of G*d and therefore must reclaim their dignity, rights and power in society and church.[52]

She is holding out a vision. Radford Ruether, on the other hand, describes a rare but present reality:

> Some of these local churches are beginning to integrate feminism into their understanding of being Church. They seek to reflect this in their language, ministerial form, and social commitments. Such churches begin not only to use inclusive language for humanity and God but also to transform liturgy to reflect the call to liberation. They take steps to overcome the monopolization of ministry by the ordained and to create shared ministry of the whole community. The Church sponsors projects, such as a battered-women's shelter or a rape hotline, that show its commitment to justice for women.[53]

For both writers, the challenge of the community is all-embracing. It reaches out beyond the achievement of equality and wholeness in the Church through a mission for justice and liberation in the community at large.

The vision has much in common with some of the foundation visions which lie behind the Free Churches. The Puritans wanted to purify the structures of the Church in England, but also the life of the nation. The Pilgrims who fled England for the so called 'New World' aimed to create godly communities, which would live entirely by divine law. The Holiness Movement sought to draw people out of the sinful world into God's new order, in which the whole of life was transformed. All these have been subject, to some degree, to institutionalization, but that was not where they started. I recognize the breadth of vision and the fervency and commitment in feminist views of the Church, as something which underlies the tradition in which I stand.

This is an important element to have in common, and does form a theoretical link with the vision of Schüssler Fiorenza and Radford Ruether. As we have seen, this is both liberating and restrictive. Radford Ruether recognizes that the lack of structure of, say, Congregationally ordered churches is conducive to change. On the other hand, there is no institutional challenge to such churches, and therefore no hard boundary along which to bring about real transformation.

Postmodern post-feminisms of the twenty-first century

While feminist theology was roaring away in the United States, borne on the tide of second-wave Feminism and the huge increase in women's ordained ministry in the churches, the picture in Britain was very different. The Society for the Ministry of Women in the Church had been formed as an ecumenical movement in 1929 following the success of women's suffrage and the disappointment that the ordination of women in most churches did not follow suit. By the 1980s, this was a small and almost forgotten organization, a victim, I suspect, of the concentration of the argument on the Church of England and the formation of the Anglican-focused Movement for the Ordination of Women.

Women in Theology arose in the 1980s as a non-denominational organization which promoted feminist theology through meetings and publications. The organization disbanded in some astonishment on 27 November 1999, on the realization that its aims, which seemed ridiculously far-fetched in the 1980s, had largely been accomplished. Inclusive language (at least for humans) had become accepted as a norm for worship in many places; most respectable theology courses included at least an element of feminist theology or Women's Studies; and – most astonishing and gratifying of all – there existed a Chair in Feminist Theology in a British university.

The Britain and Ireland School of Feminist Theology (BISFT) was formed in 1989 precisely to document and encourage the rather muted feminist theology in these islands (as we learned to call them). We were aware of significant advances in the discipline in the USA and in continental Europe, but felt that it was possible and desirable to develop a distinct British perspective. The enterprise included regular Summer Schools, the first of which was held in the University of Wales, Lampeter, in 1992, a Feminist Theology Course, validated by the same body, which was at that time pioneering new relationships with distance learning, and a series of publications. Foremost among these is the journal *Feminist Theology*, which was first published by Sheffield Academic Press, a welcome risk-taker in the field of academic publication, and has grown to be very highly respected indeed. Alongside this, BISFT published a series of books *Introducing* various aspects of feminist theology, including Christologies, ecclesiology, pastoral theology and liturgy.[54]

At around the same time, the World Council of Churches Ecumenical Decade – Churches in Solidarity with Women was encouraging women who were practising Christians to explore new writing for worship and new patterns of church life in events and conferences connected with the Decade. At the conference which marked the end of the Decade, in Durham in 1998, there was a dual sense of achievement and failure. The conference culminated with a service in Durham Cathedral, including a mass crossing of the 'line', the strip in the floor, just inside the door, past which women had traditionally not been allowed to go. We dedicated an icon of St Hilda, painted by an Orthodox woman artist, which is still housed in a chapel of the Cathedral. It was just after the ordination of the first women in the Church of England, and the future was ours.

On the other hand, the conference consisted almost entirely of white, middle-class, able-bodied, heterosexual, liberal church women, and was rightly challenged to take stock of its mono-culturalism. The term 'feminist theology' had become irrevocably linked to a white middle-class, and now middle-aged, culture. From time to time, the editorial committee of *Feminist Theology* journal has thought of renaming it 'Feminist Theologies', for example, or finding a term which would encompass feminism, womanism, mujerista theology, queer theology, thealogy and so on. The conclusion has so far been that we should not attempt to be all-encompassing, but, more humbly, take our place within a complex field of loosely grouped disciplines, whose boundaries are not clear, nor should be.

The relationship between these groups of organizations and women in ministry is also fluid. As can be seen from the stories included in this volume, some women do not see themselves as involved in a women's movement, while others want the presence of ordained women to effect radical changes in the Church. Some of the latter group have made their own journey, as I did, from a seemingly genderless call to ministry, to a growing awareness of the patriarchal nature of the Church and its patterns of leadership, and a longing to see change.

We reach out beyond the Church to join hands with global liberation movements. Nesbitt's words about the American situation ring as true in Britain, that, 'A liberationist ideal would involve movement beyond gender parity to an inclusivity that would break down the exclusivity of particular roles, races, cultures, orientations, abilities, and socio-economic status in religious organizations, as microcosms of what could be possible in human society.'[55]

Some of this is happening completely outside the declining member-

WOMEN'S LEADERSHIP AND FEMINIST THEOLOGY

ship of traditional churches. The phenomenon known variously as emerging church, fresh expressions or liquid church[56] sees groups of people with more or less adherence to traditional Christianity meeting in a great variety of settings. In a way, we have seen this before, in ventures like the St Hilda Community, but their energy was reabsorbed into traditional church when that became possible. This is different. It is not so much a re-imaging of traditional church and worship, as it is a new start. Some fresh expressions are inimical to the liberationist ideals of inclusivity. But elsewhere, you can see the bafflement of a new generation with the traditional Church's struggles over issues like gender equality. The tide of postmodern culture has swept over the churches, leaving their internal angsts like jetsam drying on the beach. Who cares about inclusive hymns, if the strange ritual of community singing forms no part of worship? And what is ordination, anyway? What kind of leadership emerges in an internet church with 40,000 casual visitors to an online act of worship?

There is also far less institutional control over beliefs or practices. For some, this is deeply troubling, and raises the spectre of syncretism, but it sits well with a feminist theology which embraces pre- and post-Christian deity as well as struggling with the patriarchal religions. Nesbitt sees this as a direct challenge to hierarchical church structures:

> The growth of movements such as women-church that transcend boundaries not only of Catholic–Protestant Christianity but also Christian perimeters by affirming spiritualities of other religious movements or traditions where women have been valued present an extreme challenge to differentiation and hierarchicalization. So do allied New Age and Wiccan spiritualities. Such noninstitutionalized movements, energized by women disenfranchised from their own denominations and traditions, have attempted to create a theological and ethical basis for reconstituting community and social relations that are more equitable across religious, cultural, racial, gender, and sexual orientation boundaries. The architecture of new forms and processes of community also represent new paradigms in the distribution and utilization of authority and the power it sanctions.[57]

This is fascinating territory. I hope that some of the liberation ideals expressed in Radford Ruether's or Schüssler Fiorenza's or Nesbitt's vision may come to fruition in some of these communities, though their diversity and fluidity means that not all will express those concerns. But maybe it is in these freest of all expressions of church that space will be found for God's liberative gifts, at least for a while, before the lure to freeze the tradition and calcify into institutionalism besets new expression.

This is, for the moment, an exciting new world, and perhaps nothing will ever be the same again. While feminist theology forms a shifting pattern with feminisms and other liberation theologies, within and outside such fluid phenomena of church, many things are possible.

Notes

1. Elisabeth Schüssler Fiorenza, *Sharing Her Word: Feminist Biblical Interpretation in Context* (Edinburgh: T&T Clark, 1998), p. 40. Schüssler Fiorenza uses a number of neologisms to capture realities in the structure of patriarchal religion.
2. Maude Royden (ed.), *The Church and Woman* (London: James Clarke & Co., 1924), pp. 167–82.
3. Catherine Booth, *Female Ministry; or, Women's Right to Preach the Gospel* (London: Morgan & Chase, 1870).
4. Royden, *The Church and Woman*, p. 9.
5. Zechariah Taft, 'A Reply to an article inserted in the Methodist Magazine for April 1809 entitled, "Thoughts on Women's Preaching", extracted from Dr James Knight' (Leeds: printed at the Bible Office by G. Wilson near the Old Church, 1809).
6. From the preface of Zechariah Taft, *Biographical Sketches of the Lives and Public Ministries of Various Holy Women* (Peterborough: Methodist Publishing House, 1992), vol. 1, p. 1, quoted in Jacqueline Field-Bibb, *Women Towards Priesthood: Ministerial Politics and Feminist Praxis*, (Cambridge: Cambridge University Press, 1991), p. 13.
7. For a good introduction to feminist biblical studies, see books in The Feminist Companion to the Bible series, edited by Athalya Brenner (Sheffield: Sheffield Academic Press) and The Feminist Companion to the New Testament and Early Christian Writings series, edited by Amy-Jill Levine and Marianne Blickenstaff (London: Sheffield Academic Press).
8. Mary Garman *et al.* (eds), *Hidden in Plain Sight: Quaker Women's Writings 1650–1700* (Wallingford, PA: Pendle Hill Publications, 1996).
9. Garman *et al.*, *Hidden in Plain Sight*, p. xi.
10. D. M. Northcroft, *Women Free Church Ministers* (London: Edgar G. Dunstan & Co., 1929), pp. 1, 14, 18, 22.
11. Judith L. Weidman (ed.), *Women Ministers: How Women are Redefining Traditional Roles* (San Francisco: Harper & Row, 1985), p. 72.
12. Weidman, *Women Ministers*, p. 73.
13. Mark Chaves, *Ordaining Women: Culture and Conflict in Religious Organizations*, (Cambridge, Mass.: Harvard University Press, 1997).
14. Chaves, *Ordaining Women*, p. 28.
15. Chaves, *Ordaining Women*, p. 49.
16. Chaves, *Ordaining Women*, p. 36.
17. Phoebe Palmer's 1859 defence of female ministry, *Promise of the Father; or, A Neglected Speciality of the Last Days*, argued the case for women's preaching from Acts 2.

18. Susan Kwilecki, 'Contemporary Pentecostal Clergywomen: Christian Leadership, Old Style', *Journal of Feminist Studies in Religion* 3.2 (Fall 1987), 57–76, p. 66.

19. Andrew Mark Eason, *Women in God's Army: Gender and Equality in the Early Salvation Army*, Studies on Women in Religion, 7 (Waterloo, Ont.:Canadian Corporation for Studies in Religion, 2003), p. 86.

20. Taft, *Biographical Sketches*, p. 178, quoted in Field-Bibb, *Women Towards Priesthood*, pp. 208–9.

21. 'The Work and Witness of Free Church Women', The Address of the President, Mrs C. R. Batten, 21 March 1955 (London: National Free Church Women's Council, 1955), p. 2.

22. Janet Wootton, sermon preached at Westminster Abbey on the Sunday after Easter, 1988, published in Heather Walton and Susan Durber (ed), *Silence in Heaven: A Book of Women's Preaching* (London: SCM Press, 1994), pp. 143–6, p. 144.

23. Patricia Wilson-Kastner, 'The Once and Future Church: Women's Ordination in England', *The Christian Century* 100.7 (1983), pp. 214–16, p. 214.

24. Wilson-Kastner, 'The Once and Future Church', p. 216.

25. Wilson-Kastner, 'The Once and Future Church', p. 216.

26. Rosemary Radford Ruether, *Women-Church: Theology and Practice of Feminist Liturgical Communities* (San Francisco and London: Harper & Row, 1985).

27. Janet Morley, *Celebrating Women* (London: Women in Theology and Movement for the Ordination of Women, 1989).

28. June Boyce Tillman and Janet Wootton (eds), *Reflecting Praise* (London: Stainer & Bell and Women in Theology, 1993).

29. Hannah Ward and Jennifer Wild (eds), *Human Rites: Worship Resources for an Age of Change* (London: Mowbray, 1995).

30. Hannah Ward and Jennifer Wild, *Guard the Chaos: Finding Meaning in Change* (London: Darton, Longman & Todd, 1995).

31. Uta Blohm, 'Women Clergy Working with Rituals', *Feminist Theology* 15.1 (September 2006), pp. 26–47. The full results of her survey can be found in Uta Blohm, *Religious Traditions and Personal Stories: Women Working as Priests, Ministers and Rabbis* (Frankfurt am Main: Peter Lang, 2005).

32. Blohm, 'Women Clergy', p. 33.

33. *The Methodist Worship Book* (Peterborough: Methodist Publishing House, 1999).

34. Blohm, 'Women Clergy', p. 34.

35. Letty M. Russell, *Church in the Round: Feminist Interpretation of the Church* (Louisville, KY: Westminster John Knox Press, 1993), p. 140.

36. See Janet Wootton, 'Books, Liturgical, Congregationalist', in Paul F. Bradshaw (ed.) *The New SCM Dictionary of Liturgy and Worship* (London: SCM Press, 2002), pp. 77–9.

37. Martha Long Ice, *Clergy Women and Their World Views: Calling for a New Age* (New York: Praeger, 1987), p. 148.

38. Ice, *Clergy Women*, p. 146, her italics.

39. See www.iona.org.uk

40. *Worship Live* has been published thrice-yearly by Stainer & Bell since its

launch in 1994 at St Martin-in-the-Fields.

41. Janet Wootton, *Introducing a Practical Feminist Theology of Worship* (Sheffield: Sheffield Academic Press, 2000).

42. Paula D. Nesbitt, *Feminization of the Clergy in America: Occupational and Organizational Perspectives* (New York and Oxford: Oxford University Press, 1997), p. 167.

43. Schüssler Fiorenza, *Sharing Her Word*, p. 40.

44. Schüssler Fiorenza, *Sharing Her Word*, p. 41.

45. Schüssler Fiorenza, *Sharing Her Word*, p. 43.

46. Rosemary Radford Ruether, *Sexism and God-talk: Towards a Feminist Theology* (London: SCM Press, 2nd edn, 2002), pp. 167–8.

47. Radford Ruether, *Sexism and God-talk*, p. 168.

48. Radford Ruether, *Sexism and God-talk*, p. 169.

49. Elisabeth Schüssler Fiorenza, *Discipleship of Equals: A Critical Feminist Ekklesia-logy of Liberation* (London: SCM Press, 1993), pp. 298–9.

50. Melanie A. May, 'Tracking the Ways of Women in Religious Leadership', in Elisabeth Schüssler Fiorenza and Hermann Häring (eds), *The Non-Ordination of Women and the Politics of Power* (London: SCM Press 1999), pp. 89–101, p. 90.

51. Field-Bibb, *Women Towards Priesthood*, pp. 201–2.

52. Schüssler Fiorenza, *Sharing Her Word*, p. 41. 'G*d' is her way of transcribing the divine noun, while distancing it from the heavily masculine word 'God'.

53. Radford Ruether, *Sexism and God-talk*, p. 169.

54. Lisa Isherwood, *Introducing Feminist Christologies* (London: Sheffield Academic Press, 2001); Natalie K. Watson, *Introducing Feminist Ecclesiology* (Sheffield: Sheffield Academic Press, 2002); Zoe Bennett Moore, *Introducing Feminist Perspectives on Pastoral Theology* (London: Sheffield Academic Press, 2002); Janet Wootton, *Introducing a Practical Feminist Theology of Worship*.

55. Nesbitt, *Feminization of the Clergy in America*, p. 176.

56. For more information, see http://emergingchurch.info, http://www.freshexpressions.org.uk

57. Nesbitt, *Feminization of the Clergy in America*, p. 168.

6. The Ordination of Women and the Ecumenical Movement

JEAN MAYLAND

In 1848 an English woman, a Mrs Dawson, applied for a divorce. Her husband had been openly adulterous, while his private pleasures included flogging her with a horsewhip and brutalizing her with a metal-spiked hairbrush. Her petition was refused.

As Rosalind Miles comments in her book, *The Women's History of the World*

> Between 1700 and 1850 the hydra headed monster of revolution had torn Europe and the Americas apart, bursting the chains that had held the human race in subjection for many thousands of years . . . But while barriers of ignorance and distance crumbled as if they had never been, one great anomaly remained. Women everywhere were still trapped in a state of sexual slavery virtually unchanged since the dawn of man-made civilisation.[1]

In 1848 also Elizabeth Cady Stanton in a declaration written for the Women's Rights Convention at Seneca Falls, USA, set out the injustices visited on woman by man:

> He has never permitted her to exercise her inalienable right to the elective franchise . . .
> He has made her, if married, civilly dead.
> He has taken from her all right in property . . .
> He has so framed the laws of divorce . . . as to be wholly regardless of the happiness of women . . .
> He has denied her the facilities for obtaining a thorough education . . .
> He has created a false public sentiment by giving the world a different code of morals for men and women . . .[2]

From this point onwards the struggle for women's equality and women's rights began in earnest. It was a hard and bitter struggle and women were often their own worst enemies with women taking a leading role in opposing the movement and resisting the ideas. This resistance penetrated society from top to bottom. Queen Victoria for example expressed her implacable opposition to *'this mad, wicked folly of human rights . . .'*[3]

The other source of the strongest resistance to the development of women's rights was the Church – especially the established Church of England working in close alliance with the judiciary.

Yet the movement grew apace. Among the women who did desire change there grew up positive alliances between secular women and churchwomen across the denominations. Those struggling with church teaching about the essential inferiority and submission of women found relief in arguments based on human rights. Increasingly it was seen that the way to improve the status of women was through political pressure. If the Church resisted this, then it resisted even more strongly pressures to give women an equal place in its own ministries. It is fascinating to see how women's ministry developed first in the churches which were locally based and non-hierarchical. It has been most bitter in the established Church of England where it still continues over the matter of women bishops. Once more issues of human rights are being dismissed and reactionary claims made about biblical teaching. In the Orthodox Church the discussion is only really just beginning while in the Roman Catholic Church – the most hierarchical of all – it is not even allowed!

The ordination of women in the Free Churches and the Church of Scotland

In September 1904 Gertrude von Petzold became the first recognized woman minister in England when she was appointed as minister of the Free Christian (Unitarian) Church in Leicester in the face of competition from no fewer than seven male colleagues. Eloquent in the pulpit and challenging on many a suffragist platform, Gertrude von Petzold grew quickly in reputation – her photo was even sold on the streets of Leicester. In 1907 she was the only European woman delegate to attend the Fourth International Congress of Religious Liberals in Boston.

On 17 September 1917 Constance Todd was ordained as the first Congregational woman minister. (The day before her friend Maude Royden began her preaching ministry – non-ordained – at the City Temple as she felt that her ministry would never be accepted in the Church of England in her lifetime. She remained an Anglican.) The next day Constance married Claud Coltman and they were appointed as joint ministers to the Darby Street Mission of the Congregational King's Weigh House

THE ORDINATION OF WOMEN

Church in the West End of London. Constance had taken a degree course in history at Oxford (she was not awarded the degree as women were still excluded from degrees at Oxford and Cambridge). She then trained at Mansfield College, Oxford and also took a London BD degree.

The Methodist Church also has a distinctive history of courageous and able women in ministry. Susannah Wesley, the mother of John and Charles, had led Bible studies, first in her kitchen and then in the church hall. Later she encouraged her sons to develop the work of lay preachers and quite early on in Methodism some of these were women. In common with other Protestant churches, Methodism also revived the ancient deaconess order. In 1972 Conference agreed that there could be women ministers and in 1974 the first women were ordained. The deaconess order was abolished but then later re-instituted as the order of deacons for men and women.

At 2.30 pm on Saturday 26 May 1963 Mary Lusk stood at the bar of the General Assembly of the Church of Scotland to present her petition which asked the Assembly to test what she believed to be her call to ministry. This was remitted to the Panel on Doctrine. In 1968, after votes in all the Presbyteries, the Church of Scotland agreed to open to women ordination to the ministry of Word and Sacrament, on the same basis as men. In 1969 Miss Catherine McConnachie was ordained by the Presbytery of Aberdeen. On St Andrew's Day 1978 Mary Lusk (who had married Fred Levison, a minister from Edinburgh, in 1965) was at last ordained herself. After serving the Church of Scotland in a faithful, distinguished ministry, both before and after her ordination, Mary Levison is now a chaplain to the Queen – the first woman to be so appointed.

Slowly therefore the Free Churches with their headquarters in England and also the Church of Scotland (a National Church) came to see the rightness of ordaining women and did so. The process was not without its struggles and there were intense discussions about the biblical texts – especially St Paul's comments about headship and the instruction to women to keep silence in church. The comments of the Revd Martin Cressey of the United Reformed Church at the World Council of Churches Conference on the 'Community of Women and Men in the Church' at Sheffield in 1981 sum up what came to be the accepted position in these matters. He said that when Paul orders the women in Corinth to keep silent in church, his hermeneutical norm was based on two desires: to build up the church and to avoid scandalizing society. If today we followed his hermeneutical norm instead of his application, then we would be ordaining women and authorizing them to speak in and to lead churches. Today society is scandalized because the Church does not give an equal place to women and its mission is compromised.

JEAN MAYLAND

Ecumenical discussion and co-operation

During these years ecumenical discussion on the ordination of women grew and the women themselves developed ecumenical friendships and alliances across the churches and also with those struggling for justice in society. In 1926 a conference of women ministers was held and out of it grew the interdenominational Society for the Ministry of Women in the Church (SMWC). Maude Royden and Constance Coltman were two of its most active members. Maude was elected as President and Constance as one of the Vice Presidents. The women realized that progress towards ordination was going to come at a different pace in each of the churches. Some could not bear this and changed churches in order to be ordained. Others felt it best to struggle on in their own church but during the process they were determined to support each other. It is one of my personal sadnesses that when the struggling for the ordination of women in the Church of England became really serious in the last quarter of the twentieth century, it was conducted as if nothing had ever happened in the Free Churches. Their contribution to the theological issues was largely ignored and the experiences of Free Church women ministers was wholly ignored by both protagonists and the media.

At least in the more recent struggles concerning women bishops, the voice of the other churches has been sought more seriously. They were invited to contribute to the so-called 'Rochester Report' – *Women Bishops in the Church of England*. Their representatives were encouraged to speak in General Synod, papers were requested and an ecumenical conference on the issues was held.

During the early years of the SMWC, there was also a close connection and co-operation between many of the women ministers with the struggle for women's suffrage. Margaret Benn (later Lady Stansgate) was a supporter of both causes. She was another Vice President of the society. In 1945 she chaired a Church of England Committee on the training of women for service in the Church. Three years later she was invited to be a consultant on the status of women at the first assembly of the World Council of Churches in Amsterdam in 1948. The experience of learning that her views were regarded as suspect by some of the Anglican hierarchy led to her becoming a convinced Congregationalist! She later became the founder President of the Congregational Federation, formed from the continuing Congregational Churches following the formation of the United Reformed Church in 1972.

The World Council of Churches and the place of women

As Susannah Herzel points out in the foreword to her book *A Voice for Women*:

> Since the 1940s there has been working within the World Council of Churches an intentional fellowship of men and women committed to restoring that mutuality between the sexes which they see as an image of Christ and his church, and which reaches back to the 'image of God' in the Genesis stories. These Christians have been seeking quietly to understand the implications of such beliefs in the light of history, particularly the history of the church. Long before many member churches showed an interest in the man/woman debate, the WCC had taken it seriously. It spent time, money and effort in facing the difficulties and providing the fora in which pioneer thinking could evolve.[4]

In the period after the end of the Second World War and the holding of the first World Council of Churches (WCC) Assembly in 1948 Dr W. Visser 't Hooft had encouraged an American woman, Mrs Calvert, to send out a questionnaire to churches all over the world to gain a picture of the life and work of women in the Church as a whole – both professional and voluntary. The response to the questionnaire far exceeded all expectations and as a result the French Reformed Church asked that the subject of women in the Church be put on the agenda for the WCC Amsterdam Assembly. At the Assembly Kathleen Bliss of the Church of England made a moving speech relating the question of women's ministry to that of lay ministry. She was then commissioned to write a book on the issues. In addition this first Assembly of the WCC in Amsterdam 'quickly supported the suggestion that a permanent commission of men and women be formed, which would relate to the general structure of the World Council and co-ordinate and encourage activities related to the question of women's ministry. Primarily this would mean an ecumenical inquiry into the biblical, theological and practical issues involved.'[5]

The Central Committee meeting in Chichester, England, in 1949 set up an official Commission on the Life and Work of Women in the Church with Sarah Chakko of India in the chair and Kathleen Bliss of England as secretary. Another person who became involved in the commission and its concerns was Dr Cynthia Wedel of the USA.

Throughout the 1950s and 1960s the WCC work on women's issues continued. In June 1974 the WCC held a conference in Berlin entitled 'Sexism in the 70s'. It was a gathering of very angry women who felt that their gifts and talents were not recognized nor adequately used by the Church.

It was at the Nairobi Assembly in 1975 that women really began to break through. For the first time they were present in significant numbers, and a plenary presentation was allotted to them.

This Assembly adopted as a priority programme a study on 'The Community of Women and Men in the Church'. Study documents were prepared and sent to the churches and many groups studied them, including many grass roots congregations. The issues studied included identity, relationships, marriage and family, ministry and worship, authority and church structures, justice and freedom. The study ended with a conference in Sheffield in July 1981. Recommendations from this conference went to the meeting of Central Committee, which was held in Dresden in August, together with a letter from Sheffield. One of the recommendations was that 50 per cent of all membership elected to sub-units and committees of the WCC be women and also that 50 per cent of the speakers, moderators and other leadership be women. After a fierce debate the Central Committee agreed that the 50 per cent should be a goal towards which the WCC should work. It did have an effect on the work of the WCC in the next two decades.

The Orthodox members of Central Committee also objected to sending to the member churches the letter addressed to them by the members of the Sheffield Conference. The two elements of the letter to which they objected most strongly were a sentence which claimed that the Holy Spirit had spoken to the people at Sheffield and also a sentence which spoke of the pain of those women in some churches who believed that they had a vocation to the priesthood which could not be tested. 'What', they said, 'about the pain of those churches which objected strongly to the ordination of women?' In the end they agreed that the Central Committee could 'take note' of the letter and send it to the member churches with a letter from the Orthodox expressing their dissent.

There was a further breakthrough from the point of view of women at the Vancouver Assembly of the WCC in 1983. At this Assembly there was clear evidence that the process begun by the study on 'The Community of Women and Men in the Church' had prompted widespread concern for fuller representation of women in all the deliberative councils of the churches and for women's voices to be heard on all the major issues. There was a large and highly successful women's pre-assembly meeting at which leadership roles were taken by women from all over the world. Women who were new to the ecumenical movement received a first-rate training during those packed days and were well fitted to make their mark in the Assembly which followed. During the assembly itself twelve of the speakers in main plenary sessions were women, and the worship, debates and whole corporate life were all influenced by the lively participation of women. In the official policy-making bodies elected by the Assembly, the proportion of women elected rose to 29 per cent.

THE ORDINATION OF WOMEN

Central Committee in 1987 decided to hold a special decade during which the churches would demonstrate their solidarity with women. Easter Day 1988 saw the launch of the Ecumenical Decade – Churches in Solidarity with Women. This encouraged the churches to take up a whole number of issues of participation and identity. Later issues of violence against women came to be regarded as equally vitally important.

In 1991 the Seventh Assembly at Canberra took place and was largely overshadowed by the Gulf War. One hot afternoon papers were to be given expressing a variety of theological views. A long paper had just been read by one bearded Orthodox on behalf of another who was absent. Heads began to roll forward. The paper ended to desultory applause. The stage emptied and was filled by figures in colourful dress carrying flaming torches and marching to the sound of drums. People woke up with a start and were electrified by a presentation of Korean feminist Christian theology rooted in ancient religions, given by Dr Chung Hyung Kyung. Her address over, all hell broke loose. The Orthodox were livid and most of my fellow Church of England delegates from George Austin onwards were apoplectic with rage.

At the Harare pre-WCC Assembly women's gathering in 1998, after a harrowing morning of presentations about violence against women, Dr Chung performed a healing action, which was rooted in the shaman tradition but drew heavily on Christian trinitarian thought. The two official Church of England women delegates left the room and would not even share the experience, condemning it as syncretistic.

After the fall of the Berlin Wall in 1989 and changes in Russia there was a backlash against the ecumenical activities of the Orthodox Church. Complex factors led to Orthodox letters and protests to the WCC about a number of activities including the Eucharist, the participation of women and women in ministry.

The WCC itself began to feel that it was losing out because church leaders were no longer giving it priority. Concern was expressed at Central Committee that the places given to women and youth were keeping away from the Central Committee church leaders who would have more influence in their home churches. In addition, shortage of money has affected the WCC and the Central Committee was reduced in size. This has meant for example that the Church of England now has only one place on Central Committee and a bishop has been appointed. When there were two places there was always a bishop and a laywoman.

Nevertheless at the Harare WCC Assembly women did play an important part and did put forward some of their issues, especially that of violence against women. From the point of view of an ordained woman, even the women's pre-Assembly regarded us as a 'problem' and Aruna Gnanadason of the Women's Desk always felt that the concerns of ordained women were of minor importance compared with the struggles of the rest of church women and the suffering of those women who experienced violence.

The World Council of Churches and the ordination of women

Among the issues raised at the 1975 Nairobi Assembly was that of the ordination of women. The WCC had begun the 1970s by holding a small Consultation on the Ordination of Women in Cartigny, Geneva, 21–26 September 1970. This meeting brought together 25 participants from six continents representing eight different traditions. They included Roman Catholics and one Orthodox bishop. A report of the consultation was edited by Brigalia Bam of the Women's Desk with the title *What is Ordination Coming To?* The British participants were Mary Levison and Margaret Forrester, both deaconesses from the Church of Scotland, and Alan Webster, an Anglican priest who was Dean of Norwich. Among the WCC staff present was Dr Ian Fraser, a Presbyterian from the Church of Scotland, who commented trenchantly,

> What seems lacking to me is a positive theological case for ordaining women. It is agreed that the negative work has been done well, but it is believed that this clearing away of the brushwood of bad biblical exegesis and bad theological thinking is insufficient. Can we then prepare a theologically argued case for ordaining women as part of the necessary pattern of the Church? I believe not. We can produce no positive theological case for ordaining Scotsmen – by a clear oversight on the part of God, they were not represented among the apostolic band: but the extension of the Church to the Gentiles cleared the way for the ordaining of people of all nations. The same extension of the Church to total humanity is, surely, the basis for the possibility of ordination to total humanity.[6]

At the back of the report a small chart set out the position on the ordination of women in the member churches of the WCC. This revealed that at that time 72 member churches of the WCC did ordain women and 143 did not. In 1970 no Anglican churches ordained women and of course no Roman Catholic, Old Catholic or Orthodox. Four Baptist churches ordained women and eight did not while one agreed to the principle but had not put it into practice. Ten Lutheran churches ordained women and twenty did not. Seven Methodist churches ordained women, while ten did not and one more had agreed to the principle but had not put it into practice. Perhaps more surprisingly, 23 Reformed Churches ordained women and 33 did not – a clear sign of the influence of cultural factors. Five Congregational Associations had ordained women, three

THE ORDINATION OF WOMEN

had agreed in principle and two did not. Behind these statistics stretched years of struggle and pain, change and joy.

A Canadian preparatory paper focused on the dynamic of the Church itself:

> On Easter Morn there were eleven men 'set apart' (but surely not formally ordained to a Ministry of Word and Sacraments in the congregation), but there were no three-level ministries, no congregations, no 'church' as we know it, no scriptures, no ecclesial structures, canons, or forms of any kind. All we have was one day proposed by or grew out of the needs of a situation in a particular age as something 'new' – was examined, prayerfully, tested theologically, and, under God judged to be, 'good' for its time; thus did tradition grow and continuity become established.[7]

As time went on and the Anglican Churches began to ordain women, the concern of the Orthodox representatives at the WCC grew as if they feared that they might be next.

At the Festival in Harare in November 1998, which ended the Ecumenical Decade – Churches in Solidarity with Women, a letter was sent to the Eighth Assembly of the World Council of Churches, which was to follow. In spite of strong objections at revision stage this mentioned the ordination of women as a problem along with ethical issues such as abortion, divorce and human sexuality. Afterwards I protested strongly about this to Aruna Gnanadason at the Women's Desk, saying that we ordained women were tired of still being thought of as a problem. She said that it was done out of sensitivity to the Orthodox, which infuriated me as I knew the Orthodox woman in question personally supported the ordination of women. Aruna did raise the matter with Konrad Raiser, the WCC Secretary, and with Alan Faulkner of the Faith and Order Commission, reminding them of their long-standing commitment to follow up on the Community of Women and Men in the Church study process. They replied that it was hoped to have a consultation early in 2002. We are still waiting!

Dr Janet Crawford, an Anglican priest from New Zealand, wrote about this matter at the end of the Ecumenical Decade – Churches in Solidarity with Women, in the special edition of *The Ecumenical Review* in which she commented on the work of the Faith and Order Commission of the World Council of Churches and the Women's Desk. She described them as working on parallel lines without ever meeting. She was well qualified to write as she had served as a member of the Faith and Order Commission and had also worked for a time at the Women's Desk, preparing for the Sheffield Conference and analysing the results of the study on the Community of Women and Men in the Church.

She pointed out that at the inaugurating Assembly of the WCC in

Amsterdam in 1948, women insisted that 'the question of women's place in the church was a theological and ecclesiological issue, that it had to do with the very nature of the Church and their membership in the body of Christ'.[8]

She demonstrated that the Faith and Order Commission had worked on a whole range of issues but had consistently failed to face up to or even to recognize the impact of these matters on women and had never encouraged the inclusion of women's perspectives on ecclesiology. The concerns of women expressed during the Ecumenical Decade – Churches in Solidarity with Women had no impact upon the deliberations of Faith and Order.

Meanwhile the Women's Desk had been following theological issues on a parallel track and had faced up to the issues of women throughout the world including, to some extent at least, those of ordination.

Janet concluded:

> When will women's ecclesiological questions and challenges be reflected with full seriousness in the ecclesiological studies of Faith and Order? Or will there continue to be two 'ecclesiological streams' within the ecumenical movement, a 'women's stream' and a 'Faith and Order stream'? Present indications are that Faith and Order is planning a consultation on 'Ministry and Ordination in the Community of Women and Men in the Church' in 2002. This consultation, hoped for since the end of the Community study, called for since at least 1984, and first mooted in this form in 1989 – more than ten years ago! – may provide an opportunity at last for the two streams to flow together and to contribute together to the understanding of koinonia and, finally, to the unity and renewal of the church.[9]

After one particularly difficult session of a Central Committee meeting in Geneva, Janet Crawford and I sat in the sun outside the railway station drinking a glass of wine and trying to recover before catching the bus to our respective destinations. 'I am tired of being regarded as a problem,' said Janet. 'I am not a problem. I am a person and a priest, trying to offer gifts to a church and an ecumenical movement that does not want to receive them.' I knew just how she felt. Much of my life has been devoted to the ecumenical movement and the unity between the churches, which I so passionately desire. Yet constantly the issue of the ordination of women has been presented as an ecumenical problem. The trouble is, of course, that the Church of England especially has always seemed only to look in one direction ecumenically – namely towards the Roman Catholic and Orthodox Churches. If it glanced more frequently in the opposite direction, then it might realize that it was its failure to give women a completely equal place in ministry, which was an affront to its other ecumenical partners. In addition of course there have been splits within the Church of England itself and within the Anglican Communion.

The Anglican Communion and the ordination of women

The struggle for the ordination of women, part of a movement throughout the global Anglican Communion, has been long and hard and bitter and still continues. The very first woman to be ordained priest in the Anglican Communion was Li Tim Oi, a remarkable Chinese woman. She was born in 1907. Her father was a doctor who had given up medicine to become a headmaster. He was a Christian although he had two wives or, rather, an official wife and a mistress or concubine who was Tim Oi's mother. Li gave his newly born daughter an unusual name: Tim Oi means 'another much beloved daughter'. The Chinese tradition tended to undervalue and despise girls. Mr Li was determined to show that a daughter could be loved and cherished. Tim Oi was educated at Belilios Public School where she learnt about Florence Nightingale (from whom she took her own English name). She taught in a church school, graduated in theology at Union Theological College in Guangzhou, and became a lay worker. In 1940 she went to work in Macao, where life became more difficult as the Japanese tightened their hold on south China. In 1941 she was ordained deacon. Macao belonged to Portugal, and as the Portuguese were not at war with the Japanese it became a haven for refugees. Some of these went on to Taiwan where they met Bishop R. O. Hall, and they told him of the wonderful work Li Tim Oi was doing in Macao. Some time later, Bishop Hall wrote to Li Tim Oi to ask her to travel to Xingxing to be ordained priest. After a difficult and dangerous journey they met and talked and prayed, and then Bishop Hall ordained her as the first Anglican priest. She then returned along the dangerous roads to Macao where she served as a priest for the rest of the war.

After the war Bishop Hall was strongly rebuked by the other Anglican bishops for what he had done. Li Tim Oi wrote to him with humility to say that she was a very tiny person, a mere worm and she did not want to cause trouble for him. She promised not to exercise her priesthood but to work as though she were a deacon. Li Tim Oi went back to China to work. She continued her ministry when the 'bamboo curtain' went down and suffered along with others in the Cultural Revolution during which all her books were burned and she had to do hard labour.

Yet her example bore fruit: in 1969 a resolution was put to Hong Kong and Macao Diocesan Synod that two women should be ordained to the priesthood. This was accepted in 1971.

In that same year Bishop Baker told the Anglican Consultative Meeting in Limuru in Kenya that he intended to conduct this ordination and asked whether, if he did so, his church would still be regarded as in communion with the rest of the Anglican churches. After a hard-fought debate by a narrow majority it was agreed that the Diocese of Hong Kong would still be regarded as part of the Anglican Communion and on Advent Sunday 1971 Jane Hwang and Joyce Bennett were ordained as priests. Joyce Bennett (who retired to England and ministered to the Chinese congregation at St Martin-in-the-Fields, and has recently celebrated the 35th anniversary of her ordination) was the headmistress of a large girls' school. Jane Hwang was also a teacher. Both had served as deacons for some time.

Gradually other provinces of the Anglican Communion followed suit. At the time of writing, women can be ordained as priest in the Provinces of Aotearoa, New Zealand and Polynesia, Australia, Bangladesh, Brazil, Burundi, Canada, Central America, Ceylon, England, Hong Kong, Ireland, Japan, Kenya, Mexico, North India, Philippines, Rwanda, Scotland, South India, Southern Africa, Sudan, Uganda, United States of America, Wales, West Africa, and West Indies. They can be ordained deacon in the Indian Ocean, Southern Cone, Congo and Pakistan.

There is no women's ordination in Central Africa, Jerusalem and the Middle East, Korea, Melanesia, Nigeria, Papua New Guinea, Southeast Asia or Tanzania. Some of the reasons for refusal to ordain are cultural. Others are connected with which missionary society first took the gospel to that country!

The issue of bishops is rather more complicated. Some provinces have voted to have women bishops but have not yet ordained any women to this position. Canada and the USA actually have women bishops at this stage. Aotearoa, New Zealand and Polynesia has a retired bishop, Penny Jamieson, but none currently serving. The following provinces have passed the necessary legislation but have not yet ordained any women bishops: Bangladesh, Brazil, Central America, Ireland, Japan, Mexico, North India, Philippines, Scotland, Southern Africa and Sudan.

There are also women bishops in the Swedish and Norwegian Churches (Lutheran), which are linked to the Church of England through the Porvoo Agreement, and in the German Evangelical Church, which is linked to the Church of England through the Meissen Agreement. The French Lutheran Church and the Moravian Church in the UK also have women bishops.

Problems within the Anglican Communion

The slow spread of the priesting of women in the Anglican Communion led to theological problems within the Anglican Communion itself. If provinces recognized the right of another province to ordain women

THE ORDINATION OF WOMEN

but did not themselves receive those women as priests, what kind of communion remained?

In 1978 the Lambeth Conference faced a situation in which Hong Kong, Canada, the USA, and New Zealand had all ordained women to the priesthood and eight other provinces had accepted the ordination of women in principle. In response the Conference passed Resolution 21: 'Women in the Priesthood', which recognized the autonomy of each province to admit women to Holy Orders. It also noted that this would be of great significance for the Anglican Communion as a whole but committed itself to preserve as great a degree of unity as possible.

In 1985 the General Convention of the Episcopal Church, USA, expressed its intention 'not to withhold consent to the election of a bishop on grounds of gender'. The Presiding Bishop brought the question to the Primates meeting in Canada and they requested John Grinwood, the Primate of Australia to head a committee to prepare a paper for the 1988 Lambeth Conference.

This recommended two options:

- to counsel restraint;
- to say that if a province went ahead with this decision it should be offered to the Anglican Communion for 'reception'.

The Conference went ahead with the second option and recommended the setting up of a commission to monitor the situation until the 1998 Conference. The Eames Commission was therefore set up and reported to the 1998 Lambeth Conference that the matter had moved forward with the maintaining of a large degree of 'impaired communion' within the Anglican Communion.

At the present moment women bishops have actually been ordained in the Provinces of Aotearoa, New Zealand and Polynesia, Canada and the United States. Other provinces have passed the necessary legislation but have not yet ordained any women bishops.

In June 2006 the Episcopal Church of the USA elected a woman, the Rt Revd Katharine Jefferts Schori, as Presiding Bishop of Nevada. She is a scientist, a theologian and a qualified pilot who flies herself around her huge diocese. All the old prejudices came to the fore.

On 20 June 2006 Ruth Gledhill of *The Times* reported that, 'the Anglican Church in America descended into ecclesiastical anarchy last night as American traditionalists refused to accept the authority of a woman and asked the Archbishop of Canterbury to lead them instead'.[10] It was also reported that Rowan Williams was seriously considering this! My blood pressure went up to new heights – when will women ever be fully accepted?

JEAN MAYLAND

The struggle to ordain women as priest and bishop in England

With the struggle to ordain women as priest in England as opposed to the rest of the Communion, the theological issues took on a new perspective. For the evangelical wing of the church, the biblical arguments, especially ones about headship, were of supreme importance. As I have already said, to the annoyance of the Free Churches, the debate in the Church of England was conducted as if no-one had ever discussed the issues before. Their experience was totally ignored. For the catholic wing of the Church, however, the arguments had to do with tradition, catholicity, the icon of Christ and relations with the Orthodox and the Roman Catholics. Somehow also the mention of 'priest' rather than 'minister' brought in all kinds of deep psychological issues and fears of women's sexuality. The whole spectre of priestesses was raised. When the Free Church women wrestled with their churches to become ministers, only one skeleton fell out of the cupboard, namely the idea of having a woman as an ordained minister. In the Church of England all the skeletons fell out at once: priesthood, ordination, inclusive language, the motherhood of God. This made the battle long and hard and bitter, but in 1994 women were at last ordained priest in the Church of England

The cost of getting to this position was, however, very high. The Measure which provided for the ordination of women had clauses protecting the right of parishes not to receive the ordination of women and bishops not to ordain them. The supporters of women's ordination accepted these provisions (sexist though they were) in order to show compassion and maintain the inclusive nature of the Church.

More was, however, to follow.

The bishops met in Manchester, ostensibly to draw up a code of practice to enable women to be ordained. In the event the bishops came back with a proposal for three bishops to be appointed to provide an Alternative Episcopal Oversight. Because they were to be members of the House of Bishops, sharing in their collegiality, it was suddenly acceptable for them to be created in order, as Prebendary Donald Barnes pointed out, 'to oppose part of the canon law which they were being ordained to administer'.[11] Moreover, the Act was moved in Synod and defended by the then Archbishop of York. Swept by a mood of compassion and reconciliation and assured that the measure was pastoral and not connected with jurisdiction, the Synod passed the Act of Synod by a great majority. The dioceses and the deaneries were not consulted.

The effect of the Act of Synod has been to give women a sense of betrayal, to harden opposition to the ordination of women in some areas, to divide the church and to raise serious issues about the position of diocesan bishops who have ordained women.

Women bishops

Now the Church of England is turning its attention to women as bishops and the Bishop of Rochester presented a report to the 2006 General Synod. It sets out a number of options as to the way forward. It also covers yet again all the ground which was argued over and fought over for forty years before women were ordained priest. The General Synod first decided that the way forward was to allow those opposed to women bishops to have 'Transferred Episcopal Authority' (TEA). The Synod was urged to accept Transferred Episcopal Authority by the Archbishop of Canterbury, who moved the motion, and the Archbishop of York, who supported him.

This decision left many women priests and their supporters angry, depressed and near despair. A woman recently retired from local government described it to me as 'institutionalized sexism'. Christina Rees, Chair of Women and the Church (WATCH)[12] objected in General Synod to the idea that people needed 'safeguards' from the faithful ministry of women priests.

Under the terms of TEA all existing provisions for the non-acceptance of women priests would be cancelled. All parishes which did not want a woman priest or bishop, nor a male bishop who was prepared to ordain women priests and join in their consecration as bishop, could ask that transferred episcopal arrangements be made.

Such provision would depend on grace and trust and mutual respect. It works in America. In England, however, the Archbishop insists that those opposed need the protection of law and measure. What a failure to show grace, respect and trust! What a witness to the world around us! Robert Key MP, said 'the danger was of sidelining the Church from God's people'. A woman churchwarden I know said that the Church is just making itself utterly irrelevant.

In the end WATCH and other groups convinced the House of Bishops that TEA would not work. The opposition, however, still demanded further legislative protection and the bishops could not agree about that.

In July 2006 General Synod agreed to set up a new group to find a way forward. They are to do so within certain parameters:

- those opposed to women bishops must be recognized as faithful Anglicans as well as those in favour;
- the church's Canon Law A4 must be accepted by all. This states that all who have been lawfully ordained as deacons, priests and bishops in the Church of England should be recognized as such by its members.

Ecumenical issues

In such a situation Anglican Communion and ecumenical issues come into play once more. As we have seen, the Anglican Provinces of Aotearoa New Zealand and Polynesia, Canada and the United States have all accepted women bishops. There are women bishops in the Swedish and Norwegian churches (Lutheran), which are linked to the Church of England through the Porvoo Agreement. There are women bishops in the German Evangelical Church, which is linked to the Church of England through the Meissen Agreement. The French Lutheran Church and the Moravian Church in the UK also have women bishops.

The Free Churches in Britain and Ireland do not have bishops as such, but have extensive experience of the ministry of women in positions of wider authority. Many Free Churches are organized into geographical areas, which have appointed or elected leaders. They also commonly elect a national leader each year, or for a two- or three-year period. These can be seen as roughly equivalent to bishops, or, in the case of national leaders, the Archbishop of Canterbury. Leadership at every level is open to women.

The Methodist Church, which first ordained women ministers in 1974, has had women as Chairs of Districts, and female Presidents of Conference. The Methodists have entered into a covenant relationship with the Church of England, but have made it clear that any failure to accept the full ministry of women (including a ministry of oversight) would constitute a serious and theological obstacle to full unity. An episcopate in the Methodist Church would necessarily be open to women as well as men.

The United Reformed Church (URC), which brought together Congregational and English Presbyterian traditions has women ministers who are Moderators of Provincial Synods and currently has had three ordained women as Moderator of its General Assembly. In 1994 the URC declared itself an equal opportunities organization: 'Equal opportunities is not an option for Christians; it is a moral, and getting to be a legal, imperative. Equal opportunities is about valuing individuals, getting the best person for the job, being the body of Christ.'[13]

The URC further stated that it believed it had come to these conclusions under the guidance of the Holy Spirit. This contrasts sharply with the position taken by the Church of England conservative evangelical group, 'Reform'. This group claims that to make women bishops and give them authority over men would be contrary to biblical teaching, and rejects modern notions of justice and human rights as against the true teaching of Scripture. However, the URC also holds a high view of Scripture. In URC worship, the Bible is treated with enormous care and respect as the basis of faith. At the beginning of worship in many local churches and at the start of each session in General Assembly, the Bible is carried in with due solemnity and placed reverently on the table. Indeed, the URC statement of faith and order declares, 'the highest authority for what we believe and do is God's word in the Bible alive for his people today'.[14]

Both the United Reformed and Methodist Churches have clearly studied the Bible most seriously and thoroughly and come to the conclusion that the essential equality of men and women in church life and ministry is at the core of their belief and practice.

Whereas the situation in the Free Churches is a great support to those members of the Church of England who want leadership at all levels to be open to women, there are more problems when it comes to ecumenical relations with the more hierarchical Churches. Opponents of women bishops from the more 'catholic' wing of the Church lay great stress on the harm it would do to ecumenical relations with Rome.

At the official level, the Roman Catholic Church opposes the ordination of women. In 1994 Pope John Paul II issued an Apostolic Letter entitled 'On Reserving Priestly Ordination to Men Alone' – *Ordinatio Sacerdotalis*,[15] making the non-ordination of women as close to infallible as possible. In theological terms this pronouncement was called 'definitive' in the light of a previous papal Letter, *Instructions*, published in 1990, despite the fact there was no consultation with the world's bishops before the Letter was issued nor any echo of agreement on this question from the faithful.[16]

An outcry in the Roman Catholic press and in personal writings followed *Ordinatio Sacerdotalis* and it can reliably be inferred that many in the Roman Catholic Church are opposed to this papal statement. In 1995, Cardinal Ratzinger (now Pope Benedict XVI) forbade discussion of any possibility of female ordination, yet it *is* widely discussed, albeit sometimes in an atmosphere of fear. The movement for Women's Ordination Worldwide (WOW) is growing and has held two international conferences, and the Catholic Women's Ordination (CWO) group in Britain is active and organizes training for ministry. Some Roman Catholic women have followed the path of 'illegal' ordinations while others have been ordained into the Old Catholic Church. The Old Catholic Churches of the Union of Utrecht have ordained women as deacon and priest for some years, but they have not yet made the decision to have women bishops.

The Orthodox Churches

Unlike the Roman Catholic Church, the Orthodox Churches do allow free discussion of the issue of the ordination of women. In 1988 the

Ecumenical Patriarch convened a special inter-Orthodox symposium in Rhodes on 'The Place of the Woman in the Orthodox Church and the Question of the Ordination of Women'. The consultation had problems with the ordination of women to the priesthood but believed that discussion of the topic should continue. It did, however, agree that the 'apostolic order of deaconesses' should be revived, concluding in its official report that 'there is ample evidence from apostolic times, from the patristic, canonical and liturgical tradition, well into the Byzantine period (and even in our own day) that this order was held in high honour'.[17] The report goes on to describe how the deaconess was ordained within the sanctuary during the divine liturgy with two prayers, receiving the orarion (the deacon's stole) and Holy Communion at the altar. It concludes, 'the revival of women deacons in the Orthodox Church would emphasize in a special way the dignity of woman and give recognition to her contribution to the work of the Church as a whole'.[18]

In 1997 the Ecumenical Patriarch gave a further statement on the issue, following Orthodox consultations on the place of women held in both Damascus and Istanbul: 'The order of women deacons is an undeniable part of the tradition coming from the early church. Now, in many of our churches, there is a growing desire to restore this order so that the spiritual needs of the people of God may be better served. There are already a number of women who appear called to this ministry.'[19]

Despite this, there are still no women deacons in the Orthodox churches, although the Church of Greece in 2005 voted to allow the ordination of women deacons in monasteries. There are a number of reasons for this: the Orthodox Church always moves slowly; there is fear of division within the Church; the Russian Orthodox Church, which in 1988 was one of the most keen on the revival of the diaconate, has faced a huge backlash from reactionary and anti-ecumenical factions since the overthrow of Communism in 1989; and other Orthodox churches are reluctant to act without the Russians.

Bishop Kallistos Ware and Elisabeth Behr-Sigel have written a book about the ordination of women in the Orthodox Church. Both fail to see any theological objections but advise care and caution. Elisabeth (who has since died) acknowledges that to ordain women as priests now would give rise to schism in the Orthodox Church and counsels that 'in view of this risk we must be patiently impatient', but she was clear that women's ordination would not represent a break with Orthodox tradition. Rather, she urges, 'we must never give way to threats from obscurantist fundamentalists, who are often Westerners who are recent converts to the Orthodox Church.'[20]

In his part of the book, Bishop Kallistos considers the issues of tradition, anthropology and the *meaning* of priesthood. In the light of these he poses the question, 'Is there any specific reason why women cannot become priests?' He does not find any convincing arguments against the priesthood of women in any of these areas. He goes on to explore the concept of priest as icon of Christ, pointing out that in Orthodox theology (unlike that of the Latin West) the celebrant speaks as the representative not of Christ but of the church of men and women. In union with the people he recites the epiclesis, asking the Father to send down the Spirit and so effect the consecration. 'At this crucial moment, as throughout the Eucharistic prayer, he is not Christ's vicar or icon, but – in union with the people – he stands as a supplicant before God.'[21] Thus, though there *is* a sense in which the ministerial priest is Christ's icon, Bishop Kallistos does not find that this in itself excludes women from the priesthood. Indeed, he argues that the debate must continue in a spirit of expectation and hope.

During the first debate about women bishops in the Church of England in July 2005 the Orthodox representative, Archimandrite Ephrem Lash, said, 'You have women priests. Obviously therefore you can have women bishops. The two cannot be theologically divided so why are we wasting two hours on a hot sunny afternoon debating the issue!' Later he also commented, 'there was no TEA [see above] at Nicea!' Opponents of women bishops have been surprised by these Orthodox interventions.

A personal comment

In the early days of the search in the British Churches for the ordination of women, there was tremendous fellowship and solidarity across the Churches. Women of all denominations found they had a common cause and worked together. The Society for the Ministry of Women in the Church (SMWC) had an enormous membership and great influence. Its membership included some wealthy and important people, and meetings were often addressed and attended by politicians. The agenda included social and political issues, such as votes for women.

In the secular world most of the battles for women have been won, at least from the point of view of the law with equal opportunities and human rights legislation – even though the struggle for hearts and minds is by no means over. The tragedy is that it is Churches – notably the Anglican, Roman Catholic and Orthodox Churches, which have sought exemption from this legislation. In areas where many of us believe the proclaimers of the gospel should be in the forefront, they are in fact in the rear. Politicians and statespeople have now often lost touch with the churches as religious influences have waned. On the other hand in its recent campaign of letters to MPs, WATCH has found considerable support for women bishops and for legislation in that area which provides real equality.

Another factor of present-day life is that women ministers no longer seem interested in groups or organizations just for women's concerns. After a long and distinguished life SMWC has been obliged to close and give its documents to the Women's Library. Other ecumenical women's groups have similarly come to an end. The Ecumenical Forum of European Christian Women (EFECW) struggles to get members in Britain although it is still very important in Eastern European countries. Even WATCH has a much smaller membership than the Movement for the Ordination of Women (MOW) used to have.

Evangelical members of General Synod now claim that biblical rules about the headship of men in marriage actually apply to the whole of life, and society is wicked to give women equality. Young evangelical women claim the right to practise 'loving subservience to the sacrificial leadership of men'!!!! I have also been devastated by the attitude of many of the younger women priests in the Church of England. They are as bossy, traditional and as authoritarian as any man. They have no time for feminist theology or inclusive language and an affirming, inclusive church. The only compensation is that there are male priests who do share a concern for those issues; our earlier dream that women might change the Church has to change to a hope that women and men together may change the Church. Together we hang on in the Church as the conveyor of good news while at the same time longing to change the institution.

Meanwhile the world passes us by.

Lauren (granddaughter aged sixteen) was with me in Hexham Abbey recently, attending church for the first time for months. The Bishop of Newcastle was present and the younger children were able to ask questions before they went out to make a collage. One of them asked 'Are you in favour of women bishops?'

He said, 'You have put me on the spot! But yes, as they can be priests it is logical that they can be bishops but it will take ten to twelve years as we have to be sure that we are meeting all the needs of those loyal Anglicans who are opposed.' Lauren said under her breath, 'What year does he think it is? When will the Church realize that it is the twenty-first century not the Dark Ages?'

When indeed?

Notes

1. Rosalind Miles, *The Women's History of the World* (London: Michael Joseph, 1988), p. 182.

2. Louise Michele Newman (ed.), *Men's Ideas, Women's Realities: Popular Science, 1870–1915* (New York and London: Pergamon Press, 1985), pp. 192–3, quoted in Miles, *The Women's History of the World*, p. 183.

3. Letter from Queen Victoria to Sir Theodore Martin, 29 May 1870.
4. Susannah Herzel, *A Voice for Women* (Geneva: World Council of Churches, 1981), Foreword.
5. Herzel, *A Voice for Women*, p. 10.
6. Brigalia Bam, *What is Ordination Coming To? Report of a Consultation on the Ordination of Women (September 1970)* (Geneva: World Council of Churches, 1972).
7. Bam, *What is Ordination Coming To?*
8. Janet Crawford, 'Women and Ecclesiology – Two Ecumenical Streams', *The Ecumenical Review* (January 2001), pp. 14–24, p. 14.
9. Crawford, 'Women and Ecclesiology', p. 22.
10. *The Times*, 20 June 2006.
11. Report of the Proceedings of General Synod of the Church of England, November 1993.
12. http://www.watchwomen.com
13. The United Reformed Church, 'The Basis of Union and Schedule D: A statement concerning the nature, faith and order of the United Reformed Church version 1 and 2' (1971).
14. United Reformed Church, 'The Basis of Union'.
15. John Paul II, *Ordinatio Sacerdotalis*, 22 May 1994.
16. Dorothea McEwan and Myra Poole, *Making All Things New: Women's Ordination – A Catalyst for Changes in the Catholic Church* (Norwich: Canterbury Press, 2003), pp. 14f.
17. Gennadios Limouris (ed.), *The Place of the Woman in the Orthodox Church and the Question of the Ordination of Women: Report of the Inter-Orthodox Symposium, Rhodes, Greece, 30 October to 7 November 1988* (Katerini: Tertios, 1992), p. 31.
18. Limouris, *The Place of the Woman in the Orthodox Church*, p. 32.
19. HAH Ecumenical Patriarch Bartholomew, in Kyriakis Karidoyanes Fitzgerald (ed.), *Orthodox Women Speak: Discerning the 'Signs of the Times'* (Geneva: World Council of Churches, 1999), pp. 15–18, p. 15.
20. Elisabeth Behr-Sigel and Kallistos Ware, *The Ordination of Women in the Orthodox Church* (Geneva: World Council of Churches Risk Book Series, 2000), p. 44.
21. Behr-Sigel and Ware, *The Ordination of Women in the Orthodox Church*, p. 85.

Stories

Kate Cotterill

Salvation Army officer

The shaping of my ministry

'Danny, what are those marks on your back? . . .'

Danny and Tracey[1] were on their way to a funeral. Danny needed a new shirt, and so I had invited him and his girlfriend Tracey into our little charity shop so that he could choose one. As he changed his shirt, the scars were unmissable. Danny looked at me through a drunken haze and staggered as he tried to point to Tracey.

'You'd better ask . . . her!'

Tracey drunkenly smiled.

'Well he did ask for it.'

I began to wish I hadn't asked, as she continued.

'I stabbed him.'

I looked from Tracey to Danny's stabbed back and then back to Tracey. I tried not to look too shocked. I tried to look as if this was normal for me, as if a daily occurrence, but I failed.

'Stabbed!'

I don't know why I should have been quite so surprised. Danny had only recently got out of prison for setting Tracey on fire using lighter fluid. These were people who regularly frequented our church. We were part of their lives and they were part of ours.

I remember once going to visit Tracey and Danny in their flat to take them a rug. I remember entering a world that you usually only see in TV documentaries. A world where almost all the furniture and household items had either been sold to fund an addiction to alcohol or destroyed through the effects of the drink. A world where the living room furniture comprised just one crate and one chair. I was there with the rug to help bolster Tracey's self-esteem that could get no lower.

I remember seeing Danny walking around the local market in a drunken mess. A huge unkempt dressing covered the left side of his face. His arms and hands showed ill-formed scabs. Angry scars to add to his collection. His injury was caused by a drinking pal burning him with scalding fat.

Danny and Tracey were some of the first characters my husband and I met after we arrived at our inner-city Salvation Army church in the East End of London. We don't see them anymore. Tracey has moved on. Danny is now dead – someone in a drunken stupor threw car battery acid over him. He died as his body was slowly poisoned.

There are other stories I could tell. I could introduce you to Mr Harley, who shuffled the streets with a big charity shop suitcase, originally bought to go somewhere, but now dragged by a man with nowhere to go. I could tell you about Donald, so lonely that no-one turned up to his funeral, except the minister and the undertaker. Stories of people who represent, I now realize, what my ministry is all about – offering respect to non-designer people that society has given up on; bringing cohesion through loving with grace; bringing stability through offering safety from a world and a fragmented way of life that I still do not understand.

I tell Danny and Tracey's story, and others like it, because their story has become my story. Their lives have shaped my life. No amount of reading or study at a ministerial or theological college could have given me what the Dannys and Traceys have given me, and I really do not know what I would be without their indelible influence on my ministry.

Ten years ago my husband and I entered the Salvation Army Training College to be prepared for ministry in the Salvation Army. Ten years ago I responded to that which I could not avoid, God's unmistakable 'call' on my life to be involved in full-time ministry. But standing in the charity shop with Danny without his shirt on, displaying his multiple stab wounds, wasn't exactly what I had expected. The dawning of reality for me had really only just begun.

We were beginning to know the fear of vulnerability.

That was a few years ago now, and both my ministry and my calling have been continuously refined by such 'Danny and Tracey' encounters. I look back on those and other seminal moments not for reminiscence, but to look at what has shaped me as I endeavour to live out the gospel as a minister within the Salvation Army. It was at 13 or 14 years old when I first realized that God wanted me to serve him as a Salvation Army officer and, like so many others who are called to full-time ministry, it was not something I initially wanted to do. But I knew for certain it was what God wanted, and I also realized that I could not evade God's call and remain true to myself or to him.

Looking back, I can see how over the years God has gently chiselled away at my rather naive and maybe even 'romantic' view of ministry. How, through others, he has guided me to understand that my involvement in ministry was going to be so much more practical and messy, and how through his own ministry to me, he has pointed out what my ministry is to be. I remember a special moment in prayer that really helped to cement my calling. 'Pictures from God' can be a loaded phrase, but that was what it was. I saw three wooden crosses: one a large ornate cross made of what looked like mahogany; another beautifully carved and polished pine; the last a plain cross which seemed to be made out of two old splintered planks of rough timber. The meaning shocked yet affirmed through its challenge – responding to a call to ministry had to move beyond the terms I was placing upon it. I knew I had to put aside my ornate or beautifully polished concept of ministry and take up the cross that had been prepared for me. I had to put aside my selfish ideals, humble myself, and allow myself to be put into a position of vulnerability, beyond any concept of what was comfortable.

During our two years at the training college, it became increasingly clear that God was directing my husband and me to inner-city ministry. We were scared. We were beginning to know the fear of vulnerability. What about schooling for our child? Her safety? Our safety? We had no experience of inner-city life; we had a comfortable, safe and predictable background where church was squeaky clean and nice. Suddenly, the reality was dawning and it was becoming apparent that for us, for me, ministry was going to take on a new meaning beyond singing nice songs and PowerPoint, a meaning to be forged in a gritty and fragmented world of those squeezed into the margins of society to be forgotten.

It happened. Our first appointment was to a busy inner-city community-based corps (church), where we have been ever since. We moved to the East End of London and entered a world where on a daily basis we were subjected to God's groaning creation. Where we were to be Jesus' hands and feet to all kinds of people. Where we had to reach out in grace to those who were used to being rejected. Where we had to live out the gospel to the mentally ill. Where we were to live lives of compassion with those with no hope. Where we were to embody the kingdom of inclusion to those who have no-one else.

We could have ended up somewhere else. A comfortable suburb, or the leafy lanes of a rural idyll. We could have ended up somewhere that would have seen us content to be custodians of Christendom, content to live our lives for our valued parishioners. We didn't and the intensity of a vulnerable inner-city ministry, and the people we have encountered, has laid some foundations for the rest of my ministry.

Through people and situations that Danny, Tracey and others like them have thrown up, there have been certain aspects of ministry that God has brought into sharp focus for me. Certain things that my involvement in ministry so far has given me that I hope will never be forgotten. For instance, I've learned that in order to encounter our community there needs to be less a concept of doing church and more a concept of being church. Robert Warren describes missionary congregations as: 'congregations that had reworked themselves to be mission focused. The congregation proclaimed the gospel as much by being church, in the quality of its spirituality, as by "doing" church through active evangelism.'[2]

'Should our church be removed overnight from our community, who would miss it?' is a missional litmus test for all that we do, as we engage and blur the encounter between church and community. Who would miss us if we as a church were not there – the Sunday congregation? If it were the community we minister to that missed us perhaps that would reflect the outward focus that we feel is essential. We've learned that the demands of the Dannys and Traceys are a gift for us to show the gospel in action, a gift of opportunity to show and embody love, mercy, grace and compassion.

Looking back, I think of occasions where divine appointments have been made. Times when I've been glad to be part of conversations, when I have been able to minister through the strength of authentic relationship where people have responded to who I am rather than what I do. I'm learning that 'Mission is not primarily an activity of the church but an attribute of God.'[3] Attributes of God can't be programmed, but they need to be lived out, attributes of God can't be measured, but they need to be shared out, and so my involvement in ministry has taught me to be more concerned about what I am, rather than what I do.

The reality of Jürgen Moltmann's assertion that 'Evangelization is mission, but mission is not merely evangelization'[4] has also shaped my ministry. Once mission for me was a mere euphemism for evangelism, a buzz word, a fast-growing fad for the Church. The things that have been asked of me, and the things that I have seen, the things I have had to encounter, have cemented the falseness and narrowness of such an understanding. I never want to forget that evangelism only makes sense within the fuller understanding of mission through the demands of *missio dei* (the mission of God). My ministry, my involvement in my community, has retained its authenticity by not allowing anything to be stolen from acts of love to the Traceys, Dannys, Mr Harleys and Donalds of this world. My ministry has been forged within the tension of refusing to allow our work for justice, compassion and love to drift into what Ann Morisy describes as a 'sequential or consecutive process, with either social action or evangelism being treated as prior to the other.'[5] The key for me is grace, loving with no buts, giving without expecting a return, keeping a no-strings-attached mindset to all that we offer through our church. Then allowing the provocation of who we are to open doors.

I've discovered in a world of *thanks but no thanks*, a world tolerant of my belief structure but happy with their non-requirement of God, that there is a need to recognize that people are not asking the questions that we want to give them the answers to. We identify with Tillich's complaint that 'it is wrong to throw answers, like stones, at the heads of those who haven't even asked a question'.[6] Consequently, a further foundation for my ministry has been that of living out the gospel in a way that provokes questions and intrigues those watching the Church in action. Bryant Myers in a similar vein to Graham Tomlin's *Provocative Church* suggests that,

> Doing development and living our lives in ways that result in the community or some of its members asking questions of us to which the gospel is the answer unites gospel-as-life and gospel-as-deed with gospel-as-word.... Our witness depends on our living lives so that the Holy Spirit may evoke questions to which our faith is the answer.[7]

I've learned that people ask questions when they see something they do not expect or understand, so a foundation for my ministry has been to live out a life of intrigue, laced with grace, in order to provoke questions to which the gospel is the answer.

I've learned so much during the past eight years, and for me one of the realities of ministry is that it is an enormous privilege. To share with people in their joys and in their sorrows, to have them confide in me, seek help and advice, is a real honour. To think that God has called me to be a signpost for him, directing people towards his love and his purposes is truly amazing. To be a voice for those who usually go unheard is so fulfilling. Yes, there have been times when trying to juggle my various roles, as minister, wife, and mother, has been tough. Times when I've wished for more hours in a day, times when I've longed for more space for devotion and prayer. But it's also been at these times when I've learned to rely totally on God to carry me through.

So far, at a local level, my gender has never impeded my ministry. In fact, throughout writing my story I have found it hard simply to reflect in the singular. My husband and I are in an unusual situation in ministry whereby we work and minister together. The Salvation Army has a long history and heritage of such joint covenants for ministry. It is important for us, it is important for me. Of course we are not joined at the hip, we defer to each other, we have distinct gifts and talents. There are some things that one of us does better than the other, but we are who we are because of us.

William Booth was once reported as saying, 'We have a problem. When two officers marry, by some strange mistake in our organisation, the woman doesn't count.'[8] Within our local setting, my experiences so far tend to run contrary to his claim, for my ministry has always been known and respected. People don't refer to me or see me as an 'add-on' extra to my husband. I have learned to hold my own as an individual. I stand up against violence and aggression – even when my knees wobble! I make decisions. I am an individual respected for who I am. But I am also aware that for other married women officers, William Booth's statement continues to ring true 118 years on.

Other tensions exist too – I sometimes wonder why it is my husband who can show assertiveness and forthrightness without being labelled, but why when I show the same qualities I am seen as being a 'scary' woman! Why when I refuse to be the pathetic – hands thrown in the air – fragile lady, we get the smiles and the 'We know who wears the trousers in that house!' Why when my husband takes a back seat on an issue or simply takes up a supportive role to my ministry, he has to live with the potential of the 'mousey husband' label.

Mostly we smile – sometimes we feel like compromising to the culture that cultivates such thinking. But then the next time a Danny or a Tracey comes into our centre with their demands and needs, do I say, 'Wait here – I'll get my husband'? No, I don't. I roll my sleeves up and wade on in!

Notes

1. Names have been changed to protect anonymity.
2. Robert Warren, *Building Missionary Congregations* (London: Church House Publishing, 1995), cited in Michael Moynagh, *Changing World, Changing Church* (London: Monarch Books, 2001), p. 133.
3. David J. Bosch, *Transforming Mission: Paradigm Shifts in Theology of Mission* (Maryknoll, NY: Orbis Books, 1991), p. 390.
4. Jürgen Moltmann, *The Church in the Power of the Spirit: A Contribution to Messianic Ecclesiology* (London: SCM Press, 1977), p. 10.
5. Ann Morisy, *Journeying Out: A New Approach to Christian Mission* (London: Continuum, 2004), p. 13.
6. Quoted in B. L. Myers, *Walking with the Poor: Principles and Practices of Transformational Development* (Maryknoll, NY: Orbis Books, 1999), p. 210.
7. Myers, *Walking with the Poor*, p. 18.
8. William Booth, 'The May Meeting Addresses: Summary of the Year's History', *The War Cry*, 12 May 1888, p. 10.

Susan Durber

Minister of St Columba's United Reformed Church in Oxford and of Cumnor United Reformed Church

I have a memory from childhood of kneeling at the communion rail in the parish church I attended every Sunday. I must have been waiting to receive a blessing. And I can remember thinking that I wanted to be a priest. I don't know if it's possible to judge whether this was a childish need to emulate a hero, or whether you could call it the call of God. But it is my earliest recollection of the thought that I might serve the Church in ministry. I know that at that moment it had not crossed my mind that all the priests I knew were men, just as it hadn't really dawned on me that the Ladybird book about the call of Samuel that I had treasured from a very early age was about a boy and not about a girl – and that there was no parallel story about a girl. I was innocent then of the gender politics of the Bible, the Church or the world, though I would learn fast. When I was confirmed in the same parish church, at the age of ten, in a white lace dress (secondhand from a cousin), my church sponsor gave me a book about Gladys Aylward,[1] and I began, albeit unconsciously, to understand that the Church had a view about which ministries were appropriate for women. But I did notice how unfair it was, that though I could sing solos at school, the church choir was for men and boys only.

At school I had many friends who were Roman Catholics. I was fascinated by their devotion to Mary, that they prayed to her and expected that she would both understand and soothe the traumas of female adolescence. While something did trouble me about the impossible pairing of virgin and mother even then, I found it somehow exciting and intriguing to contemplate a 'goddess', a divinity who could share or at least understand my own gendered experience. This was, you might say, my first foray into feminist theology, though it felt furtive, exotic and strangely ill-matched with the faith I had so far learned. In my early teens I met some young people from a United Reformed church and went along, out of curiosity at first. I discovered a church that seemed to me then more 'open' in all sorts of ways I could barely name. I found the sermons more thoughtful and more intellectually challenging than anything I had met before. I remember that for a while, I took notes, so keen was I not to miss anything! I think the truth was that I was ready for a change, ready to test the faith God was nurturing in me in a setting which was unfamiliar. I discovered that I was welcome in the choir and that the major decisions about the church's life were taken at Church Meeting, to which all members of the congregation were welcome. I found elders who took a deep interest in me and my questions about the faith and who encouraged me in learning and thinking. For a while I went to the URC in the evening and my parish church in the morning, but eventually I decided to become a member of the URC congregation and to live out my Christian life there. As teenage rebellions go it was hardly huge, though the parish priest was determined that I should understand what a big deal it was. I hope I was generous enough to say how grateful I was for the grounding in the faith I had received from him, but I fear not!

By the time I was in my late teens I had also heard that, in the United Reformed Church, there were ministers who were women, though I had never actually seen one. And, I have to admit, at a time when it was revolutionary to have a woman reading the news, I wondered myself what it would be like to have a woman lead the congregation. But, this knowledge did allow me to reopen the question of my own future, away from politics or journalism or marrying someone like Peter Ustinov(!), towards ministry again. With the encouragement of a good minister I began to explore what it might mean.

I know that for a lot of people who feel called to ministry, or perhaps for those who look on and ask what inspires someone to become a minister, it's often thought to be about 'helping people', the ministry being one kind of caring profession. I don't think I ever really felt or thought that. I did want to be caring and to make a difference to the world, but that wasn't what drew me towards ordained ministry. I knew that if I had wanted to enter a caring profession there were other routes – and routes much more favourable to women. (Even as a naive teenager I recognized that a church which would in principle ordain women would not always and in every place make them welcome.) That initial childhood 'call' had come as I knelt at the communion rail, and what called to me then was the significance and the privilege of creating 'spaces' in which worship could really take place, times when the 'beyondness of things' could be felt, acknowledged and explored – and occasions when people might encounter the reality that I knew I met in the holy space of worship. I was a child with a huge sense of the 'holy' (when I later read Otto's famous book[2] it was with a great sense of recognition!) and I intuitively sensed that ministry was about making spaces for the holy to enter into ordinary life. I was also a very thoughtful child and teenager. I wanted to 'know the truth', to find the interesting questions and to awaken thought. At school I loved texts, history, and ideas – and I felt called to a life that could be spent exploring these things with others and connecting them with daily life. I think I saw ministry then as being something like a cross between being a priest and a rabbi! I had no sense then, I think, that the future of the Church was insecure or uncertain and I thought little about mission to those outside the Church. My sense of call was about being within the community of faith and resourcing it and serving it. I was studious and scholarly, with a rather mystical turn, and that was the 'me' that I believed God was asking to be used in the service of the Church. I was excited by that and keen to do it. I had little sense that my being a woman would make much difference to any of that. In fact, if anything, I was determined that it should make as little difference as possible (given that the difference I thought it might make would be to disadvantage me in finding access to ministry). But I also, I confess, got a kind of thrill from feeling that I was, in even a small way, a kind of pioneer at a time when women ministers were few and rather rare. Please remember that I was all of eighteen!

I told the school careers teacher that I wanted to be a minister. After a brief misunderstanding about a possible ambition to achieve a Cabinet post, I dutifully studied Latin O level, along with my A levels, and set out to read theology at what I understood was the URC college at Oxford. I did go to Oxford, to Mansfield College, and, while still an undergraduate, candidated for the ministry of Word and Sacrament. I can remember little about that process and sometimes wonder what on earth I said at my interviews, but I was accepted. I took a year out to study in a Lutheran seminary in Minnesota before returning to Oxford to complete training for ministry. Meanwhile I had married another ministerial student, who was preparing for ministry in the Congregational Federation. I knew that this would likely complicate things, but I was only twenty-one, and had an indefatigable sense that I wouldn't be beaten. My sense of call was strong, and coupled with a huge surge of what I can only really describe as ambition. At my best I wanted to be a really good minister. At my worst I wanted to be well known. What I dreaded was being in any sense second-class because I was a woman.

As it turned out, I was the only student in my year to leave college without a call to a church. My husband was called to a Congregational church in Greater Manchester and so I went with him and hoped that something would be found for me. A hard and bitter year followed. I threw myself into doing practical things like learning to drive and getting some experience alongside the local hospital chaplain, but I was in turmoil. What if no congregation would 'take' me? Looking back, I lacked the spiritual maturity to cope well with this situation. I had excellent support from the Synod Moderator, and that kept me going until, after a year, I was ordained and inducted into my first pastorate, in south Manchester. I waved aside the cautions some gave about the effect living in two manses might have on my marriage (probably unwisely I see now), so determined was I to fulfil the ministry I believed God was calling me to do.

It was a wonderful pastorate in so many ways (three congregations – all very different). I am sure I have never worked so hard and in such a variety of situations. I reflected very little about either the fact or the significance of being a woman in ministry, though looking back I can hardly believe I was so naive. I was amused when, in the local pub in my dog collar (now abandoned), I was mistaken for a stripper-gram. It was sometimes rather wearying when people outside the church found it puzzling that a woman had been asked to take the funeral or preside at the wedding. And on a church trip to Taizé I found I couldn't join the other clergy visiting Brother Roger. But mostly I just got on with things, or so it seemed to me. I was doing it 'just like a man', even joining in the traditional male clerical jokes about the women's meeting and encouraging the benign and kindly (but still predominantly male) leadership in the churches. I remember one moment when I did notice what a difference it might make for women to be ministers if we could find a distinctive voice. In the ministers' fraternal (*sic*) I longed to be able to share struggles, disappointments and vulnerabilities. I was saddened to find that, in a male culture (as it seemed to me), the talk was mainly about sharing triumphs and a certain kind of optimism. I learned to speak a different language.

When I left my first pastorate, I was hugely pregnant and about to start a PhD! The study stretched and fulfilled me and certainly reinforced the 'rabbi' side of my understanding of ministry. But it was the experience of having a baby that changed me radically and rendered me what I would now call 'woman-identified'. I had spent much of my life and ministry struggling to get into and to hold my own in what you might call a 'man's world'. My heroes in ministry were men – wonderful men, but still men! I did not question the models of ministry I had been taught or admired. It had not really occurred to me that there was more to women being ministers than simply being the same as the men. And I was really very naive about issues of gender. I suppose I imagined that my brief stay on the maternity ward would be quickly over – and that I would return to the world of 'work' as fast as I could, having been a reluctant visitor in the world of women. But the maternity ward proved to be a gateway into a new world, a world I have not left but have been glad to belong to – like coming home.

I began to value women's lives and experience in a way I had not allowed myself previously. I began to read feminist theory, feminist biblical criticism, biographies of women and women's history and writing.

I was grateful to God for this 'conversion' experience and my sense of ministry was transformed. The sense of striving to 'succeed' in a male-dominated Church and world was gone (well, mostly!). I wanted now to be in the Church wherever women were and wherever women's voices were heard. And I understood that it was no use my being ordained and a woman if it made no difference to the lives of other women. I left behind my desire to be an 'exceptional' woman in a man's world, the kind of exception that only proves the rule. I wanted, I felt called, to be with women, to share their lives and to do whatever I could to shape a Church (and world) that could invite women to flourish, affirm their lives and speak with their own voices. I wanted to continue to work in the Church (though for a while I wondered whether models of ordained ministry are so deeply patriarchal that it would be better to leave them behind completely). But I wanted to work for change and to begin so much of what I had always done from a very different place. I was blessed with wonderful women friends and colleagues who patiently opened for me this new world and let me find my own voice within it. Gifts I had learned to suppress came forth; creativity and empathy, for example, and a new kind of courage.

After a time combining teaching in a wonderfully innovative and brave theological college with part-time ministry in a challenging inner-city pastorate – and finishing the PhD! – I was called to a church in the centre of Oxford. I was returning to one of the places where I had begun, but as though for the first time. The ministry here combines city-centre ministry and university chaplaincy and, since I came, I have also been called to serve as a minister to a village congregation just a few miles from the centre of Oxford. I have acquired more responsibilities within the URC and have been part of the Faith and Order Commission of the World Council of Churches, but, however exciting they are, those kinds of extra things are really not where I believe the centre of my ministry has been. The heart of my life as a minister is as I preach the gospel and break bread at the communion table in the midst of the two congregations I serve. And I sense God's presence most powerfully in my ministry when I am able to use the 'rabbi' side of my vocation in the local church – in leading Bible study, for example – and perhaps the 'priestly' side when the worship services really do somehow make a space for people to encounter the holy. But it is certainly true that I *strive* much less than I did, that I am much more willing to wait for God to decide what's urgent, and I'm more content that the Holy Spirit will find a way to be known and to change the Church which doesn't depend on me! In a time when the Church is facing many challenges – numerical decline, loss of status and voice, a tarnished reputation and new internal conflicts – I think it is hard to be a minister. Even in my own twenty years as a minister things have changed beyond measure. Ministers have to be ready to change and to serve the Church of today. But, I ask myself, is there anything that is absolutely core to the meaning of being a minister?

Along with talk of 'new ways of being church' there are, rightly, questions to be asked about new ways of a being a minister. My 'conversion' and identification with women gave me a new perspective on what it is to be a minister. It means that I no longer bracket out, but include in, women's experience and reflection as I read the Bible or teach, as I engage in pastoral care, pray and conduct worship. It means that I am much more aware of the implications of my gender both for the ways I act or speak and the ways in which my actions or words are received. It means that I am more concerned to be a minister who is a servant of the women of the Church than to be a guardian of the institution and its traditional forms. But none of that means at all that I have turned my back on my ordination vows or that I see myself as a kind of interloper now in foreign (or even enemy) territory. In fact, I hold what many would see as a rather traditional view of what a minister's life should be about. I have found nothing among some of the recent attempts to redefine ministry which can compare with the life I promised to lead, and the roles I promised to fulfil with God's help, at my ordination and at inductions since.

At its heart, ministry is about proclaiming the gospel, breaking bread and sharing wine at the communion table, praying and leading worship, and offering pastoral care and leadership to the Church. I don't dissent from any of that and my whole ministry, at its best, has been about continuing those tasks – even if with a renewed understanding of how some of those things should be done, and with whom. Among the questions about ministry is the one about whether it should be considered functional or ontological. Is it a question of what you do or who you are? Are ministers set aside by the people to fulfil particular roles, or are they called by God to be in a particular relationship to the people? This is not just a debate that divides 'high' from 'low' church, but it emerges in various ways within the traditions. I don't believe that when I was ordained my status was changed before God and I would resist those who want to say that to be ordained is somehow to enter a different order of being. But equally I want to resist those who argue that it's only about function. Experience in other parts of my life tells me that what I do affects who I am and vice versa. I don't stop being a mother, for example, when I'm not actively 'doing' it. There is something about my being that is touched and changed because I have to do something differently. I think that women's lives often testify to a way of living that cannot and does not divide work and leisure, status and function, into different and separate categories. Though I think ministers should act and behave in a professional way, I want to resist the professionalization of ministry. It's not a job, it's a way of life. It is not done best if done with too much attention to hours and rotas. But equally, ministry is not at all about a status that carries no obligations actually to do anything! My experience as a woman and my reflection as a feminist suggest to me that this traditional dichotomy deserves undoing.

Perhaps the greatest challenge with which I wrestle now, at this stage of my ministry, has to do with integrity. The denomination of which I'm a part now gives me work to do beyond the local pastorate, offering me both amazing opportunities and the privilege of wider service and responsibility. I have had cause to be astonished and moved by the trust given me. I belong to a Church which, in many ways, recognizes and affirms the ministry of women. But it is also true, nonetheless, that in every part of the great Church women still face exclusion and sometimes abuse, their experience is not listened to and the truth of their lives is not visible. I know that I am in danger of being tempted to secure my own now sometimes privileged position within the Church by closing my eyes to that reality and by letting go of the hands of my sisters. I believe that God asks me to remain attentive to my own body, to continue to hold to my identity as a woman and to give the best of my scholarship, passion for truth and creativity to a ministry that will bear witness to the God who loves and creates women (and men).

There is a certain indulgence in telling your own story. I spend most of my days with the wisdom of Jesus ringing in my ears that the path to life lies in the loss of self. So it's hard to bring my self to the fore in this way. I have also, naturally, edited the story. The reader does not need to know the details of a personal life that does not conform to the kind of straightforward narrative that a minister's life 'should'. There is cause for shame, sorrow and regret there, as well as deep wells of joy. I hope, however, that the narrative of the ministry to which God continues to call me and coax me, is as honestly told as a chapter of this kind will bear. It may not have the charm of Samuel's tale, but I hope that, though I too sometimes mishear the voice that calls, God finds a way to bring me again to the holy places where people gather, where the Bible is open and where bread and wine are shared. For that is where I can most truly answer the call.

Note

1. Alan Burgess, *The Small Woman* (London: Pan Books, 1957).
2. Rudolph Otto, tr. John W. Harvey, The Idea of the Holy: An enquiry into the non-rational factor in the idea of the divine and its relation to the rational (Oxford: Oxford University Press, 1926).

Fleur Houston

Minister of the United Reformed Church, currently serving the Church of the Holy Family, Blackbird Leys

God calls the most unlikely people to the most unlikely tasks. When I first discerned a calling to the ministry of Word and Sacrament, I reacted in disbelief. My life was happy and contented. Our three children were at school; we already had one minister in the family and I believed then as I still do that the ministry of lay people is vital to the Church.

But the calling was insistent and when I finally decided to let it be tested out by the channels of the Church, it was with a sense of relief.

God leads us through events and encounters that we only recognize later to be a calling. I see now that much of my life up till then was a preparation for this. My childhood in Aberdeenshire was played out in an area of great natural beauty, dominated by Bennachie, the 'mountain of light'. Monymusk was an early monastic settlement, a little village in the crook of the river Don, nestling around an eleventh-century parish church. There were also ruined castles, stone circles and inscribed Pictish stones to nourish a child's historical imagination and develop her religious awareness. The world Church had a presence in the village too; in the camp for displaced persons, there was a magnificent Orthodox chapel with icons and gilded chandeliers made from beaten marmalade tins.

I internalized from my parents the assumption that church and community were bound up with one another. My father was headmaster of the local school and intensely involved in the life of the village where he was well liked and respected. He was also, for over fifty years, session clerk of the parish church, and from my early childhood, he took me to church every Sunday.

My mother encouraged a growing aesthetic sensibility. From the age of five, my brother, sister and I took part annually in the speech and drama sections of the Aberdeen Music Festival. Every year, my mother taught me to deliver poetry in Scots and English, and by the time I was in my teens I knew by heart large sections of Shakespeare as well as most of the great poetic passages of the Bible in the Authorized Version.

At secondary school, I developed a love of Greek, for the sophistication of thought, the beauty of language and the insights into human brilliance and frailty and for art, where I learned to trace character and personality from the lines of face or body and developed a sense of the rhythm and pattern of things. But at Aberdeen University, I studied for an honours degree in French – that was, I thought, more 'relevant' – and obtained a scholarship to forward friendly relations between France and Scotland, spending a year at the Sorbonne, Paris. My enjoyment of French language and literature led to a research degree at Lady Margaret Hall, Oxford, and an assistant lectureship at Queen's University, Belfast, followed by a lectureship at Manchester University.

By then a new phase of life had begun. I married Walter. And in due course Sara was born, then Amy. My knowledge of God, grounded in an awareness of beauty, matured with the companionship of marriage and the rich textures of family life. But there were also deeper cadences that sang of human fragility. For we went to live in Nsukka, Nigeria, just after the end of the Biafra War and, although we have lasting memories of the loyalty and friendship of those we met, water and western medicine were in short supply, malaria was endemic and armed robbers in evidence. And then, four years after our return to live in Liverpool, our third daughter, Laura, died shortly after her birth.

My personal understanding of God became increasingly bound up with an awareness of the Church as agent of God's purposes. When Elisabeth, our youngest child, was an infant, we moved to Cambridge; and over the years, I became more and more involved with service to Emmanuel Church, as Junior Church leader, then as elder, then as Church Secretary. Around the same time, I was invited to attend the Colloque Franco-Britannique and discovered that I enjoyed theology. My personal knowledge of God, now firmly rooted in service to the Church, was taking on another dimension: an urgent awareness of the gap between the world as it is and the world as God would have it be. And I derived energy from the awareness that this gap is not inevitable and that God does not want us to live in it.

And so when I began my training at Westminster College, it was with a sense of rightness that has only increased as the years have gone by. There were times of testing, before and after my years of training. First, I had to tell my parents. And a letter or phone call wouldn't do – I had to tell them in person. For I anticipated that they would be deeply distressed. The Church of Scotland of their generation was imbued with the normativity of male ministry. They had little experience of women ministers and had found my election to the eldership very hard to take. But when they learned that I was about to train for the ministry, contrary to my expectations, they were greatly thrilled and continued to provide the most loyal encouragement and support over the years. The second time of testing was the year I had to wait after the end of my training before receiving a call to a local church. Introductions there were, and in each case there were obstacles. But I knew that God's timing is right and I waited on a deeper understanding of his purposes.

Then two things happened: First, I received a phone call from Geneva. The World Council of Churches was looking for a minister, bilingual in French and English but not English by nationality, with experience of living in West Africa, and I more or less fitted the bill. Could I go to Cameroon with Archbishop Desmond Tutu in a week's time? The aim of this mission was to do what could be done to prevent civil war in a country which was cascading into anarchy following recent elections. And so I went. The diplomatic work was intense, we met with the president, we met with the leader of the opposition parties, we met with politicians. We talked, we prayed, we preached. We met too with church leaders who were disturbed by the 'disappearance' of ministers who had challenged the policies of the régime in power. The level of fear among the people we met was very high – but so too was their courage. The experience sharpened vividly my awareness of the urgent need to proclaim a gospel of peace, justice and reconciliation.

Then, on my return, I received an invitation from the Church Secretary of St Andrew's United Reformed Church, Sheffield, to lead worship. I didn't know the church, but several people had already suggested that we might have something in common, so I was curious. I went and immediately felt at home. The vacancy committee convened that afternoon and asked if they might give my name to the Moderators. As the formal process of introduction got under way, I responded to the warmth and vitality of the worshipping congregation, the respect for the living traditions of the past, the desire to apply the gospel to the present and the zeal for mission. I shared their aims and it was with joy that I responded to their call to minister among them. The 'inward constraint and the outward call' answered each other. As if in confirmation of the rightness of this, the post of tutor in Old Testament Studies in Luther King House, Manchester, became vacant shortly after. Walter was appointed and we made our home in Sheffield.

Calling is a continual process; there are several other calls within the overall framework. Sometimes there is the inner certainty that it is God's will that one should move to serve another pastorate. After eight years in Sheffield, this certainty was brought home to me in two ways: first, through circumstances, and second, through the quality of relationships with the Church of the Holy Family, Blackbird Leys. I knew that 'circumstances', in this case the fact that Walter had been appointed to the post of Chaplain-Fellow in Theology at Mansfield, were God's hand directing me to Oxford. It was clear to me that the appointment was right – and it was equally clear to me that we should make our home together in Oxford. So I told the Synod Moderators that I was available to exercise ministry nearer Oxford and prepared elders and members of St Andrew's for that eventuality. But I had to wait for eight months before I could enter the process – there was a moratorium on vacancies in the Oxford and Reading District.

In due course the name of the Church of the Holy Family appeared on the list of vacant pastorates. I made enquiries and, interested in what I heard, asked the Synod Moderator if I might explore the situation further. I met with the Church Officers' Group and the reasons for my initial interest in the pastorate became clearer to me. As a minister of the United Reformed Church, I have always been interested in pushing back ecumenical boundaries. This pioneering Local Ecumenical Partnership (LEP) had come into being in the 1960s as a product of the Nottingham Faith and Order Conference. A new housing estate, it was felt, needed a new kind of church. So it evolved and today there is one united congregation sponsored by the Anglican, Baptist, Methodist, Moravian and United Reformed Church traditions. To minister in this situation with all its challenges and opportunities was attractive. I also saw Christian faith as being firmly rooted in everyday life and I noted the many ways in which this church was involved in service to the community. The preparation of services has always been important to me and I warmed to the fact that the members were clearly anxious that the new minister should develop further the worship of the church. I discerned too from what I observed and heard the great pastoral need of the estate and found myself responding to that need. I responded to the theological rigour of those I met and to their openness and friendliness; and the call when it came was expressed in such warm terms that I had no alternative but to accept.

Each of the churches I have served as minister has beautiful worship space; each presents excellent opportunities for developing the use of music in worship. The Church of the Holy Family is particularly distinctive in both respects. Its liturgical space, with great swooping parabolas focused on the table and font, enhances the drama of the sacraments and lends itself to creative use in worship. It also enables effective crowd control. This is particularly useful in the case of the large congregations, usually numbering hundreds of people, whom we attract frequently for occasional services. We have a splendid gospel choir and we use in worship musical settings for hymns and responses composed by one or other of our members. We draw upon the liturgical resources of our five different sponsoring traditions and the congregation encourages an emphasis on exegetical preaching. I have learned to value and respect the traditions of the Caribbean community and am honoured from time to time to lead Black Pentecostal services.

The LEP is also the parish church, and an important part of my time is spent in working with people on the estate who have little or no church connections but who do have religious sensibility. The work to 'bridge the gap' is as creative as it is intense. Ministry around funerals is particularly significant and often has long-lasting ramifications. Preparation for baptism or for confirmation and church membership can tax one's hermeneutical skills and imagination but the effort is worthwhile.

When I was ordained, I knew that I was called to proclaim a gospel of reconciliation in Christ, and that this involved preaching and pastoral care. But such ministry often leads me in quite unforeseen directions. The two following instances illustrate this.

A church member had struggled for years to maintain the fiction of a marriage that had died. And this was because of the great seriousness with which she held the marriage vows. But the day came when her husband put pressure on her to apply for a divorce and she knew she had to give in. She was distraught. Deeply religious, she felt she had betrayed her relationship with God. I gradually became convinced that the only way of addressing that situation with integrity was to hold a service in church after the decree absolute was awarded.

When the time came, there were some things about which she was clear: she wanted to honour her wedding and include some material from the wedding service and she wanted to affirm the intention that marriage is a life-long union. And so there was a thanksgiving for marriage and the gift of children, with a recognition that this marriage had nonetheless ended. There was also an acknowledgement that in marriage breakdown each partner has a share of responsibility, as does the wider family and friends, an expression of penitence and assurance of God's forgiveness and, finally, an offering of this home and its future to God in blessing.

It was a simple pastoral liturgy but it had far-reaching effects. It was cathartic. Virtually the whole congregation, including the organist, wept unrestrainedly. The person involved felt she had honoured her vows and didn't feel a failure any more. The effect on her has been long-lasting.

What I hadn't bargained for was that one of the congregation would send a brief account of the service to the local newspaper. An extraordinary media circus got under way. Some newspapers used language carelessly – 'celebration of divorce' was not what it was about! Radio and television interviews were particularly interesting – the interviewers often had little or no religious experience but asked good questions. Not only 'What does one do in an act of worship?' but 'What does an act of worship do?' On breakfast TV, that is an opportunity not to be missed! Many people with little or no church connection tuned in to their local radio stations, and found themselves thinking about these things. They would write and tell me; and for a year, I received accounts of painful situations chiefly, though not exclusively, connected with marriage breakdown. The one common factor was a need to express confession and receive forgiveness, to be released from contemplation of failure, to turn about, released into hope for the future.

My second instance also stems from an act of worship. A local resident was brought to church one Sunday by his landlady. He wanted to explore the Christian faith. We were impressed by the strength of his conviction and his growing involvement with the life of the church. So in due course, he attended instruction classes and was baptized on Easter Day. At home in Iran, he had been intimidated because of his interest in Christianity and had fled to the UK where his initial application to remain had been refused. I accompanied him to two successive Appeal Tribunal hearings.

In neither case did I feel that justice was well served. The questions asked to test the credibility of the appellant's Christian faith were unfair and inappropriate; the assumptions made about the non-evangelical ethos of the Church of the Holy Family had no basis in reality. The appeals were not upheld.

With three colleagues who had similar experiences, we drafted a dossier which assembled a number of cases from a wide spread of different church traditions. We listed improper questions used by immigration authorities to test whether or not a claimant had genuinely become Christian. We also chronicled the experience of clergy who had given evidence only to have this swept aside by the adjudicator. On our behalf, this dossier was sent to the Home Office by the Churches Main Committee. This led to continuing correspondence with the Home Office and meetings with the Parliamentary Under-Secretary of State, officials from the Immigration Nationality Directorate and the legal services. Our concerns now are wider in scope and negotiations with the government on behalf of the churches are ongoing.

In the quality of pastoral relationships I enjoy, I am greatly privileged. I have known many fine relationships in which I have been able to give much and in which I have also received a great deal. I am deeply thankful, for in such instances one gives and receives something of God.

I am all the same aware of the risk of transference. It is not uncommon for unhealed emotions regarding a parent to be transferred onto a minister of the same gender and I have occasionally been confronted by abnormally high energy levels in the way people respond to me as a minister. I might instance the man who maintained with passion that 'women are all heart and no head' or the woman who protested vehemently (but not to the minister!) that I did not regularly 'help in the kitchen'. Such criticisms may or may not have been deserved, but the energy levels that sustained them had to be significant.

An extreme example was a young woman who stalked me without remission for two years. She had, we learned subsequently, briefly stalked other women: there was nothing I could have done to prevent it. She attended one or two services which I led and then asked if I would baptize her son. I arranged a visit. And then the letters started, followed by threatening or abusive phone calls, pizza deliveries and expensive bouquets. I advised the elders. Silent phone calls became insistent, up to seventy a night. Then one day, she ran amok. Diagnosed with a personality disorder, she was regarded as mad by the police, seen as untreatable by the psychiatric services. No-one could help.

In the associated trauma for all concerned, one stark and sobering fact was clear: the nature of this person's psychiatric condition meant that she was incapable of authentic relationships. She lived with fantasies which she came to believe were true. Her exaggerated expressions of penitence were short-lived. This, combined with the intensely personal focus of her attentions, made it impossible for me, or indeed the local church, to minister to her the grace of God.

It was a salutary warning against any tendency to rely on what is humanly possible instead of trusting wholly in the all-sufficiency of God.

Is there any sense in which my experience of ministry as a woman is different from that of male colleagues? The answer has to be no. I find that I cannot address that question on the basis of personal experience. Successive male colleagues with whom I have collaborated in team ministry have been as different from one another as they have been from myself.

The Church is set in a broken world that needs to be healed. The mission is by definition ecumenical, and I have always known it important to foster ecumenism. I could cite the bringing to fruition of a local Churches Together in Sheffield. I could cite the work I did for the Yorkshire Synod in fostering relations with the Church of the Palatinate or for Wessex with the Eglise Réformée de France and the United Church of Zambia. Or the service I gave to the Assembly Doctrine, Prayer and Worship and Ecumenical committees. My awareness of other traditions was enriched by my work with the Methodist Faith and Order Committee and the Joint Liturgical Group. I currently sit on the ecumenical bench on General Synod and am listed in the Textbook among Moravian ministers.

But there is a particular dimension of this that has become increasingly focused for me over the years. To begin with, the ecumenical movement saw questions of doctrine and church order as problems of Faith and Order, whereas questions of politics, economics and the significance of the Christian faith in the life of the world were treated as Life and Work. But now it is increasingly recognized that the two cannot be separated. This gradually became apparent in my own experience.

My lengthy engagement with the Sheffield Churches Homelessness

Forum and the St Andrew's Child Contact Centre was based on theological grounding and continuing reflection with elders. My involvement with the Reuilly doctrinal conversations between the Anglican Churches in the UK and the Reformed and Lutheran Churches in France would have meant little without its embodiment in 'witness and service'.

The work I do as a member of the Council of the Community of Protestant Churches in Europe (CPCE) brings these two strands of ecumenical experience together and has become an increasingly important element in my ministry. The CPCE is founded on the Leuenberg Agreement, which crossed boundaries that had been a feature of church life since the Reformation and enabled pulpit and table fellowship between Reformed, Lutheran, United and Methodist Churches in Europe and South America. With a compelling vision of the imperative of church unity, doctrinal conversations continue to be a major feature – with the European Baptists, with the Orthodox, with the Anglican Churches in Europe. As the new Europe emerges with all its social and ethical challenges, there is a fresh imperative to cross social and inter-religious boundaries.

There is a sense of movement, of dynamic, as I have responded to the calling to minister. And this has been enabled by the generosity of my husband and children, who have given me space to dream dreams and discover God's vision for the Church.

Jane Leach

*Senior Tutor and Director of Pastoral Studies,
Wesley House, Cambridge*

Ordination by the laying on of hands

embodied –
now we are become what we have been
in flesh – at last we know the gentle hands
of choosing, blessing, breaking, giving,
laid on us.

hands,
heavy, measured, deep with meaning –
often unawares the means of grace –
now grave, with all the weight of life and faith,

impress
upon us deep and wait upon the echo sound
of answering deep – the 'yes'
of flesh and blood
to incarnation.

(poems by Jane Leach)

I was ordained a presbyter at the Methodist Conference of 1998 after five years' training at Wesley House in Cambridge and two years' probation serving as a minister in a circuit of nine churches in the Cambridgeshire Fens. The day was a momentous one and marked a significant step in the journey of becoming who I am.

I felt called to ministry in my late teens, but those who knew me best say that they knew my life would be bound up with the life of the Church. From about eleven onwards I had made a strong identification with our local church as a place where I felt safe and heard and valued for myself; it was a place in which I was taken seriously in all my (doubtless) peculiarity; and it was a place in which I encountered God, identifying with the Christ who was not afraid to take up his cross.

When I offered as a local preacher at the age of nineteen, I knew that answering this call was responding to God's invitation to me to be fully myself. I knew that without the discipline of an office I would find it hard to find the motivation to keep myself faithful to those routines that would be life-giving: the close and regular reading of Scripture; the wrestling with questions of faith; the struggle to bring myself, honestly, to prayer.

Like the seasons of the church year, the discipline of preaching has provided me a structure through these (almost) twenty years, to keep me within the means of grace – something which I first experienced in the Methodist Covenant Service once I had been confirmed at thirteen, but which I articulated for myself most clearly on the occasion of the ordination of my friend, Michael.

Covenant

A gift this life has been, this
fixed frame life, bound close
with promises: (I bind unto myself today the strong name of the
 Trinity.)

Bound I have been,
begun in baptism, swaddled in the grace of Christ,
from which there has been no escape, nor need.

Bound by choice within this chosenness,
at times, I beat against the chest of such a steadfast, strong embrace
and wrestled with the angels who would not let me go till
dawn has found me standing at the altar, limping

and yet holding out to others in my out-stretched arms
this fierce-fired grace that burns and bubbles in my voice,
'Lift up your hearts,'
And leans to hear the bound, Amen,
'We lift them to the Lord.'

When life has been hard, it has been the disciplines of preaching and presiding at communion which have kept me faithful in trying to be real with myself and before God. When I was a circuit minister (from 1996 to 2001) I would read the lectionary readings on Monday morning, and live with them through the week, as I chaired meetings and led assemblies and visited the dying and dug the garden. By Sunday, it would be a question of what not to say; by Sunday the readings would have come alive with resonances from my own life and from the lives of others and this was essential to me: the sermon needed first to have spoken to me and called for my own repenting, my own turning back to the truth that I am held in being by grace, and not by any skill or knowledge or device of my own. The necessity for this grounding came home to me when preaching as a visitor in the church in which I was brought up in River near Dover.

On preaching at River

self spent
I kneel, to voice the prayers
of beading, bright, beseeching eyes, too grateful
for the magic touch of rhetoric,
like stardust sprinkled liberally
on ancient longings buried deep; too grateful
for the mirror-glimpses of themselves
as precious souls, whose lives, embattled yet,
are held between the stars; and I,

self spent,
kneel, head in hands –
the image of their piety – and wonder
if I've spun them lies and whether they would know – or care?
as long as I can touch their dreams
and weave them to reality.

I guess, like other women, I have been reluctant to claim the authority that belongs to the office of presbyter. Disturbed by abuses of power, within the Church and beyond it, it has taken me a long time to realize that ministry can only be empowering if the leader takes the power that is theirs, acknowledges it and uses it wisely. This was something I first learnt in liturgy.

I was presiding at a baptism and there were many more visitors in the church than regulars. Preaching about being beloved of God, I offered to bless anyone who wanted to come forward, using the baptismal water and the words, 'You are much loved'. Having issued the invitation the silence was deafening. No-one moved. Standing by the font I felt exposed, embodying God's invitation in a far more vulnerable way than I normally did behind the communion table. I began to accommodate the possibility that no-one would come. And then they came:

STORIES

These little ones . . .

To hold in my hands the power
to bless or withhold my hands,
is this what you meant:
'The sins that you loose are forgiven, but those
not forgiven remain?'

The choice – to loose sins, or not –
I'd thought to be yours, alone, and yet
here I stand, hands soothing with water (none other)
each brow after furrowed-deep
brow, eyes searching for peace.

And had I not offered this birth-water sign,
what would they have carried away,
these little ones, caught in the tide
of the teeming world's pain, streaming the aisle
for the touch of my finger-tips, firm
on their faces, still glistening with grace, wet
from the font of new life, fount of rebirth?

I began to realize that to hold the office of presbyter is sometimes a lonely place to stand. Although ministry is always relational, a leader needs to be able to stand apart and speak, not just as 'we' among 'us', but as 'I' to 'you', for words of grace to be heard and heard deeply.

The learning came partly through standing in that lonely place, and partly through receiving the ministry of others who were prepared to embody grace for me.

Rembrandt Petite: Return of the Prodigal

Uncorking her story
She thought it would outburst –
A torrent of tears
Until she was drowned.
But the flood-words just faltered
And fractured a silence,
A deafening, soul-wrenching
Chasm of sound;
Till into the life wound,
Not words, but a presence,
Of softness and stillness
Was bold to contain
The prodigal longings

Of one lonely daughter,
Returning, at last,
To remember her name.

The poem describes a pastoral encounter which happened on the retreat before my ordination. Nine months before I was ordained, my three ordained colleagues in the Fenland circuit – Neville, Herbert and Adrian – had died within three weeks of each other. Extremely inexperienced, I was left, largely on my own, to work with eight churches. In a state of shock myself, I did my best to help the churches grieve, and to enable all those churches to continue their work of ministry in their respective communities. By the time I reached the ordinands' retreat, I was exhausted. Some of the feelings of the time are expressed in this poem, written after a visit to St Cuthbert's tomb in Durham Cathedral.

Retreat to St Cuthbert's Tomb

In the shade of the altar six steps high lies Cuthbert,
Sleeping in the hallowed cool of centuries.
Long past, the grasping hands of church and state;
The hasty flight from Viking grip; the preying eyes on saintly flesh,
Long dead. Your last translation leaves you be
In peace to gaze this next one thousand years
On Christ, transcendent, mirror for your hard-earned poise,
Cruciform above. And O what bliss one summer afternoon,
In flight from preying twentieth century eyes,
To press my hollow cheek on silent stone,
And rest between your gaze on gaze –
Hand to hand and soul to soul adoring.

Sitting with Dorothy in a small room at Ushaw College, three days away from my ordination, I had no such words. Yet Dorothy had the insight and the courage to read my suppressed anger; to apologize on behalf of the Church; to weep tears I could not find; and eventually to hold me. In doing so, she enabled me to come to myself. When, later that day, she lifted the chalice at the communion, I felt my exhaustion and grief and anger lifted with it, and in the lifting of that chalice I recognized the work I am called to do and to which I was about to be ordained.

Communion

Presiding at communion wholly centres
Me in who I am; requiring me through presence
To draw in past and future through this point

In time; demanding sinewed concentration – Re-
Membering the body in each wondering
Pair of eyes; each pair of hands outstretched
And longing to receive – not me, but life
In all its fullness, channelled here if
I can firm my feet and ground myself
In love itself that grace might flow.

The ability to stand firm in myself and in the love of God for me and for all creation has come largely through friendship with the living and with the communion of saints. A series of poems which brings together these two strands consists of variations about the statue of Mary by Josef Pyrz, which also stands in Durham Cathedral.

Theme & Variations on Annunciation by Joseph Pyrz, Variation V

Mary,
We allow you
No history; no name;
No growing, rebelling,
Insisting or choosing,
Only yielding, submitting
In your women's clothes.

But young though you were,
It was not angel innocence
That chose you to be saved by child-bearing –
It was the elusive, hard-earned truth
You'd already grasped with two hands –
That any who would gain the world
Must sculpt a place within themselves
To bear, embodied,
All the depth of human pain, until
Both host and guest, together,
Are transformed.

Mary,
Who was it who taught you
To open yourself to the pain of the world?
Who held you and rocked you, caressing
Your need in her gaze till you knew
Beyond doubt you were loved; loved
Beyond time and all hoping?
And who was it that you held

Close to yourself, shaping
A space for the angels'
Embrace for the first time?
Finding through simple attending a healing
Transforming the whole inner-scape
Of the known world?

All hail Mary, full of grace
And she who taught you,
Held you, let herself be held and changed . . .

To some degree these poems are the story of growing into a conferred authority to be a representative person – to minister Christ's compassion – as the Methodist ordinal puts it. The focus of this journey was upon worship leading and pastoral work and the relationship between the two. Moving back to Cambridge to take up the role of senior tutor at Wesley House highlighted for me the ecclesial nature of ministry and the need to represent the authority of the Church which was much less comfortable.

Initially confused by the loss of key pastoral and worship leading roles when I moved to college from circuit ministry, it took some time to realize that exercising episcope is ministry too. Although I spend a good deal of time one to one with students it is very different from pastoral work. The student and I are bound to a covenant in which they must address profound issues of life and faith. Members of congregations and communities come to the minister by choice. Students come because they must, and sometimes there is painful and difficult work to be done in which hard things must be said and heard.

Engaged in this work I have become painfully aware of the need for supervision; the need to know my own self and to keep my issues separate from those of the students; and the continuing need to make my own journey of faith so that we can meet, when it is appropriate, not just as tutor and student, but as fellow disciples.

The college women's group which is organized by women students but open to staff has been one important venue for re-membering myself as a disciple person alongside some of those among whom I exercise authority. It is not possible in that context to tell all of my story, but it is possible to allow important aspects of myself to be known. Identifying together common issues of ministry and gender has been a helpful reminder of my belonging in the body of Christ and my responsibility to be a shaper of the tradition as well as one who represents it. This poem arose out of the collaborative making of a cloth corpus for the college chapel and the group's meditation on the role of women as witnesses to the resurrection.

STORIES

Easter Vigil

like women, we kept vigil; the air spiced with frankincense,
sandalwood seasoning our grief;
in these lost moments mouthing a last fare-well
to a body we had loved; given birth to; now
leaving behind who knows what vestiges of life
to which we'd clung – too blind and fearful yet to stumble on.

and then a sign from deep within that time
had shifted on its axis; that devotion now needs work
and thought and care through hands outstretched, untying,
releasing, receiving this crumpled, collapsing corpus of cloth –
all tension gone. Like women, laying out their dead,
embodying love in our bare hands.

and as we straightened, smoothed and folded,
lingering, still clinging to a life we knew,
some courage dawned to dare release this golden thread
that grace might come. And a loosened knot eased
and broke the silent waters of the aching heart and like women,
going to the tomb while it was yet still dark
we found in our arms these grave clothes and a stranger, shining.

Allowing myself to be known in ministry has been a difficult issue. I believe that ministry happens when I am able to be real with others, and yet it is not always appropriate for everything about me to be spoken. Sometimes this surfaces in anger as it did recently listening to a lecture by Professor James Dunn.

In response to Jimmy Dunn

You tell me,
'According to Paul, nothing may be added to faith as a requirement for others' justification.'

I ask you,
'Not even being heterosexual?'

You tell me,
'In Romans 14 Paul makes it clear that if you can give thanks to God as you eat idol meat, by extension, being able to give thanks in good faith for your sexuality and relationships is the test.'

I ask you,
'When I've been silenced and taught to hate who I am.
When people like me have been criminalized and sent to gas chambers,

Where is the community in which I shall learn to rejoice in who I am
and whom I love,
When what I have learned in the Church is to be grateful for crumbs?'

You tell me,
'As Romans 14 suggests, "Give thanks, but limit your freedom
for the sake of others who cannot stand where you stand."'

I ask you,
'Is it really the same to keep quiet about the butcher you use
As it is to be silent about who you are; where you see beauty
And what it is to share your deepest self in love?'

You tell me,
'Don't ask; don't tell.'

I tell you,
'Silence is the stealthiest form of persecution. It breeds
isolation, suicide and despair. Have you seen the statistics?
It is this from which I am saved by faith.
Where is the community who will rejoice with me
In the God of our salvation and come with me
Into his courts with thanksgiving?'

You tell me,
'Authentic faith is that which propels us to bear witness to the resurrection.'

I tell you,
'You never ask. You have told me not to tell.'

The truth, however, is not so stark. The Church is both a life-giving place for me, providing a framework for the deepest things of my life in which I have grown and become more nearly myself, and, simultaneously, the Church is a place which cannot always cope with the full reality of who I am. The important learning is that this is true, not just for me, but for all of us who make up the Church and struggle to receive God's grace.

As I have needed to learn to love, not a fantasy of myself, but the self I am, so I have need to learn to love the body of Christ as it is, flawed and in need of redemption.

Psyche et Eros: reflections on reading Mary Grey

And nothing is withheld and yet
There are constraints; not because of moral bonds
Imposed upon us by the odd and chancy creeds we inherited
When we were not looking but because we choose
To love with our eyes open, refusing a reduced identity,

Even for the sake of passion whilst the passion lasts.
Instead we seek intelligent loving: love that does not select
What to see and what to rue at leisure when it's all too late;
Love that opens wide the heart to otherness in all
Its full dimensions, alongside all life's other claims.
And love that will not close its eyes to history – the scars
Of each one's journey towards the truer self are precious,
Marking wounds that may not fully heal in this life.
And never willing otherwise, rejoicing
Through our tears that things are as they are.
No fantasies. For fantasy divides the self from presence
To the self and grace – leaving us bereft and separated.
Instead we choose real presence: laying, at last,
Responsible claim to relatedness.

In the end, ministry, for me, is about relationship. It is about being attentive to the other in all their otherness, whether the other is an institution or an individual; it is about being attentive to my own heart – to its distortions and its wisdoms – and to those who know me well; and in and through it all, it is about being attentive to the God who has called me into this particular relationship with the Church as an ordained minister. This final poem celebrates both the particularity of the ministry of the ordained, and its embeddedness in the ministry of the whole people of God, worked out in the fullness of our humanity.

Ash Wednesday – In memory of Ruby Scott

Between showers, bright with rain, the earth sunk
Beneath our purposed feet. Clumping, each along
Our chosen track to the farthest part
Of the farm, the cloying soil webbed our feet,
Reminder of our earth-bound fate,
And weighed our gait like swans returning
Burdened from the fields in sodden Spring.

And our hearts, this bright March day, were wet
With tears, and our tracks, like those of wading birds
Along the shore, marked for all to see our path to this,
The long appointed place. And pausing, here,
Beneath the trees – ivy-clad and bone-dry
Dead – the rooks to call the last lament,
We scattered, white, our sister's dust,
Cruciform, on Adam's clay, and prayed,
That we, like she, in life and death, might yet enrich
God's given earth, even, on this least fertile part of the farm.

Margaret Mwailu

Probationer Minister with the Methodist Church of Great Britain

I was brought up in a Christian home, and can never remember a time when I would not attend church regularly. My parents taught me what it meant to be a Christian and how to establish a personal relationship with God. I became a Christian at an early age and was baptized. My baptism was a particularly meaningful event in my life. Preparation for baptism was intensive and grounded me well in basic Christian beliefs.

Like many Kenyan families, my father worked some 300 miles away, and came home only during his annual leave. As a family we looked forward to dad coming home, because he brought us gifts and, if extremely good, we had added pocket money. As the last born in the family, I was always good and got extra pocket money as the baby of the home.

At the age of six I felt compelled to give part of my pocket money to God. I did this during Sunday school offering. I did not understand what I was doing, but I felt happy that I was giving God something more than what I had been given by mother for offering. I shared with mother what I was doing; she was overwhelmed and commended me. She enquired how long this had been going on for and explained to me that God was calling me not only to give him my pocket money, but also, to give my self fully to his ministry. She explained how God called Samuel at a very early age. The story sounded so real to me that I decided when I grew up I would work in the Church.

I continued faithfully giving God some of my pocket money, until my early teens, when I started to save my money to buy material things. Also because I was not keen in attending church any more. Peer pressure influenced me to a point that my dad had to caution me. And before long, something frightening happened to me. I vividly remember reading a book while walking, when suddenly something bit my right heel – a puff-adder snake. I started crying and calling for help, at the same time cutting the hem of my dress, to tie my leg before the poison spread. Someone arrived within minutes, and scraped the teeth of the snake from my heel. The evening felt long before dad got back from work (by now he had retired from his job as magistrate and owned his own business nearer home). When he came, he took me to the nearest dispensary, which was about ten miles away. I was treated and sent home. During the night my leg started hurting so much, and by morning it was very swollen, with many blisters on the heel; when I stepped out of bed, it started bleeding. The poison of the snake had taken its toll. My parents took me to the district hospital, which was about twenty miles away, and I was admitted. The blisters got infected and I could not walk for nearly two weeks. It was during my stay in hospital, as I lay in bed, that I felt a deeper desire to serve God, and my thoughts went back to the time when I was giving God some of my pocket money. On leaving the hospital, I promised myself to serve God full-time, when I completed my secondary school education.

After my O levels, I did not seek employment, neither did I desire to proceed with further education, but my mind was set to train for Christian ministry. One day there was an open day for interviews to recruit teachers. I joined a group from my village, and we went to the education office for the open day and interviews. I had no peace about what I was about to do. Surprisingly, a large group were not interviewed, and I was one of them. I was not upset but willingly accepted the outcome. I felt an inner assurance that teaching in a secular school was not for me. A few weeks later, there was a letter from the local Government Secretarial College inviting me to go for training as a secretary. I turned this offer down, although it offered a lucrative salary and highlife of the type a teenage girl would long for.

I attended a Christian youth camp, and shared with the director of youth ministry my desire to serve the Lord. He advised me to share with my local minister and the elders of the church. Meetings were arranged for me to go through the process of candidating. My parents, siblings and friends encouraged and supported me as I went through this process. After consultations the leaders of the local church, district and connexional panel told me that they all sensed God's call in me, and that they were willing to encourage me to go forward to train for full-time ministry. The idea of ordination was not an issue for discussion because my church, the Africa Inland Church, Kenya, did not ordain women at the time.[1] Nevertheless, I had the conviction to obey God's call.

With the recommendation of the District Synod, I was invited for an interview at a theological college, some 400 miles away from home. I attended the interview, after which the college principal (Dr Gehman) noted that I was slightly under the recommended age. Many of the students were mature men and women, over the age of twenty-five years, and I was only seventeen years old. However, the principal informed me that after listening to my testimony they would offer me a place to train for Christian ministry. I was overwhelmed and looked forward to starting the training. I had peace of mind about my vocation. This marked the first phase of my long journey – scary, but I had peace and assurance of God's presence through his Holy Spirit.

In 1975, I started my training, and graduated in 1979 with an honours Diploma in Theology, second overall in four years, only topped by one male student! I also had found a fiancé in college. I left the college full of excitement and looked forward to serving the Lord. We had planned to marry shortly after my graduation, but my fiancé received a scholarship to study in England, plus my mother advised me to work for a while before marrying. We postponed our wedding and my fiancé left for England, with the hope that he would return the following summer.

I was appointed to teach in a bible institute, the only ministry open at the time to female graduates. Besides teaching, I was a matron to the females in the institute, and also heavily involved in preaching at women's meetings, and Christian youth camps. I enjoyed my ministry for a very short time, and then things turned sour. Some of the tutors and church leaders had opposed my appointment. They held Victorian views imbued with African culture and felt that it was not suitable for a young female to teach male student ministers who were older than her. Fellow tutors influenced a few students who started to abscond from my classes, just because I was a young woman teaching them. Some of the male tutors would walk into the classroom while I taught. They made life a hell for me. Some of the leaders who wanted me to stay argued that for many years the church had been accepting young white missionary girls, to teach in bible institutes; how come when it came to a black intelligent woman it was not acceptable? The conflict escalated, and as the saying goes, *where two elephants are involved in a fight, the grass suffers*. This time, I was *the grass* that suffered. I had to stop and leave, with feelings of rejection! The first phase of my journey ended with conflict between church leaders and missionaries, and left me with a deep sense of rejection. Thankfully, my fiancé returned in the summer, and we got married in August 1980.

The second phase of my journey started when I arrived in England in October 1980, as newly married bride. Life was exciting in a new country, and I looked forward to taking up ministry. Little did I know how much the events of the previous phase had affected me. That experience had a profound impact on my outlook on ministry. My self-confidence was crushed, I had become very timid, frightened, and became very shy. I brushed off any thoughts of church-related ministry, although there was always 'a small voice' that kept assuring me of God's call to ministry.

In response to this small voice, and with the encouragement of my husband, I enrolled at Trinity College, Bristol, for a two-year Diploma in Higher Education (DipHE) leading to a BA degree. I did not complete the course because of the arrival of our first-born. We agreed with my tutor that I would change from the DipHE course to a one-year missiology course. I transferred my credits to this course. After two years, I graduated with a Diploma in Science of Missions (DSM). The following three years were spent at home looking after the child. My husband and I found ourselves 'de-churched' as we struggled with the racial tensions of the 1980s as black people in Britain. Inwardly, I feared venturing to try ministry in case I faced rejection again. I convinced myself, being a housewife was a ministry in itself. However, I had a tug of war within me; I could not wipe away the desire to serve God. Occasionally things would happen which reminded me that I was not only a woman, but I was a black woman in a white country. I was frightened that church leaders in England might treat me the same way I was treated in my own country by white missionaries.

When our son turned four years, I went back to college for further theological studies, feeling this would give me some credentials, perhaps, making me somebody! I vividly recall praying, 'If, God, you want me to serve you, please provide finance for my studies ... I am yours, gold and silver are yours and the ministry you have for me is yours as well.' Miraculously, I was awarded a grant for three years to take a theology degree course at Birmingham University and started in 1985.

After graduation, I did not envisage church ministry as my earlier experiences still haunted me. I was fearful, timid, and could not stand in front of a fellowship meeting and speak. I decided since my husband was in the ministry, I will be consumed in him and give him moral and spiritual support, and this way, I would be serving God. As I continued in what I call 'home-based ministry', I again enrolled at Manchester University for biblical studies, still seeking further studies, trying to address feelings of inadequacy. This took two years; by this time I had spent eleven years studying theology and biblical studies. Having dismissed in my mind full-time ministry, I found myself asking 'What about social work?' thinking that I could become a faithful Christian social worker. I walked to the Social Services offices in Birmingham, seeking information about training as a social worker. I was informed that experience of working in a specified field was a requirement. I was advised to work as a volunteer alongside social workers. I started visiting elderly people in their homes. I did this for some time, and as I was about to convince myself this was God's calling, I was expecting our second son! This blew me into pieces, not so much the forthcoming child, but because I was very ill and was in and out of hospital for the entire nine months. Following the birth of our second son, I suffered severely with postnatal depression, which lasted several years. After recovery, I was still wondering what God's will for my life was. The Chair of York District, Stuart Burgess, encouraged me to be involved in church work, to which I firmly said, NO. I did not feel confident to work in church ministry again. My husband also tried to encourage, telling me I was as qualified as some of his female colleagues, to which he received the same answer.

At this stage, I had started wondering whether God was calling me to serve him outside the Church. I remembered the invitation letter from the Government Secretarial College in Kenya, early 1975. Without hesitation I started looking for colleges that offered administrative training. I imagined if I trained for secretarial and administrative procedures, I would work as personal assistant either to a bishop or at the Methodist Connexional office. I contacted York College of Higher and Further Education, and the door was wide open. This again worked very well, because I got a job as a care assistant in a residential home for the elderly for two nights a week. This enabled me to pay the college fees. Within a year, I was awarded the Royal Society of Arts Diploma in Administrative Procedures. I tried several Christian organizations, and the only interview offered was with National Children's Homes, in Harrogate. I had very high hopes for the job, since it was a Methodist organization.

To my shock, I was not offered the job. I tried several other Christian organizations, but all doors were closed. As I contemplated and wondered what God was saying in all this, I saw an advert in a local insurance company. I called and was offered an interview straightaway and a job offer followed in the afternoon on the same day. For three months I worked in that office, until one day, I clearly heard a voice speak to me, 'This is not what I called you for.' I looked around, and saw no-one around me. A chill ran through my body, and I said, 'All the theological and biblical training was to end up working as a word processor, typing equine insurance claims?' To make matters worse, the desk where I was working from faced a big blank wall, while my back was turned to others in the room. As I continued to ponder my situations, I broke down; I could not control my tears, they became like a bubbling spring. I went home, and after a day I was admitted to hospital for three weeks. This was to be a turning-point back to the call into full-time ministry.

The third phase was full of self-questioning because my health deteriorated. This caused great concerns and I was in and out of hospital for tests. I travelled to the USA and visited my sister Esther in Rochester, New York. She introduced me to her minister. The minister invited me to speak at her weekly fellowship group. I accepted the invitation, but afterwards I was very nervous. At the same time, I appreciated the minister's gesture to invite me. In the meeting I shared what the Lord had placed in my heart; the response was overwhelming. As a result of this, my thoughts went back to the desire I had to be involved in ordained ministry. I remembered the eleven years I had spent reading theology and biblical studies. The following day after the meeting we travelled to visit my cousin in Maryland. As we caught up with family news, my cousin's daughter asked me why I was not involved in ministry. I went numb, and had no answer to give her. It sounded as if an angel had asked me this question because two different people at the fellowship meeting at my sister's church had asked me the same question. These questions were very much in my thoughts as I returned to England. A few weeks went by, still reflecting on my experiences, and the reasons why I was not involved in ministry. As I positively considered going into ministry, a big weight dropped off my shoulders; the frequent chest pains that I had been experiencing reduced daily.

Following my return, I shared with my husband about my challenges whilst in America. I told him that I was willing to do whatever is required to be actively involved in the ministry of the Church. In October 2001 I started training as a local preacher in the Methodist Church, and after a period of eighteen months, I was accredited as a local preacher. My ministry as local preacher was widely accepted. Churches in the circuit were a blessing to me, as several people, particularly Mrs Winkley, whom I refer to as 'my mother', were a tremendous encouragement. She greatly encouraged me to take a further step into ministry and not to stop as a local preacher. I began to feel a renewed zeal to ministry. It felt as if I was going through metamorphosis like a butterfly. I started emerging from my cocoon of fear and timidity. God took away my shy personality and transformed me into a woman who was willing to challenge the culture in which I grew up, and church tradition that believed and taught that women should not be presbyters, or teach men! I did not care what friends back in Kenya would say if they heard that I was a minister like my husband! I believed that I was accountable to God for what I did with eleven years that God had deposited in me by way of biblical studies and theology.

As the months went by, the call to ministry became a passion burning within me. I made an appointment with the District Chair and confided with him about my call, struggles and fears. To confirm this call, the circuit meeting and the district meeting voted for me to go forward for foundation training. Although I had gone through the candidating procedure in Kenya, I had to go through the process again. I felt encouraged that other people in the church in this country concurred with those in my country of origin in discerning God's call for me. After completing foundation training, I went through the process of selection for presbyteral ministry. Through this process I was deeply moved by God's presence, and assurance that I was obeying God's call. More than ever, I trust God that whatever battles I face as I pursue ordination, he will be with me, as he has been in the past.

As I move to the fourth phase of my long journey, I am filled with great peace and joy but also fear and trepidation. Peace and joy because I know I am at the centre of God's will. I have experienced God's presence and love throughout. I am full of joy as I finally reach this remarkable phase of my journey, convinced that, 'he who began the good work *in me* will carry it on to completion until the day of Jesus Christ' (Phil. 1.6).

It has taken me 31 years to be where I am today; my call to ministry feels as though it has been through fire refinery, and now I am emerging refined, and trusting God to help me challenge the intimidation and prejudice that I faced in my early days of ministry. By the time I get ordained it will be 33 years since I took the first step to train for ministry. My journey has been long and hard, but it has been worth it, I have met many challenges, but I have learnt and am still learning that the journey is not easy, but one that is enjoyable because of God's presence, and assurance that he is always with us. I am delighted for the opportunity to serve the Lord God, who embraces all people, and believe he welcomes all those willing to minister in the capacity that he calls them. At the time of writing this article, I look forward to my appointment as a probationer in the Manchester circuit hoping to be ordained in June 2008, when the fifth phase of my life-long journey starts. Please pray for me.

Notes

1. This is the third largest Church in Kenya after the Roman Catholic and Anglican Churches and was started by missionaries from both America and Europe, from a variety of denominations, including Baptists, Methodists, Presbyterians and Anglicans.

Suzanne Nockels

Minister of Market Harborough Congregational Church

I can't remember a time when God was not someone I knew. There have been times when God was little more than an annoying acquaintance but I've always known of God's existence. From being a toddler to the age of eight my mum took my brother and me to a small Baptist chapel in Colchester, which seemed miles away from our house. My dad dropped us off and picked us up and as a child I never wondered why he didn't come in with us. My dad was very strict about us going to Sunday school. At the age of seven I asked him why and his response was 'so that you learn how to be a good girl'. I suspect I am the last generation for whom Sunday school was part of a social upbringing. My impression of the chapel was warm and welcoming. I can remember the giant fan heaters in winter, being surrounded by loud singing, the outings to Malden, the annual prize giving and the length of the services. I'm sure they were just an hour long but time passes differently for children. I can remember being so moved by one sermon that it made me cry. I wish I could recall what it was about.

I loved the stories of the Bible and I still do. Communicating them is one of the central features of my ministry. They have a power to speak into our human experience and transform them. The people in the stories I heard as a child had great adventures and did amazing things. One of the lines I heard a lot at the chapel was the need 'to be useful for God'. I so wanted to have an adventure like the people I heard about and I think I saw God as some sort of superhero with me as a sidekick. I'm sure there was also the desire for people to point at me and say 'Look at that girl, see how godly she is'. However, the people at church just seemed so ordinary so I tried to think of the most spiritual people that I'd heard about. While my mum was doing the washing up I asked her if I could be a nun when I grew up (at that stage I'd never met a nun). She can't remember her reply, but I can; she said, 'You can't, you're a Baptist!'

When I was nine we moved house to Haverhill so my dad could

become a partner in his father's business. My mum went to the Baptist church but she found it a bit narrow and there were few children there so she went to the Congregational church. At that stage it didn't matter because my brother and I were not going with her. Sunday morning kids' TV was the more attractive option. We did go to the church's social events and I can remember the minister Janet Wootton teaching us to dance to the song 'Jubilate'. I thought it was great that you could dance to hymns. It honestly didn't strike me as odd that my minister was a woman at the time. Some years later I was in a Sunday school class when one of the girls who attended St Felix Roman Catholic school said that her classmates had taunted her that she wasn't really baptized because she'd been baptized by a woman. The teacher floundered a bit. I thought the idea was nonsense and still do.

Sometime during the interregnum between Janet Wootton leaving and a new minister arriving, while I was in my early teens I started attending church again, this time without my brother who stayed at home with my dad. I think it became a 'mother and daughter' thing. We used to discuss the service at great length while mum prepared Sunday dinner. My mum has been the central Christian influence in my life. Looking back, I think my faith looked a lot like curiosity then. God was the most important person in the universe and so other areas of interest paled into insignificance. I asked a lot of questions, not only the usual ones about life, death and ethics, but things like 'How do I know that my dreams are not reality and what I think of as reality is not a dream?' The new minister after Janet, Stephen Haward, coped with my adolescent intellectual posturing very well. He says that my favourite word at the time was 'patronizing'. I found everyone and everything 'patronizing'. A great deal of it was teenage angst, but I never found him patronizing. He was a great encourager during difficult times at school or worrying about exams. He also introduced me to theology. We were talking about the existence of God, and I came out with something about even if God didn't exist God would be a good idea, and he said Voltaire had said that. I felt chuffed that I had independently come up with the same idea as a famous philosopher.

I didn't originally intend to study theology at university, I wanted to do English (again the love of stories and drama). I'd never had an RE lesson at school let alone any formal study of doctrine, but I liked the sound of it. Funnily enough it was an old film about the life of Francis of Assisi that was on BBC2 during study leave that made me change my mind. I thought, what is there more important to learn about than God? So I tore up my UCCAS form and wrote out a new one with only two days to spare.

I guess everything sounds quite 'head' based rather than 'heart' or 'soul' based, but I find it impossible to separate those things out. I am quite an emotional person who wears her heart on her sleeve (not always a good place in ministry) and my reaction to the film was an emotional one. If I talk of 'the arts' it sounds a bit highbrow but I've always been moved and inspired by music, pictures, TV and film. Many of the crucial moments of my life are wrapped up in a piece of pop music or a scene in a movie. I suspect it's a Generation X thing and it is a big part of my ministry. I enjoy the challenge of finding new illustrations in popular culture to communicate the ancient words and stories. At times it has been frustrating, as ministerial colleagues have belittled a window into God's world that I value. At times I've got it hopelessly wrong, as people haven't connected in the way I connected to something. I hope it has made me realize and be more tolerant that people live and move among different 'cultures'. I also hope that when I look at present-day cultures I do so critically, finding what does illustrate the truth of the gospel and what doesn't.

It was at university that my faith began to change and I began to get a sense of my calling. I struggle with some of the language of calling because I don't think there has ever been a one-off moment for me. I prefer the idea of growing into something. Neither do I think I'm fully grown yet and I'm not sure I ever will be. What I look like and do now might not be what I'll look like and do in the future. God can call me into a pastorate of a church, but God can also call me into something else entirely. I think it was at university that I got to know Jesus; up to then God the Father had been my main focus. Jesus made the difference between looking for things that provoked the mind or stirred the spirit, and a way of life. I don't mean that I hadn't thought about Jesus before but he wasn't the person I had an ongoing relationship with. Later, I discovered the Holy Spirit or rather the Spirit discovered me. I remember walking down the Strand after a lecture on the Trinity. Again, not something I'd thought about much before, and just in the middle of that noise and grime having a tremendous sense of the love of God. It felt like being surrounded and filled up at the same time. I laughed in the middle of the street and more than one tourist thought I was mad. When, years later, I heard charismatics talk of the baptism of the Holy Spirit, the experience made more sense to me.

It was also a time when all sorts of things opened up to me. I found the feminist, liberation and literary readings of Scripture exciting and new. My favourite hymn is 'We limit not the truth of God',[1] which has the stirring chorus, 'The Lord hath yet more light and truth to break forth from his word'.

I didn't study theology with the idea of becoming a minister, in fact I wanted to be an RE teacher. I've always enjoyed working with children and it seemed the obvious thing to do. I flippantly said to a London minister that I could always go into the ministry later on once I'd had some life experience. He became the minister of his church at 18 and told me that if I had any thoughts regarding pastoral ministry I shouldn't put them off.

My choice of university was made for mostly romantic reasons. My boyfriend Keith lived in London and we had been dating for a year. Keith is a lot older than me and I found his maturity very attractive. Keith was brought up in a Congregational church but he's really a Quaker who likes singing. He has a very strong Quaker sense of social justice and the need to work for peace, and both have influenced me. We married while I was at college in London and after completing my studies I had planned to do a PGCE, but I discovered I was pregnant. Certain stories in Scripture make me smile because God can still use unexpected pregnancies to change people's lives. There was no way I could cope with an intensive course and giving birth two weeks before the final exams, so I had to let the place go. At the time it felt like my world was over. It's funny, young women are told so often that getting pregnant is the worst that can happen that when it does in a secure and loving relationship you can still feel like you've messed up. In fact my son Joe is great on so many levels and I love being a mum. I'm not a very mumsy mum, in fact often I'm the one who lays down the ground rules, but it is such a joy to watch a child grow and have the privilege of seeing things through their eyes.

One of my friends who is a minister in London suggested I did our denomination's training course. The way our course works is that you can take different routes through it. It is not aimed solely at those who want to be ministers. Although I'd done previous study I originally wanted to do as much as possible. I can remember writing essays in the middle of the night when Joe wouldn't go to sleep. At that time we moved to Witney in Oxfordshire and I had the job of being a church caretaker and doing some youth work. My church involvement there and the course helped to confirm a growing feeling that that was where my future lay. The best way to describe it is as a missing jigsaw piece, and the feeling that I would always have something missing if I didn't at least explore the possibility. I went for various interviews and carried on studying and found that at each stage the doors didn't shut but were opened. It's not very dramatic, but then compared to my childhood hero sidekick fantasies that is probably a good thing! I did pray long and hard about whether this feeling was genuine or my attention-seeking personality. I came to the conclusion that God can use different personalities, even mine, and if there was potential there I hoped others would see it. I think the final affirmation really was a church in Scotland issuing a call to me in 2001.

However, my first church was hard going. Only looking back now can I admit to how hard it really was. It took Keith over a year to find a job in Aberdeen and so we only saw each other every other weekend or once every three weeks – difficult when you have a young child. I was very green and naive and didn't fully realize the true state of the church before I went. The last minister had left after making good a threat to resign, and the church had lost its way without him. The majority of the congregation wanted to escape the mess and the hurt and saw me as a way of handing on the problem to someone else. At my induction there were thirty church members there; the following Sunday there were eight. I would walk the mile from my home to church with Joe every Sunday morning whatever the weather, and in Aberdeen the weather could be horrible. We were rarely offered a lift home. Joe was going through the terrible twos and he would kick-off in the service, which was all the more noticeable when there were only a few. He really needed another adult to take an interest in him and sit beside him, but I was told quite firmly that people didn't come to church to baby-sit. The church was also heavily in debt, so much so that I would dread opening the mail for fear of another final demand letter, a fear that has not quite left me.

In short, I was definitely the wrong person in the wrong place. The formality of the church didn't suit my informality. Still, I smiled at the Conferences and said how well things were going when really I was failing there. I've been quite a high achiever and not really encountered failure, at least on this scale. It was good to learn that failure doesn't kill and the role of minister is not all that I am. Now I can see that first difficult pastorate as a gift from God, but it has taken a few years to get there. Was being a woman part of the problem? In part, yes, I was treated a bit like a novelty but I think my age at the time was more of an issue and being somewhere where I didn't understand the rules. It was hard to move because I couldn't see what would happen to the church if I did and those that were still there had become close friends who I loved dearly, but another friend pointed out that I wasn't helping them if I stayed. If I left it would free them to move on to other churches with a less hurtful history and that is what has happened to the people who worshipped with me. It wasn't all bad, we had some great Bible studies and it was while visiting a residential home I began to understand more about the elderly, but it wasn't enough to make up for the rest.

In 2003 I accepted the call to Market Harborough Congregational Church in Leicestershire, my present pastorate. It is a fellowship that likes putting on productions. We've done dramas and also organized other events in and for the community. It's a church that can use what I have to offer; my love of Scripture and the arts. It's a church that has the confidence to ask questions of Christian faith and itself. It feels like a church wondering what will happen next, not mourning what has been. I must be careful not to paint a too rosy picture, as it has not all been great. There have been times when I've disagreed strongly with Church Meeting and grieved the decision that was made. Yet this church has the ability to maintain friendship despite difference. Often ministry is only seen as what you offer a church, but a church offers a minister different things as well. So far Harborough has been a healing place and an honest place. I can be Suzanne in pastoral ministry here.

Note

1. 'We limit not the truth of God', William Walsham How (1823–97).

Ann Peart

Principal of Unitarian College, Manchester

Although my family was nominally Unitarian, they identified themselves by the chapel they did not attend, so it was left to an aunt, with whom I occasionally stayed, to introduce me to chapel attendance in my early teens. I became interested, not least because of the discussions we had in RE lessons at school. As I was the only Unitarian in the class, I had to know something of what I was supposed to stand for in order to argue my corner. Actually choosing to go to chapel was a form of teenage rebellion, but I soon got hooked, and had my first taste of 'ministry' when the minister invited me to become May Queen for a year when I was eighteen. In our chapel community in the north-west of England the May Queen's duties centred on the chapel, unlike the Rose Queen, who was more concerned with the Sunday school and with social events. My main tasks were helping to lead junior chapel on Sunday mornings, and taking the chapel flowers to the sick and elderly in the evening. During my year of office the minister was often away, carrying out duties as the national president of the Unitarian General Assembly, so I had a lot of freedom to interpret and develop my role, and I soon developed a taste for the pastoral visiting. On one occasion I even conducted a service (though it was in the evening, and so carried less prestige than did the morning service).

When I left home to go to university I gradually become involved with the wider Unitarian movement, initially through the Foy Society of young adults. The Sunday services at Cambridge and the minister's weekly 'at homes' showed me a fascinating world where people of all ages took religious and philosophical debate seriously, unlike home, where religion was considered a private matter, not to be discussed in polite society. I even had thoughts about becoming a minister, but dismissed these on two grounds, first because, as someone straight from school, I did not have enough life experience to be a wise guide to middle-aged and older people, and second because I fell in love, and wanted to get married and have children. So after graduation I opted to train as a teacher and got married a fortnight after my last exam.

For the next thirteen years I fitted in an enormous amount of voluntary activity with the church, conducting worship when there was a need, serving on a variety of committees and working groups, from local congregational level right up to national General Assembly. My theology developed too, following the different ministers of the congregations I joined. The assumption of liberal Christianity, based on the teachings of Jesus rather than stories about him after his death, was succeeded by a humanist phase; and then an interest in 'non-realist' language propounded by Don Cupitt enabled me to use more religious language again. The lack of life experience was remedied by marriage, with two house moves, the births of four children and the deaths of three of them under the age of two from different illnesses, the adoption of a nine-month-old London-born Indian boy, and finally divorce. It was at this point that the question of what to do with my life asserted itself. While I had been married I had known that our partnership could not cope with my having a demanding career and looking after the children. But now I needed to start earning again. I returned to some part-time teaching, but found it difficult to fit in as much church work. As I learned to find my own identity separate from that as wife and mother, I become involved with second-wave feminism, and joined a consciousness-raising group that was an important part of my life for two years. I started reading what feminist theology there was available in the late 1970s and early 1980s, and helped to found a feminist Unitarian Women's Group, while getting involved with the ecumenical Women in Theology.

The possibility of ministry re-emerged; it seemed logical to try to earn my living from what I had already chosen to do with much of my spare time, though the logistics of training with two children, Jill and Michael, not yet in their teens, seemed daunting. I didn't so much think of it as a 'calling', but a way of continuing to serve the movement that was so much a part of my life. For a couple of years I kept my aspiration to myself, but enrolled on a distance-learning course for lay preachers, for which I could study at home, and a four-year counselling course run at a local centre one evening a week by the Westminster Pastoral Foundation. When the proprietor of the small private school in which I was teaching announced that the school was to close to new pupils and wind up in five years when she retired, I took the plunge, and applied for ministry training. The friends and ministers I consulted were all encouraging. One of the women ministers I knew assured me that ministry was quite compatible with bringing up children, as one could arrange to be home after school.

At that time, training for full-status ministry was only available full-time; part-time training only led to associate status. I needed to train part-time in order to be able to look after my children, and didn't want to move them from their schools or our London home, where I had a network of supportive friends. Manchester College in Oxford was the nearest place to train, but normally ministry students were resident in college. In spite of these problems, the General Secretary encouraged me to apply, but warned me that I might have to settle for associate-status training initially. The college principal told me he did all the ministry training on Mondays and Tuesdays, so theoretically part-time training was not a problem. When I got to the residential interviews, I found that there was only one person out of the six on the interviewing panel that I did not know. The other five seemed to think that they knew me quite well; one had assessed my written work on theology for the lay preachers' course, and knew I could work at degree level. The one person I didn't know, a lay woman, had clearly heard of my reputation; she slipped in a casual question as I was leaving the room after my interview with her, and asked 'Does God have to be a woman?' My immediate reply was, 'Of course not', and I think I went on to elaborate about inclusive images of divinity. The outcome of the process was better than I had dared hope; I was accepted for training for full status with training at Oxford for a total of 200 days, to be fitted in when I could manage it.

Two supportive women friends with children the same age as mine offered to have Jill and Michael overnight on Mondays during term-time; this made training possible, and gave me a clear evening in college to study. Other friends helped with a rota of chauffeuring to and from school and other activities, and continuing to baby-sit on Tuesday nights while I finished my counselling course. Without this network of help, mainly but not exclusively from women, I could not have got through the two and a half years of training. It worked beautifully when everyone was well, but if just one person had a minor illness, reorganizing the rota was a nightmare. Fortunately this rarely happened, and Jill and Michael coped with the arrangement very well; my friends produced better meals than I did!

Compared with my complicated domestic arrangements initially training seemed straightforward. I audited a variety of university lectures, but was not required to obtain an externally validated theological qualification. The principal undertook all the ministerial formation work and taught Unitarian thought himself, and allowed me to produce essays at the rate of one a fortnight rather than one a week. The Unitarian thought/theology course consisted of preparing a series of essays on theological topics such as 'God', 'Jesus', 'Man' (sic), etc. in which we were to trace the development of Unitarian ideas by reading and quoting from whatever Unitarian sources we could find, from the seventeenth century onwards. This of course led to an over-reliance on the writings of male ministers, as few lay men, and very few women, had published works which were still on the college library shelves. Out of seven students there were two women, but gender did not seem to enter the traditional way in which we were taught. When we looked at the traditional models of ministry, with the addition of scapegoat, mascot, and some other current dysfunctional roles, I suggested adding mother, and was told no, mothers are not powerful enough! My first year went smoothly enough, but during the summer the principal apparently had a disagreement with the college governors, and we got back in October to find a different acting principal and an interim ministry tutor. This meant more freedom to arrange tutorials with a variety of staff: I ended up doing process theology, and relevant topics in sociology and philosophy. The downside was the lack of systematic coverage of all a new minister needed to know. However, I regarded the formal training as a means to an end, and although I enjoyed much of it, and took advantage of what Oxford had to offer on the days I was there, I think much of my ministerial preparation came from my long experience of working for the movement in lay capacities. I had been a committed feminist before I began training, and had a clear vision of how I wanted to change both ministry and the movement in general. It was hard to keep hold of that feminist vision while going through what was at that stage a comparatively gender-blind process, but the support of my feminist friends helped. Though I was aware that this support was patchy, and that some feminist Unitarians were either unwilling or too busy with their own lives to offer much practical help. This may have been partly because there were no other Unitarians living in my immediate neighbourhood. The two families who had Jill and Michael to stay on a regular basis were Roman Catholic and Methodist, yet more evidence that sisterhood paid little attention to denominational boundaries.

At the time I finished my training, recognition as a minister was dependent on having a ministerial position. Unitarian churches are organized on a congregational basis, with each congregation choosing and paying their own minister. During the final months of my training there was only one vacancy which was near enough to my home to allow my daughter to continue at her secondary school, and although I came a creditable second in the candidating process, I ended up without a post, and so could not get ministerial recognition straight away. However, there was an administrative post at the Unitarian central office advertised, which would qualify for recognition; I applied, and eventually got it, on the understanding that I would do four days a week and add to it a part-time ministry in the London area. I lived in Wembley, north-west London, and my congregation, at Catford, was 20 miles away on the other side of the city, but the arrangement worked fairly well for nearly three years. The small congregation was very tolerant of my feminist approach, as their previous minister had also been feminist, though they resisted any attempt to meet for week-night activities. As I was fully occupied with my administrative work, this was not really a problem.

After a couple of years a vacancy arose in my old congregation at Golders Green, and I was eventually selected as minister. This congregation had a lively witness on a variety of social issues, and was sensitive to both feminist and lesbian and gay issues. This suited me very well, and I threw myself into the work with enthusiasm. The congregation was very diverse, with a good mixture of ages, sexualities and theological outlooks. It included Jewish humanists, members of the Brahmo Samaj, a liberal Hindu movement with strong Unitarian links, and had been involved in supporting the foundation of the lesbian and gay bereavement group, a telephone helpline service. So when, after a year as minister, I came out as lesbian, it was largely a supportive community. The one person who was concerned was a closet lesbian who did not want the congregation to be known as a gay community. It was never a single-issue congregation, and I enjoyed participating in groups such as Friends of the Earth, Amnesty International and a Tai Chi class, all of which the congregation hosted, as well as developing a worship style that was not only inclusive in language (a development that had taken place before I became minister), but more participatory in style. I expected to spend the rest of my working life there, but I acquired a partner who wanted to move out of London, so we left for Manchester.

I knew that I was unlikely to find a congregation as satisfying as Golders Green, so settled for a quarter-time ministry with a small congregation. This was something of a struggle, as there was not really a good fit between me and most of the members, who were much more traditional in their attitudes. I had become increasingly aware of the need to uncover some of the stories of women in the Unitarian movement, as all the standard histories and theologies were very male-centred. Manchester is home to Unitarian College, and the principal asked me to spend some time checking the college manuscripts in the university library. This gave me a splendid introduction to possible resources for research and, encouraged by my partner, who was an academic, I enrolled for a PhD on a part-time basis. During the next ten years I worked somewhat intermittently at the research, with interruptions for the illnesses and deaths of first my father, then my mother, and the break-up of my partnership. I gave up the part-time ministry, and after a gap of a year, became principal of Unitarian College. This was the first ministerial post I had in which I was the first woman holder. I had already done some teaching both in the college and in the ecumenical partnership to which it belongs, as well as serving on various college and partnership committees, so knew a fair amount about the setup.

The college is very small, often with fewer than five ministry students, and the principal is the only full-time employee. A part-time administrator and finance officer, together with two visiting tutors, made up the staff. Of course as a new principal I set about making some changes. These included developing the training to take greater advantage of the partnership courses, though this did create problems in my first year, especially with the inclusion of Unitarians in ecumenical worship. I also integrated more work in congregations into the course, and developed college procedures so that decisions were no longer the prerogative of a dictator, however benign, but were shared with staff and students. Recognizing that ministry training in mature life causes considerable stress, I work at creating a supportive atmosphere, with (mainly non-alcoholic) drinks and food part of the regular routine. Fortunately the staff in the other colleges in the partnership are both welcoming and able, and had already developed ecumenical courses which take account of gender and to some extent of sexuality. Within the Unitarian courses, I encourage students to include the work of women when preparing history and theology assignments; this often means going beyond the usual texts and looking at Sunday school material, for example. In practical theology, except on issues of safety, I don't labour the difference gender makes, but an awareness of gender and other power issues is very much part of the discussion, especially in areas such as visiting, role and perceptions of the minister, social pressures, etc.

During the twenty years since I entered the Unitarian ministry the proportion of women has increased from about one-eighth to approximately one-third. Alongside this, women have become more numerous on the various committees and power structures of the Unitarian General Assembly. Of the five national commissions appointed in 2003, four were chaired by women – this includes the ministry commission on which I serve as chair. In 2006 the main governing body, the General Assembly Council, which had been composed of about one-third women to two-thirds men, was replaced by a smaller directly elected executive committee, which happens to have exactly equal numbers of men and women. I serve on this, and have been delighted by the collaborative way in which it is beginning to work. However, the convenor is male, as are the national treasurer and general secretary, so there are still some areas of considerable power which are dominated by male experience. Overall, though, the desire to work for equality of men and women, and to work in a co-operative manner rather than a hierarchical one (taking into account many of the principles of feminist theology), has been one of the great joys of my professional life as a Unitarian minister.

I still find much inspiration and support from women in other denominations and women's groups. A local women's spirituality group provides an outlet for creativity and expression which is denied in my local congregation, where divinity is still too often for my taste associated with maleness, at least in the words used by the male minister on

Sunday mornings. Over the past ten years living in the north of England, I have perhaps become more tolerant of, or resigned to, a certain lack of willingness to use inclusive language in local congregations. It seems important not to lose touch with the grass-roots, and to demonstrate that I can practise what I teach, so my role as chair of the congregation committee keeps my feet firmly on the ground, though I have to be careful not to interfere in the work of the minister. In 2005 I completed my PhD, and now am in some demand to talk on the history of Unitarian women; I enjoy being able to increase awareness of our heritage of women's activism, and in my year as national president of the Unitarian Women's League, the more traditional of our two denominational women's groups, I had the opportunity to do this in most parts of the British Isles. This current year, as president of the Unitarian Historical Society, I shall be able to focus on women in my presidential address, thus in a small way starting to redress the discounting of women's witness that has been the characteristic of Unitarian history over the years. My ministry in its widest sense still holds challenges and possibilities.

Angela Robinson

Head of the Girls' Section, Bangladesh International Tutorial, Gulshan, Dhaka, Bangladesh, and in pastoral charge of the only English-speaking congregation of the Church of Bangladesh

I was born in Southport, Lancashire, in 1938, the third generation Congregationalist both sides of the family. My paternal grandfather, Revd Joshua Pedlar, came off a Cornish farm in 1884 to a mission church at Rock Ferry, Merseyside, and my maternal grandfather was received into membership by Dr Dale in Carrs Lane Church, Birmingham, and went on to build up a department store in Southport which now enables me to do some rather interesting things with my life. Thank you to both of them!

I felt called to the ministry at fourteen and spent the next 26 years fighting it. After all, despite the fact that I was given the best education that money could buy – the excellent Huyton College and Lady Margaret Hall, Oxford – I was under the enormous psychological and emotional influence of a family dominated by its male members.

My mother was anxious to get me out and away in the five-month gap between school and university. She fixed up for me to be a 'Blue Angel' at the Ecumenical Institute, Bossey, Switzerland, run by the World Council of Churches and the venue of summer conferences. We did the lighter domestic work, attended some of the lectures and events – and I caught the ecumenical bug.

My first job was in Hemel Hempstead at an inspirational new school, The Cavendish, which I left after three years, partly because there was someone called John Robinson, a travel agent, who wanted to marry me, but he did not go to church so that was not 'on', was it?

My aunt died and left me £200 and I decided that, after a year as an assistant stage manager in the Sheffield Rep. and while I was out of teaching, I should go back to the Ecumenical Institute and join their Graduate School of Ecumenical Studies, offering a diploma from the

University of Geneva. As in most courses there, a handful of lay people were included to keep the parsons down to earth, and I was one of them. There were ministers, priests and theological students from all over the world, from Protestant, Orthodox and Roman Catholic churches.

Afterwards, there was the opportunity to do three months' fieldwork on a World Council of Churches' scholarship. I enquired and was asked, 'What are you interested in?' After a long discussion, we narrowed it down to, 'What is a community?' The secretary said, 'We have just got permission to send one person to an Israeli kibbutz; would you like to go?'

It turned out to be one of the few religious kibbutzim – an Orthodox Jewish one. It was one of the formative experiences of my life. Later, my RC friends would be highly amused to discover this particular Protestant had come to an interest in Christian monasticism via an Orthodox Jewish kibbutz. I had been inspired by these two experiences but got almost no reaction from other Christians and very little interest. I showed my slides to a few ladies' groups in church halls. I applied to the local Moderator, saying I was prepared to do any job, however lowly, including domestic work for overworked ministers' wives, and teach for four days a week to support myself – but it was obvious he had no idea what to do with me. When parsons complain to me that they want more dedicated lay people in their churches, I ask, 'Have you ever tried to be one?' Do Protestant churches have no idea how to use their celibates? I think not . . .

I took myself back to Oxford to read theology in order to be a theologically equipped lay person. Towards the end of my two-year degree, I heard about a group of people in Stanbrook wanting to start the first ecumenical community in the country to involve Roman Catholic nuns officially allowed 'out'. We started in Witney, in Oxfordshire, in 1970, in the home of the remarkable Clementina Gordon, who had been a research scientist and theologian and, after the war, the Anglican Church had not known what to do with her and she had become a Congregational minister. She made room for her church in her house as well as us, because it was temporarily homeless. The Congregationalists of Witney and the Benedictines got on extremely well. We discussed this and decided that, before the Reformation, those who decided that what was going on was Not Good Enough formed or joined a monastery or convent; afterwards, the same type formed or joined a chapel. In the ecumenical 'excuse-me' dance, we were dancing together and kindred spirits.

We agreed that each of us should do our own 'thing' while living together. I taught religious education at a local grammar school that was becoming comprehensive. I had come straight from Oxford theology back into the classroom and the difference between being a history teacher and an RE teacher was startling. It was the secular 1970s and I did not know how to translate what I felt so passionately about into words and concepts that schoolchildren could get hold of. It was totally humiliating and excellent training. I used to go home crying some nights and could not contemplate going full-time. Thus I lost my job three weeks before the end of the school year and the only job going in Oxfordshire was at the excellent Banbury School, 23 miles away. I felt the Lord's boot in the small of my back. It was the step I needed. The subject had status and support, the school was a good one and I saw the comprehensive system at its best. I began to put my act together. Oh, those golden days, of creating one's own syllabus around the needs of the pupils!

By that time, the remaining Stanbrook nun, Sister Jane Scott-Calder OSB and I, the rump of the ecumenical community, had moved into our own home in Witney. Jane, a wise woman, doctor and widow of a doctor, did a lot of counselling work on me as well as the others who beat a path to our door to talk with her. Thus, as my fortieth birthday approached, I was open to what was happening to me. I could almost hear the Lord saying, 'Angela, I called you when you were fourteen. Next year you will be forty. What about it?' However, my whole family background and culture had given me the conviction that, really, leadership was a 'man thing'. This was despite all the positive 'vibes' I got from my denomination that had been ordaining women since 1917, although not many of them. Besides, one of the reasons I had always given myself for not going into the ministry was the matter of baptisms, weddings and funerals. If I could not be a member of the congregation without tears pouring down my face, how could I possibly be 'up at the sharp end'? I was a woman and too emotional for the job!

I was active in my area of the Congregational Federation and, at one meeting, took the devotions and, as I was going down the aisle afterwards, a minister grabbed my arm and said, 'Have you ever thought of being Revd Angela Pedlar?' I muttered that I had been thinking of it since I was fourteen and beat a hasty retreat, but he cornered me over tea and challenged me to have my interview with the Pastoral Care Committee. The result was that I was told, 'For heaven's sake, Angela! You have knocked around the Church and the world for long enough. Get straight in!'

I had assumed that I would be asked to do a year's pastoralia and 'going straight in' meant that Jane had still a year to go before she returned to her monastery at sixty. I pondered. One evening, before our prayers, I wondered aloud if I could go into the ministry and take her with me. She promptly said that she felt our time in Witney had come to an end and she was ready. That's Benedictine 'detachment' for you! I got a list of Congregational churches wanting part-time ministers, she borrowed a Catholic directory, and we spread the map of England on the kitchen table and went down the list. There was a church at Grassington, near Skipton. No Roman Catholic church there but Jane saw there was one at the neighbouring village of Threshfield. 'That'll do!' I said. 'Good,' said Jane, 'it's the Yorkshire Dales.' 'What are they?' I said.

On a glorious spring Sunday morning in 1978, I motored north to Grassington and discovered the Dales – and the little square stone Congregational chapel. I sat in a pew during the service and knew it was All Right. I met the retiring minister and church secretary over lunch and returned some weeks later to 'preach with a view' – with Sister Jane. The sensible Congregationalists of Grassington saw immediately that there was no reason at all why there should not be a Benedictine nun in their manse . . .

It was one of those church/parson relationships that was made in heaven. Having Jane with me for my first year was very helpful in settling in. I came to know later that the church had been on the verge of closure. They offered me the manse and £840 a year and half the electricity and heating oil bills, and we lived on Jane's pension. There were only three members under sixty and no children, but they were mature Christians and loved one another and we grew together. 'I am a student minister,' I said to them. 'You are training me. Do not see me advancing towards a banana skin without saying "Oops!"' They did just that. I preached in Bradford Cathedral, in the absence of a deaconess who fell ill for a weekend, celebrating 'Julian of Norwich and the Ministry of Women in the Church' – a good combination, that! I preached in Liverpool Cathedral on the anniversary service for my old school, Huyton. It is amazing what God can do when you have been busy telling him you cannot do it!

My relationship with John Robinson had had a nine-year gap but had come to life again and, this time, I was able to discuss matters of faith with him much more positively. I discovered that he had lots of pieces of the jigsaw puzzle of faith – some better than I did, but he had not put it together into any commitment to a church. He said, in his quiet honesty, 'I have never known a church where it worked!' We were married on 29 September 1979. Having been inducted in November 1978, I was ordained in June 2000, standing on the same spot where I had made my wedding vows also.

I was in Grassington until 1986, and all sorts of things that were waiting for my sort of encouragement got it and happened. After I had been there a year, some young families arrived, and thanks to the wonderful welcome they received from the members, we became a family church. I busied myself up and down dale, finding out who were the people who made things happen in about fourteen little churches, and the Upper Wharfedale Fellowship of Churches came into being, with me as secretary – and also the Youth Praise. We got a village choir going and out of that grew the Grassington Festival. The eight allotments next to the church were sold to the Anchor Housing Trust and a care home for those in the village who could no longer be cared for in their own homes materialized a year after I had left – a major decision that was not easy for the church or the village but has proved a great blessing.

We went to Seaton in East Devon, for John's work, and I became an unemployed housewife, with many local churches not knowing what to do with me and the (mainly small) Congregational churches obviously finding me deeply threatening. I fought depression and then, challenged, in that Thatcher era, by the number of issues that had a moral and religious dimension, and by the fact that the Jubilee Centre and Care Campaigns had emerged as pioneers of major social responsibility issues, like Sunday trading, alcohol issues and debt, I pioneered the Honiton Constituency Christian Core Group. We were treated with some respect by the local MP after he had walked into Sidford Social Hall and found 250 Christians ready to nail him to the floor with well-researched questions. I became Social Responsibility Officer for the Congregational Federation. Otherwise, I wept about the fact that the churches of my denomination barely used me.

John's job did not work out well, and he decided to take early retirement and let me go into the full-time ministry. A church in Essex called me, but by that time, John was walking badly. Six weeks after we arrived, in an area where neither of us had friends or family, the diagnosis of motor neurone disease was made. It was thirteen months between diagnosis and his death in April 1992.

I was minister there until 1998, when I was sixty and 'retired'. A wise friend said I should make no decision about my future until I had had a total rest. When I was ready to look for a role in life again, I went for a job advertised in Bangladesh, through the Council for World Mission, involving teaching English to nurses on a mission compound in Rajshahi, which sounded like something I could do – for just one year. Instead, the Bishop/Moderator placed me in St Andrew's Mission, Haluaghat, founded in 1912, when it was just the jungle and the Garo – the tribal people. It now has a high school where I taught English. I was the only permanent resident foreigner for miles around. Most experienced Mission Partners were absolutely horrified that, untrained and inexperienced in mission in the tropics, I had been 'thrown in the deep end'. I stayed for two and a half years and loved it – except when the local mosque microphone said things like, 'Kill the Christians! Support the Palestinians!'

Every three months or so, I would take the four-hour bus to Dhaka, stay at a hostel and – balm to my soul! – worship with the English-speaking congregation, a small group of people, varying from 15 to 30 in number (fewer in the holiday season) but the sort of fellowship that inspires great loyalty. The need to meet with, and worship with, those of one's own 'culture', should not be underestimated. There was also the Bagha (British) Club . . .

I had refused to be Principal of the Mission High School, wanting to be in the classroom with the children and all too aware of my limited Bengali. But the powers-that-be probably felt I was not being useful enough, so I was told to go home in the summer of 2002. I completed my two-language version of the history of the mission and sent my trunk and boxes of books back to the UK by sea.

I had been writing letters to the main English newspaper, the *Daily Star*, and, unknown to me, the management of the British School in Dhaka were looking for a principal and were told, on the basis of these letters, that they should interview me! I was astonished! I went to see the school, which was, like so many of the English-medium schools, in a block of flats with a small yard and the ground-floor garage for play. However, I liked what I saw, recognized the Lord's boot once again in the small of my back and, at 64 years old, accepted this radical career change. My almost entirely Bangladeshi Muslim pupils, parents, teachers and management welcomed me with delight and supported me wholeheartedly.

The school ranged from Nursery (three and a half) to Year 11, when they took O level. We continually fought the accusation that we were 'training our children to be foreigners' – highly dangerous in the present political climate which is getting more and more hostile to anything that is 'non-Islamic'. I protest that I sing the Bangladesh national anthem every morning in assembly! My assembly talks have recently been published here – *Five Minutes with Mrs Robinson*. 'Moral values in a prestige setting' as one of my lecturers at Oxford said.

The new Bishop-Moderator asked me to be in pastoral charge of the English-speaking congregation – and presented me with a stole which this Congregationalist wears with pride. I do this 'Friday job' with much pleasure, arranging the preaching rota and caring for the fluctuating congregation of some very remarkable and dedicated people who come to work for and visit – and revisit – Bangladesh. Not a few of them leave with broken hearts. It is a tough place to work . . .

In August 2005, the school moved into new rented accommodation in a lovely old Dhaka house, to the annoyance of a property company that wanted it for 'lakeside apartments'. They began to harass us, claimed the property as their own and marched against it, wounded three guards, broke the wall down and put their gang into the building to claim it. I cancelled my plans for Eid and went to sleep on the floor of my office and, deliberately, put the fear of God into them. Lay a finger on me and it would have been a diplomatic incident – and they knew it! I read the Psalms with a new sense of the reality of the harassed and persecuted. How could we get them out before school was due to start? The parents would see the lack of security and remove their children!

I had to take two days out to go and take the Remembrance Service at the Commonwealth War Cemetery where I met the British High Commissioner (Anwar Choudhury, Bangladeshi-born and himself the object of a terrorist bomb on his eighteenth day at work here), and told him what was happening. He was horrified to hear what I was going through – and acted. The police were instructed to get the gang out. By that time the staff were back from their Eid holidays and it was two days before school was due to open. All was cleaned and swept – and two days later, the school opened!

Being a principal is a bit of a middle-management job here, but I worked happily with the young superintendent and the owner until there was a sell-out to an educational consultancy in January 2006 which augured well but totally changed the character of the school. The superintendent and I and most of the staff left. He and I have suffered harassment, legal activity and serious attempts to drive me out of the country! At the time of going to press, things are not totally resolved but I have a new visa and work permit for a new job – as headmistress of another, more prestigious school. At 68, I have signed a three-year contract and wonder if I am mad!

I now live in the part of Dhaka where most of the foreigners live, so I have much more of a social life – and the opportunity to try and find a new worship venue for the English-speaking congregation – plus the Garo (tribal) people who come here for work. They are predominantly Christian – and much in demand by foreigners as ayahs, guards, and so on, because of their loyalty and honesty. There are no churches 'between' the Roman Catholics and the Evangelicals to serve the embassies or anyone else.

The political situation, before the planned General Election in January 2007, was appalling and bode ill for the future. It has been rescued by a firm caretaker government that has taken over and is 'cleaning up', with astonishing success and popular acclaim. Being the headmistress of a school entirely of girls (I miss my boys!) means I have to face up to the many ways in which life here has special challenges. Education for a woman can be a way out, not only of the country (many educated women emigrate, often by arranged marriages) but also out of some cultural restrictions via getting into the job market. But it is still not easy. The children of the rising middle classes in the developing world need a lot of help to develop properly, in health and wholeness – but I guess that goes for everywhere today.

Madge Saunders[1]

Kingston, Jamaica
(Recorded by Janet Lees, Sheffield, UK)

The story of Madge's ministry is in some ways familiar but has a twist. A lifelong dedication to the mission of the Church took her away from home to work overseas. A period of work in the mission field was completed, and after ten years she returned to resume ministry at home. The difference was that Madge was one of the first partners in mission to come to Europe rather than go from there. It is this twist, its origins and repercussions that make Madge's story compelling. It has been an inspiration to three generations.

Madge was born in Galina, St Mary, on the north coast of Jamaica in 1913. She was from an ordinary family: her father was a wharf manager for the Carron company. As members of the Presbyterian Church in Jamaica, they were part of a Christian tradition that had been brought to the island from Europe by Scottish missionaries in the late 1790s. Indeed, she was very nearly born during the meeting of the Synod at Port Maria, when the visiting Moderator, the Revd T. V. Prentice, was presiding. Her mother had felt her labour pains begin and had left the meeting. Madge was born about an hour later. A devout woman herself, her mother had dedicated Madge 'to the Lord', thinking the child would be a boy. It was unusual for women to play a prominent role in the work of the Church at the time. Even Prentice expected a boy. On hearing a baby had been born he suggested it should be named after him, which accounts for Madge's middle name: Marjorie Prentice Saunders.

From that moment on, all of Madge's life was spent in the embrace of the Church, to which she felt a lifelong attachment. She attended Sunday school as a child and, whatever was happening locally, her family took part in the life of the local church. It is therefore not surprising that at the age of twelve, at an evangelistic meeting at Port Maria Baptist Church, she responded to the invitation issued by the preacher and made a full commitment to Christian discipleship. She went on to become a full member of the Presbyterian Church of Jamaica.

Her early work in Jamaica was primarily with children and young people. The development of basic education in the island owes much to her and grew out of her work as a local Sunday school teacher. The first 'play centre' for young children had been opened by the Revd Henry Ward in Islington, St Mary, in 1938. Madge later called this centre a Basic School. She attended the Bethlehem Training College and later, in 1948 after her return from further training at St Colm's College, Edinburgh, Scotland, became a travelling youth organizer for the Presbyterian Church. St Colm's was a training college for women missionaries. Students were both 'home' and 'overseas'; in other words from those churches around the world whose origins were due to the missionary activity of the Church of Scotland and other Scottish Free Churches. Madge studied there in 1946: her signature survives in the chapel book.

Her first initiative was to invite local women teachers, who were often very devout but essentially untrained people, to take part in a six-week programme in basic education, which included visiting a well-known school in Kingston to observe trained teachers at work. This was among the first training for teachers in many of the rural parts of the island. Her commitment to the development of early childhood education in Jamaica was recognized in 2004 when a book by Myrtle Daley and Joyce Thompson told the story of 'a vision for the children of our country'. The book is dedicated to her.[2]

One of her early projects in Jamaica, which from the start looked less than promising, was at the Falmouth United Church. This had been one of the first Presbyterian churches established in Jamaica, but its glory days were long gone and it had fallen into disrepair. Madge was persistent in her request to revive the church at Falmouth as a training centre for the local youth and as a way of regenerating the local community. After a bequest from a wealthy local woman, the Kelly-Lawson Centre was opened as one of the first centres to train women to work in the tourist industry.

The history of the churches in Jamaica is of course completely linked with the history of the island. Churches like the Falmouth United Church had had separate areas for the worship of slaves and masters. Shocked by this, Madge was to say, while a student in Scotland, that it was the one building in Jamaica that she would burn down if she could. However, it never came to that. Rather, the regeneration of the building reversed the old structures, both physical and social, so that where the slaves used to stand was transformed into the platform and the pulpit, and where the slave owners sat became the place where the congregation sat. Madge saw this as much more fitting.

She was also involved in the foundation of a number of schools in Jamaica including Meadowbroook High School, Mona Preparatory

School and Iona High School. She was on the board of governors of a number of schools at different times and considered education to be a fundamental part of the work of the Church.

Indeed, much of her ministry was devoted to the development of young people, like her work with the Girls' Brigade, formerly the Girls' Guildry. The Girls' Guildry had come to Jamaica from Scotland in 1923 under the leadership of Mrs Summerville, who was the daughter of a Scottish minister. Madge's work revived the struggling organization and it was spread to a number of other Caribbean islands. Madge saw it as essential to the training of young women for leadership roles in the society. It later amalgamated with the Girls' Brigade.

As the 1950s gave way to the 1960s the number of Jamaicans leaving the island for a life in Britain increased. Churches in Britain had a variety of responses to these newcomers. Some found it hard to accept black Christians. Others tried to find ways to offer support and aid integration. There was racism to overcome in other aspects of life as well: housing and employment were two areas in which the immigrants often encountered significant prejudice. Some church leaders began to recognize that they needed the skills and experience of ministers from the Caribbean in Britain. Madge recalls that 'a request was made for a man from Jamaica to work with the immigrants'.[3] This request had come through John Wint, a Jamaican minister who had been visiting Britain. He recommended Madge, then a deaconess in Jamaica. She must have had a significant reputation even then and clearly all her previous experience would be valuable in this new initiative. So Robert Gillespie, an Ulsterman working in Sheffield, made a formal request to the Church in Jamaica for Madge to come to Britain. Somewhat frustrated by the delay caused by the letter getting held up in the official channels, Madge was dedicated and commissioned in December 1965, at the meeting to mark the union of the Congregational and Presbyterian Churches in Jamaica.[4]

Madge recalls being undaunted by the prospect of working in Sheffield. God's presence was very real to her and she was used to travelling all over Jamaica and to other Caribbean islands. Her connections across the Caribbean stood her in good stead and helped her to make links with the immigrants she met in Britain. Yet the challenges in the churches were not insignificant. There were tensions in most churches when black newcomers tried to join. Madge was quite clear that she was not 'there to start a church' but 'to strengthen the existing one'.[5]

Even so, there were basic problems to solve, not least where to live. Reading between the lines of the official records, hearing the stories many years on, it is clear that Madge received a mixed reception. Some local white church members were wary of a 'ministry to coloured people', believing that they might be missing out on something. It was important to make it clear that the community-based advice service, for example, was available to everyone, regardless of colour.

Her work was long and varied and she tried many strategies to break down the barriers that the black people encountered. She spoke at meetings and conferences, participated in committees and held classes for black children in her flat on Saturdays and organized international evenings for church members to get to know each other's cultures. She later wrote, 'Often barriers between people have been brought about because of fear, the repetition of rumours, misconceptions and misleading propaganda. Because of these negative attitudes, conflicts and tensions on both sides have been the result. I have been called upon at all hours of the day and night to act as mediator on numerous occasions.'[6]

She wrote a booklet called *Living in Britain* which was published by the British Council of Churches. Its purpose was to introduce the immigrants to British life, but it probably also provided insight into the assumptions and expectations of the host community as well. It was later translated into Urdu and Gujurati for a subsequent group of immigrants from the Indian subcontinent. She was a member of the Race Relations Committee and a regular speaker on the local radio in Sheffield.

Madge reflected that she had enjoyed her work as a deaconess. The order was a small one and its members knew each other well, receiving support and encouragement at the annual conference as well as from the friendships they made with each other. She served on the executive of the World Federation of Deaconesses for three years and also attended some World Council of Churches consultations in that capacity. She was very much in favour of ecumenical work, writing, 'The Church is more and more moving into an ecumenical role and finding new and exciting dimensions as it experiences the vitality of other Christians . . . No one denomination can go it alone as we tackle the evils of racism, injustice and the moral and spiritual breakdown of our time.'[7] She had direct experience of ecumenical ministry in the Sheffield Ecumenical Mission, of which St James' Presbyterian Church was one of the early partners.

About halfway through the time she was in Sheffield, Robert Gillespie, minister of St James' and Madge's co-worker there, died. She went on to lead the congregation for the next five years. On her return to Jamaica after nearly ten years in Britain, she offered for service as an ordained minister and she was ordained at St Mary in Salem in 1975, the first woman ordained in the United Church of Jamaica.

Madge believed the Church should be involved in challenging and changing public and national attitudes and options, both in respect of race but also the global status of women. She wrote, 'Let us not be afraid to break out of the past and venture with Him who goes before us into the future to do great things in the building up of our lives.'[8]

She served the rest of her ministry in Jamaica, building further on her earlier experience on the island, and in Britain. Among other highlights was the completion of the Madge Saunders Conference and Youth Centre at Ocho Rios on the north coast. It was named after Madge after she encouraged the Synod to pursue its vision and raise the funds for the centre.

Even after retirement she continued her full involvement in the life of church and society. Recognizing that her own material needs were small by comparison to the educational needs of the children of Jamaica, she sold her house and bought a smaller one in order to fund bursaries for secondary school children. At the 25th anniversary of the United Church of Jamaica and the Cayman Islands, Madge's work in the Caribbean and the UK was once again highlighted. Although not then full-time in ministry, she clearly was still in 'active service'. Her advice to young Christian women was, 'You have to make a choice and live up to your Christian principles.'[9]

In 2002 Madge was reunited with some of her 'Sheffield people' when a small group from St James' Church made the journey to Jamaica to see her and the work of the United Church. She recalled many of the highs and lows of her time in the city: the work with children and young people was especially dear to her. But she also remembered the racism, graffiti on the walls and door of her flat and her response on the local radio to remarks about immigrants by Enoch Powell. She had kept the scissors, made of Sheffield steel, which the Lord Mayor had given her as she left to return home. She had made a mark: many people both in Sheffield and other parts of the UK remember her inspiring ministry. Her name is often spoken with affection at meetings and her work was documented in the book *Daughters of Dissent*, published in 2004.[10] Although only ten years of her long life had been spent in ministry in Britain, she was a pioneer. The partnership in ministry that she embodied forty years ago has become a familiar pattern among the churches of the Council for World Mission of which the United Church of Jamaica and the Cayman Islands is one.

Notes

1. This narrative is based on material in the Daughters of Dissent archive at Westminster College, Cambridge, from the St Colm's College archive, Edinburgh, and from meetings with Madge herself.

2. *The Early Childhood Movement in Jamaica: Building Blocks for the Future*, by M. Dayley and J. Thompson, was published by Chalkboard Press, at the University of the West Indies in 2004. It was reviewed by A. W. Sangster, in the *Jamaican Gleaner*, on 6 February 2005: this quotation is taken from his review.

3. Words from Madge herself in her interview with Barbara Nelson, in the Daughters of Dissent archive, Westminister College, Cambridge, p. 4.

4. This formed the United Church of Jamaica. In this respect Jamaica was ahead of Britain. A union of Congregationalists and Presbyterians, called the United Reformed Church, did not take place in Britain until 1972.

5. Madge's interview with Barbara Nelson, pp. 5–6.

6. Madge Saunders, 'The Challenge of Service', in the 10th anniversary brochure of the United Church of Jamaica and Grand Cayman (1965–75), p. 5.

7. Saunders, 'Challenge of Service', p. 6.

8. Saunders, 'Challenge of Service', p. 6.

9. *Rev Marjorie Saunders, Sojourn as a Missionary*, from the 25th anniversary brochure of the United Church of Jamaica and Grand Cayman (1965–90), p. 27.

10. Elaine Kaye, Janet Lees and Kirsty Thorpe, *Daughters of Dissent* (London: United Reformed Church, 2004).

Nezlin Sterling

*National and International Secretary,
New Testament Assembly
(Interviewed by Janet Wootton, 14 September 2006)*

'Tell me a bit about your background and upbringing.'

I was born into a religious family in Jamaica. My mother and father were joint founders and senior leaders of a local Congregational church. I am the second of three girls and we had a good and memorable childhood which we often recall with great delight and laughter. We, however, experienced the usual pressure as pastors' children.

We lived in a relatively poor area, but my father owned a lot of land, and employed labourers to cultivate the farms. Our home was one of the first well-built houses in the area, so it was central to the community. Visiting ministers and politicians stayed there, and local people came for food, clothes and – during one hurricane – for shelter. This meant that we didn't have our parents exclusively – they belonged to everyone.

We had to walk three miles to and from school. Often when we came home from school we would be given a snack and then sent on a mission to deliver food parcels to the poor, the disabled and the sick. We would then have our dinner when we returned.

I passed my Jamaica first, second and third examinations three years prior to the age when one could enter any of the professions. I then went to a secondary boarding school where I pursued O level subjects. I knew I wanted to do nursing, though my father would have preferred me to do as my sisters did, and become a teacher. I did my nursing training, and did extremely well, gaining the highest marks throughout. On graduating I staffed at my training school (which was unusual) for two years. I always wanted to travel, and so in 1966 I came to England to continue my nursing career.

While at boarding school in Jamaica, I went to a Baptist church, where I made my own profession of faith and was baptized by full immersion. Later, while I was in nursing, I joined a Pentecostal church. In 1966 when I came to England I went to a recommended Pentecostal church, where I met my husband. He was already in training for ordination, and we were married just a few months after he was ordained, in 1967.

I spent the next few years as a pastor's wife, teaching in the Sunday school, working with the ladies' group and giving general support to my husband. I took on the role of National Secretary for the New Testament Assembly Women's Forum in 1979 and, later, became Vice President.

'How did you receive your call to ministry and how did your ministry develop?'

In the Pentecostal churches, you are expected to grow and develop in your faith. This spiritual journey is aided by good mentoring from local pastors and bishops who help you to discern your gift(s). Following recognition of my gifts, I was ordained in 1982, and soon afterwards I was appointed as the Assistant General Secretary of the New Testament Assembly.

This was a period of development for the Assembly. At that time, there were two wings: the Jamaica wing and the UK wing, which included churches in Canada, the USA and Ghana. I was instrumental in 1994 in drafting a 'Unification document' as both parties were desirous of being under one management umbrella. After consultation, a single international organization was formed, and I became the first International Executive Secretary in 1994.

In 1997, I was also appointed to the position of National General Secretary – UK, and I have since then held both positions. As the UK General Secretary, I represent the organization on Churches Together in Britain and Ireland, Churches Together in England, and I am a member of Christian Aid's Board of Trustees, Chair of the African and Caribbean Evangelical Alliance and serve as the black majority Churches representative on the Church of England General Synod.

Internationally, it is my responsibility to call together the annual meeting of bishops and their secretaries, and disseminate information between the seven constituencies.

These roles are voluntary, and I have carried them out alongside bringing up my three sons – now adult – combined with a successful nursing career, which culminated in the post of Director of Nursing in Hillingdon (West London) Hospital.

'Has being a woman made a difference?'

From its origin in Jamaica in 1954, the New Testament Assembly has had women in senior leadership positions. In fact the National Trustee Board – UK is 40 per cent female, and women pastor many of our congregations, preside at communion, preach and carry out all other functions. Women tend not to baptize. This is because the men protect them from having to go into the water.

To date there has not been a woman bishop. There are some reservations about this from our older senior male ministers, but gradually these reservations are being worked through. There is a strong possibility that the first woman bishop will be appointed in Jamaica within the next two years when the current bishop is due to retire from the position.

I regard my husband as the head of our home, and submission to this biblical edict is important and not an issue for me. I support this and propagate it. I see my husband as my priest, and I like this. I want him to protect me, care for me, hold my hands (physically and emotionally) and pray for me. I see much of society's dysfunction as a result of women usurping men's position. Men seem no longer to have confidence in their role.

This is in no way a contradiction to women's leadership in the Church. A woman may be a pastor in the church in which her husband is a member or deacon, and that should not be a problem or an area of conflict. It will all depend on the relationship the couple has with each other.

Pauline Webb

Local preacher and broadcaster, former Vice President of the Methodist Conference and Vice Moderator of the World Council of Churches

Some people are clearly called into the ordained ministry; others are simply pushed into other forms of ministry they might otherwise never have dreamed of. I am one of the latter. I feel as though all my life I have been prodded along like a donkey into paths that others, or perhaps just One Other, have chosen for me. Kicking against many pricks, chafing against many restraints and stumbling over some rough ground I was yet led eventually into a far wider ministry than I would have ever found on a route of my own or my family's choosing.

It would have seemed that the path was pretty well marked out for me right from the beginning. I am told that my mother, having already had two much-loved daughters, confidently announced when she was expecting her third child, 'This one is going to be a son. Moreover he will become a minister like his father and one day he will be President of the Conference.' When I arrived to complete the trio of sisters, she was quite unabashed and said, 'Never mind! By the time she's grown up they will have women in the Methodist ministry.' Her prophecy on this matter proved to be as inaccurate as her forecast about my own gender. But maybe that increased her determination that neither I nor either of my two sisters should ever feel that their lives were in any way limited or disadvantaged because they were women.

From our earliest moments we felt valued and loved for our own worth and we were expected to fulfil all the potential born within us. Our home was a Methodist manse, and my first journey from home was to Park Lane Methodist Church in Wembley, where my father was the minister. There my infant head was signposted with the mark of the cross, the way chosen for me by my parents whose whole lives were lived under the direction of the way of Jesus. It's hard to deviate far from that way when all one's upbringing is directed towards it. In my childhood games I played at being a minister, imitating my father as I preached sermons to my dolls and even on occasions persuaded my sisters to take up a collection! Yet I also sometimes kicked against the restraints that life in a manse inevitably imposes. Even a little child soon learns that the Christian way is no easy path. Commitment to Christ's Church makes special demands on a minister's time and energy, and yet also brings its own rewards.

In our home we never seemed to have as much money to spend as other families and yet somehow we always seemed to have more fun. Home for me was a hilariously happy and safe place to be. My mother had a quick wit and a keen sense of humour which enabled us to see the funny side even of some of the things that were happening in the church! My father, by contrast a quiet man, had a serene temperament which taught us the value of daily prayers, and of the weekly time of fellowship in prayer we shared as a family. Our home always seemed to be full of people with all kinds of needs and requests. There were times when I even felt that mother Church demanded a disproportionate amount of my father's time. It was a family joke that my father's response when we asked for some new luxury was always, 'We can't afford it!', but we learned to laugh about the shabby manse furniture and the handed-down clothes. Yet I secretly envied those school-friends whose fathers had chosen more lucrative and less time-consuming ways of earning a living.

Being the family of an itinerant Methodist minister we were always on the move, once every three years during my childhood. For me this proved to be an exciting and enriching adventure. I always hated leaving old friends behind, but that meant also leaving behind a reputation for bad behaviour at school and having the opportunity of a new start! I soon learned from experience that wherever one goes in the world, there are always new friends waiting to be discovered. I loved the old, familiar places but I learned to live happily in such a variety of surroundings – a village, a city, a seaside resort and an industrial area – in Lancaster and London, in the Midlands and the south – that now I find it easy to settle in any environment. I can feel at home everywhere because I have had no 'fixed abode' anywhere. In fact the whole concept of what 'home' means became much fuller to me when I realized it had nothing to do with the bricks and mortar of a particular building or with possessions and places that stayed permanent, but just being together with people who loved me. That love led me through the rebellious teenage years and eventually set me free to go out to find my own vocation in the adult world.

When I did at last arrive at King's College, London University, I felt that now I could choose my own path and would not be branded with any particular image or expectations. True, I found myself on my first day in the college chapel attending the opening of term service. But from that moment I determined to try and free myself from the restraints that a religious view of life would seem inevitably to impose on me. Yet as I became more aware of the entirely secular views of some of my fellow students it seemed to me that many of them lived in some ways a more confined life than I did, living as they did within the limited dimensions of their own familiar surroundings and the excitements of the immediate moment. Among several women students I found that what they called 'free' loving meant little more than becoming entangled in an entirely human bondage in which, as in Medea's description of women in love, 'their whole vision had become enchained on a single soul'. I wanted love, but I wanted liberty too.

It became more and more clear to me that without some basic direction and commitment I would have neither. As I have told in testimony elsewhere (in my memoirs, entitled *World Wide Webb*),[1] I came into contact eventually with a group of Christian students who did have a sense of direction. It was one of them who finally persuaded me to go with her back into that same college chapel and make there a personal commitment to Christ which would determine the direction of every other decision I would ever make. From then on, I felt that I was 'firmly bound, forever free'.

There followed then the search for a way of expressing that commitment in some form of full-time ministry. Because my own father had been such a faithful minister of the Word and Sacraments I felt that there could be no greater privilege than to be called to share in a ministry such as his. It seemed a providential coincidence that in the very year when I graduated, the Methodist Conference was debating the question of the ordination of women, which had once been agreed in principle but which had been postponed from coming into practice during the Second World War. In 1948 it was confidently expected that Conference would now agree to accept women candidates for the ministry. Yet to my astonishment and dismay, the proposal was rejected and the door to full-time ordained ministry remained firmly closed to women.

I had little idea then of what else I wanted to do. My two sisters had both had a clear sense of vocation – my sister Joy to the teaching profession and Muriel to nursing, both of which were regarded as wholly suitable careers for women. But I wasn't really attracted to either, and all the spheres I did find attractive – journalism, law and politics – were all regarded as difficult for women to enter. Living in Dartford as I did at the time, I even heard the (failed) Conservative candidate, by name Margaret Roberts, speaking on the hustings. She once declared that she did not think she would ever see a woman rise to be Prime Minister in her lifetime. After she married and became known as Margaret Thatcher, she eventually became Britain's first, and so far only, female Premier, which shows how wrong even political prophecy can be.

Undaunted by my mother's prophecy having been proved wrong, I continued in my determination to serve the Church in some way to the best of my ability. After a short period of teaching I went to work on a short-term contract as an Education Secretary and later as Editor with the Methodist Missionary Society (MMS). It was a bit of a shock to discover that in church circles then women missionaries and employees of the MMS were still paid considerably less than their male colleagues. It was only because of the requirements of the Equal Pay for Equal Work legislation that the Church eventually had to come into line with the requirements of the rest of society! But for many years, shamefully I felt, the Church as an employing body was still exempt from the law banning discrimination on grounds of gender because of its refusal to accept women for ordination to the ministry of Word and Sacraments.

However, there was nothing really to deter me from a ministry of the Word except the prejudice I still encountered on occasions against women preachers. This sometimes took an obvious form, when people who objected to females in the pulpit merely stayed away when women were appointed to preach. In my job at the missionary society I had often to speak in church on behalf of overseas missions. It was one day after I had made an appeal of this kind that my own class leader, a lay man, who had heard my advocacy, asked me why I had not ever responded to a call to preach and become, in Methodist terms, a 'local preacher'. 'Do you really think women are called to preach?' I asked him. 'Where in the Gospels,' he asked me, 'is it ever suggested that Jesus told them not to?' Certainly even though throughout the nineteenth century the Wesleyan Methodist Conference had refused to allow women to preach to any but their own sex, John Wesley himself had recognized that there were women with what he called 'extraordinary gifts' whom he couldn't prohibit from preaching!

For over fifty years now I have been a local preacher and have shared in training many other women as preachers. It is worth noting that by far the most effective and well organized ecumenical event in the calendar of most churches is the Women's World Day of Prayer. Yet I remember on one occasion when the service had been most expertly prepared and rehearsed by a group of women from all the churches in the area, I who had been invited to preach was warned by the vicar not to stand in the pulpit, as it was not a suitable place for a woman's presence! So I stood at the altar steps instead, but pointed out that that unfortunately simply made it more difficult for the congregation to hear what I had to say!

I have to admit that, despite such occasional examples of prejudice, I received the greatest support and encouragement from men colleagues who were determined to open up new paths of opportunity for me. Though obviously I did not qualify to go to a Methodist theological college, Philip Potter and Harry Morton, both colleagues of mine at the Methodist Missionary Society, encouraged me to apply for a year's scholarship to study at the Union Theological Seminary in New York. There I was invited to be one in an ecumenical group of students from four different continents, eleven different countries and twelve different churches. We were only a small group, fourteen in number, three of us women, and yet it seemed to me to be a prototype of the coming great Church in which there really were no barriers of race or gender, sect or culture as we discovered our true oneness in Christ. We became aware of the great winds of change blowing through the Church across the world. An evidence of that wind of the Holy Spirit sweeping across the Church was the growing number of churches which were beginning to recognize and accept the ministry of women.

So I came back to Britain emboldened to campaign for the ordination of women in my own church and received great support from the Society for the Ministry of Women in the Church, of which Lady Stansgate was in those days the President. I also subsequently joined the Movement for the Ordination of Women in the Anglican Church. At present I am still supporting our Roman Catholic sisters in their efforts to persuade their Church to be aware of the gift I believe God is waiting to bestow upon the whole Church. For, despite all the argument, I have never seen the campaign for the ordination of women as necessarily impeding in any way the ecumenical movement towards the unity of the whole Church which ought surely to represent the whole of humanity in its priesthood.

Eventually I became aware that there was still also a very real lay ministry to be developed among both men and women in and beyond the Church. So when I was appointed by the Methodist Conference to a pioneering post as a Director of Lay Training I emphasized the important role women had to play at all levels of church life as well as in all kinds of lay professions. At many of the lay training conferences we held I was impressed by the wealth of the talent among women that was still lying untapped both within and beyond the confines of the women's organizations within the Church.

As for my own vocation, God in his wisdom by closing one door to me opened a door to a world wide ministry I could never have dreamed of. Again it was a male colleague, Colin Morris, who suggested to me that I apply for a job as Organizer of Religious Broadcasting Overseas in the World Service of the BBC. Through my membership of the Central Committee of the World Council of Churches I had had unique contact with the leadership and the life of all the major religious denominations. This meant that I would have many resources on which to draw for programmes to be broadcast across the world. So, despite my initial lack of experience of radio production, to my astonishment I was appointed to the World Service. Even the BBC had been affected by the winds of change! I was the first woman and the first non-cleric to be appointed to this particular post, one which gave me a daily congregation countable in millions and one in which I learned to work with colleagues of both genders, of many faiths and of all races. So, though when I first graduated I thought I had missed my vocation when the Church seemed set on rejecting me, simply on account of my gender, I found a greater fulfilment than I had ever dreamed of when God called even me, to 'Go and preach the gospel to the whole world' and gave me the opportunity to do it!

Note

1. Pauline Webb, *World Wide Webb* (Norwich: Canterbury Press, 2006).

Afterword

This is our story. It is a story worth telling, and one to engender both pride and regret. It has historical depth, a great breadth and range of experience, and it is striding on into the future. Some of the women who have told their stories have participated in the tectonic movements in opinion and practice in society and church in the past half-century or more. Others are at the beginning of their careers, and who knows what changes they will see and bring about?

Some have suffered greatly in their journey to the fulfilment of their calling. The most painful stories, of course, have been withheld, and I know of them only from phone conversations, explaining why a story cannot, at this stage, be made public. Others, on the other hand, have found the way open before them, often because of changes in social mores or because they are entering into ministries that other women have exercised before them.

I am immensely proud to have known many of the women who have contributed to this book. I can remember, before the ordination of women in the Church of England, attending a conference on women's ministry, and being encouraged by the black women present not to be afraid. There was no bar to women's equal leadership with men. It was only a matter of time. I can remember sitting on a panel at a fringe meeting during the 2001 Methodist Conference, with Jean Mayland and Pauline Webb, in a discussion on women bishops, 'Should women wear purple?' Of course, we had very different opinions on the matter, but I recall the pleasure I had in these women's company. When God calls such wise, energetic and powerful women to speak prophetically, we do well to listen!

And people are listening. Despite our frustration at the unjustified predominance of the Church of England in the press, the ordination of women in that Church has raised the profile of women in church leadership in Britain. From *The Vicar of Dibley* to *The Archers*, women church leaders are now widely accepted, even preferred, by those who receive their ministry or work with them.

Besides this, the patient work of women and men on liturgical commissions and hymn book editorial committees has brought inclusive

AFTERWORD

language into the main stream, at least when it comes to speaking about human beings. Even female images of God are finding their way from the pages of Scripture to the songs and prayers of the Church. Slowly, church structures are beginning to change. Leadership is more often shared in team ministries, and is less often autocratic. Models of church are changing, with new patterns of church emerging, though these are not uniformly receptive of women's leadership. Most training for ministry includes at least some reference to gender studies and a recognition that the theology and history written by an unbroken line of white men has its own biases!

Liberation theologies, which were by and large exclusively male in the 1960s, have broadened to include a great variety of feminist, womanist, and other gender-based theologies. Such theologies are necessarily based in praxis, and interact with a growing recognition of the oppression and abuse of women, in domestic violence, trafficking, unfair treatment in the workplace and in many other ways. Churches have (usually) followed in the wake of social and justice movements to combat some of these injustices.

It is there that the regret and frustration lie. The main chapters in this book reveal a tentative history of women's leadership in the Church, but it is more like a series of matches lit in the dark than a steady burning light. And yet the writers are clear that the stories of the women who encountered Jesus, told in the Gospels and Acts and reflected in the Epistles of the New Testament, open up a radically new view of the relationship between women and men: that Jesus invited women into the circle of his disciples, and held astonishingly open conversations with them; that women both hosted and led some of the early house churches; and, by the evident backlash in some of the Epistles, that women were taking roles in those churches that were radically new and shocking to the society of the time.

It is a matter of untold regret, centuries of regret, that the Church has systematically and deliberately excluded women from ordination and leadership. The loss to the Church and the world is incalculable, and the loss to the particular women tragic.

Knowing the strength of my own vocation, and its deep rootedness in my identity, I cannot imagine the pain of living a whole life called, but unable to fulfil the calling. To be told that you cannot answer the fire of vocation burning within you, which becomes part of your identity, because, by identity, you are female, gives rise to an existential contradiction which is impossible to bear. And yet I know many women who have borne that pain, and I have read of countless others.

What would the history of the past two millennia have been, if the Church had maintained and built on Jesus' counter-cultural inclusion of women in the apostolate, in close discipleship and in theological debate,

AFTERWORD

instead of ratifying and justifying men's right to control women, by concentrating on patriarchal aspects of Scripture and Tradition? This is not to say that women have an entirely benign influence, but that women and men working together have a greater chance of creating wholeness in humanity and the world, and that working counter-culturally gives rise to radical questioning that can bring about change. If they had dared to live and demonstrate a different way, we might be living in a very different world now.

Even worse is the existing backlash against women's leadership. I remember sitting at a Church Representatives Meeting of the Council of Churches for Britain and Ireland (as it was then) discussing the theme of the proposed Lent course shortly after the end of the World Council of Churches Ecumenical Decade – Churches in Solidarity with Women. One representative suggested that it should include a section building on the Decade's work on violence against women. With a sigh, another rose to his feet. 'Surely,' he said, 'surely we have *done* women.' The chapters in this book not only celebrate the biblical precedents for women's calling and leadership, they also recognize that the situation is still precarious.

The present Pope is the one who, as a cardinal, banned discussion of women's ordination in the Roman Catholic Church. The right-wing fundamentalist Protestant churches are equally adamant in their opposition to women holding positions of leadership. Their electoral ascendancy in the USA gives them a very strong power base, from which they have a global reach. This finds a strong echo in some of the churches in the southern hemisphere, where, of course, the Church is growing more strongly than in the North. From time to time, chillingly, we hear of churches rescinding their former decisions to ordain women, and depriving those women they have ordained of their standing.

The present situation feels extremely precarious. It is not possible to predict the future stability of the advances made since the 1970s in equality of access to leadership in the Church, and all the dazzling changes that have accompanied them. This generation could be the vanguard of unstoppable change. Future generations may look back with wonderment at a time when women were systematically excluded from leadership in the Church, as we now look back with sadness on the age that accepted the enslavement of Africans as natural, or the destruction of indigenous peoples as divinely ordained.

On the other hand, history teaches that women's equality is not normally continuously recognized, and advances are followed not only by retrenchment, but even by the denial and concealment of the fact that they happened at all. It may be that we are about to enter a period of repression, during which any equality that women have achieved is withdrawn and forgotten. In that case, the women of a future generation will

AFTERWORD

need to pioneer change again, and may uncover our stories as we have uncovered the long but intermittent stories of the past.

But while the present and the future are in the hands of women of the calibre of those who have contributed to this book, and while we can hear the voices of those foremothers whose stories are contained in its pages, we must retain hope for an inclusive range of ministries for women and men, and a Church which dares to run counter to the dominances and inequalities of the cultures which have so much influenced it in the past.

Bibliography

Aldred, Joe (ed.), *Sisters with Power* (London: Continuum, 2000).

An Anglican-Methodist Covenant (Methodist Publishing House and Church House Publishing, 2001).

Bam, Brigalia, *What is ordination coming to? Report of a Consultation on the Ordination of Women (1970 Sep)* (Geneva: World Council of Churches, 1972).

Baptism, Eucharist and Ministry (Geneva; World Council of Churches, 1982).

Bartholomew, H.A.H. Ecumenical Patriarch, in Kyriaki Karidoyanes Fitzgerald (ed.) *Orthodox Women Speak: Discerning the 'Signs of the Times'*(Geneva: World Council of Churches, 1999), pp. 15–18.

Batten C. R. 'The Work and Witness of Free Church Women', The Address of the President, Mrs C. R. Batten, twenty-first March, 1955 (London: National Free Church Women's Council, 1955),

Behr–Sigel, Elisabeth and Kallistos Ware, *The ordination of women in the Orthodox Church* (Geneva: World Council of Churches Risk Book Series, 2000).

Belleville, Linda L, *Women Leaders and the Church* (Grand Rapids: Baker, 2000).

Benvenuti, Sheri R, 'Pentecostal Women in Ministry: Where Do We Go From Here?', in *Cyber Journal for Pentecostal-Charismatic Research*, 1 (January 1997), accessed at http://www.pctii.org/cyberj/cyber1.html.

Blohm, Uta, 'Women Clergy Working with Rituals', *Feminist Theology* 15.1 (September 2006), pp. 26–47.

Blohm, Uta, *Religious Traditions and Personal Stories: Women Working as Priests, Minister and Rabbis* (Frankfurt am Main: Peter Lang, 2005).

Booth, Catherine, *Female Ministry; or, Women's Right to Preach the Gospel* (London: Morgan & Chase, 1870).

Booth, William (1888) 'The May Meeting Addresses: Summary of the Years History', *The War Cry* May 12, 1888, p. 10.

Bosch, David J., *Transforming Mission: Paradigm Shifts in Theology of Mission* (Maryknoll: Orbis Books, 1991).

Boswell, James, *Life of Dr Samuel Johnson*, vol. 1 (entry for 31 July 1763).
Bowman, William, *The Imposture of Methodism Display'd* (London: Joseph Lord, 1740).
Bradshaw, Paul F, *The Search for the Origins of Christian Worship* (New York: Oxford University Press, 1992).

Called to be One (London: CTE Publications, 1996).
Chapman, Diana, 'The Rise and Demise of Women's Ministry in the Origins and Early Years of Pentecostalism in Britain', *Journal of Pentecostal Theology* 12.2 (2004) pp.217–46
Chaves, Mark, *Ordaining Women: Culture and Conflict in Religious Organizations* (Cambridge, Mass.: 1997).
Chilcote, Paul W, *She offered them Christ: the legacy of women preachers in early Methodism* (Nashville: Abingdon Press, 1993).
Classen, Carl Joachim, *Rhetorical Criticism of the New Testament* (Tübingen: Mohr Siebeck, 2000).
Clifford, Anne M., *Introducing Feminist Theology* (Maryknoll, New York: Orbis Books, 2004).
Collins, John N., *Deacons and the Church: Making Connections between Old and New* (Harrisburg, Pennsylvania: Gracewing, Morehouse Publishing, 2002).
Commitment to Mission and Unity: Report of the Informal Conversations between and the Church of England (Church House and Methodist Publishing House, 1996).
Constitutional Practice and Discipline of the Methodist Church, vol. 2 (Peterborough: Methodist Publishing House).
Cox, Harvey, *Fire From Heaven: The Rise of Pentecostal Spirituality and the Reshaping of Religion in the twenty-first Century* (London: Cassell, 1996).
Crawford, Janet, 'Women and Ecclesiology-two ecumenical streams', *The Ecumenical Review* (January 2001), pp. 14–24.
Cullmann, Oscar, *Early Christian Worship* (London: SCM Press, 1953).

Davis, Angela, *Women, Race and Class* (New York: Random House, 1981)
Delling, G., *Worship in the New Testament* (London: Darton Longman & Todd, 1962).
Dill, Bonnie Thornton, 'The Dialectics of Black Womanhood: Toward a New Model of American Femininity', *Sign: Journal of Women in Culture and Society* 4 (Spring 1979), pp. 543–55.
Dodd, C. H., *The Apostolic Preaching and its Developments* (London: Hodder & Stoughton, 1936).

BIBLIOGRAPHY

Donaldson, Gordon, *The Faith of the Scots* (London: Batsford, 1990).
Doriani, Dan, *Women and Ministry* (Wheaton: Crossway, 2003).
Douglass, Jane Dempsey, *Women, Freedom, and Calvin* (Philadelphia: Westminster Press, 1985).
Drane, John, *The McDonaldization of the Church* (London: Darton Longman & Todd, 2000).
Drane, Olive M. Fleming, *Clowns, Storytellers, Disciples* (Oxford: BRF, 2002).

Eason, Andrew Mark, *Women in God's Army: Gender and Equality in the Early Salvation Army*, Studies on Women in Religion 7 (Waterloo, Ont.: Canadian Corporation for Studies in Religion, 2003).
Eisenberg, Azriel, *The Synagogue through the Ages* (New York: Bloch Publishing Company, 1974).

Fell, Margaret, *Women's speaking justified, proved and allowed of by the scriptures*, first published 1666 (Amherst, Mass: New England Yearly Meeting of Friends, 1980).
Field-Bibb, Jacqueline, *Women Towards Priesthood: Ministerial Politics and Feminist Praxis* (Cambridge: Cambridge University Press, 1991).
Fiorenza, Elisabeth Schüssler and Hermann Häring (eds), *The Non-Ordination of Women and the Politics of Power* (London: SCM Press, Maryknoll, N.Y.: Orbis Books, 1999).
Fiorenza, Elisabeth Schüssler, *Discipleship of Equals: a Critical Feminist Ekklesia-logy of Liberation* (London: SCM Press, 1993).
Fiorenza, Elisabeth Schüssler, *Sharing Her Word: Feminist Biblical Interpretation in Context* (Edinburgh, T&T Clark, 1998).
Forster, Faith and Roger, 'Women's Spiritual Gifts in the Church', in Keay, Kathy (ed.), *Men Women and God* (Basingstoke: Marshall Pickering, 1987).
Foster, Elaine, 'Women and the Inverted Pyramid of the Black Churches in Britain', in Sahgal, Gita and Nira Yuval-Davis (eds.), *Refusing Holy Orders: Women and Fundamentalism in Britain* (London: Virago Press, 1992).

Garman, Mary et al. (ed.) *Hidden in Plain Sight: Quaker Women's Writings 1650–1700* (Wallingford, PA: Pendle Hill Publications, 1996).
Giddings, Paula, *When and Where I Enter: The Impact of Black Women on Race and Sex in America* (New York: William Morrow, 1984).
Gilkes, Cheryl Townsend, *If It Wasn't For The Women: Black Women's Experience and Womanist Culture in Church and Community* (Maryknoll, New York: Orbis Books, 2001).
Gouldbourne, Ruth M.B., 'Reinventing the Wheel: Women and Ministry in English Baptist Life' (Oxford: Whitley Publications, 1997).

Greaves, Richard L, 'The Role of Women in Early English Nonconformity', Church History 52.3 (1983), pp. 299–311
Guy-Sheftall, Beverly (ed.), *Words of Fire: An Anthology of African-American Thought* (New York: The New Press, 1995).

Hattersley, Roy, *Blood and Fire: William and Catherine Booth and Their Salvation Army* (London: Little, Brown and Company, 1999).
Herzel, Susannah, *A Voice for Women* (Geneva: World Council of Churches, 1981).
Hudson, Wade & Valerie Wilson Wesley (eds), *The Afro-Bets Book of Black Heroes From A – Z: an introduction to important Black achievers for young readers* (Orange, NJ: Just Us Books, 1988).
Hunt, Mary, 'We Women Are Church: Roman Catholic Women Shaping Ministries and Theologies,' in Fiorenza, Elisabeth Schüssler and Hermann Haring (eds), *The Non-Ordination of Women and the Politics of Power* (London: SCM Press, Maryknoll, N.Y.: Orbis Books, 1999).
Hymns and Psalms: A Methodist and Ecumenical Hymn Book (London: Methodist Publishing House, 1983).

Ice, Martha Long, *Clergy Women and Their World Views: Calling for a New Age* (New York, Praeger, 1987).
In the Spirit of the Covenant: Interim Report (2005) of the Joint Implementation Commission under the Covenant between the Methodist Church of Great Britain and the Church of England (Peterborough: Methodist Publishing House, 2005).
Isherwood, Lisa, *Introducing Feminist Christologies* (London: Sheffield Academic Press, 2001).

Jackson, Anita, *Catching Both Sides of the Wind: Conversations with Five Black Pastors* (London: British Council of Churches, 1985).
Jamieson, Alan, *A Churchless Faith* (London: SPCK, 2002).
Japinga, Lynn, *Feminism and Christianity: an essential guide* (Nashville: Abingdon, 1999).
Jensen, Anne, *God's self-confident Daughters: early Christianity and the liberation of women* (Louisville: Westminster John Knox Press, 1996).
John Paul II, *Ordinatio Sacerdotalis*, 22 May 1994.

Kaye, Elaine, Janet Lees and Kirsty Thorpe (eds), *Daughters of Dissent* (London: United Reformed Church, 2004).
Keay, Kathy (ed.), *Men Women & God* (Marshall, Morgan & Scott, 1987).
Keay, Kathy (ed.), *Men Women and God* (Basingstoke: Marshall Pickering, 1987).

Keller, Rosemary Skinner & Rosemary Radford Ruether (eds), *In our own Voices: four centuries of American women's religious writing* (San Francisco: HarperSanFrancisco, 1995).
Kienzle, Beverly Mayne and Pamela J Walker (eds), *Women Preachers and Prophets through two millennia of Christianity* (Berkeley: University of California Press, 1998).
Kim, Eunjoo Mary, *Women Preaching: theology and practice through the ages* (Cleveland: Pilgrim Press, 2004).
Kim, Eunjoo Mary, *Women Preaching: theology and practice through the ages* (Cleveland: Pilgrim Press, 2004).
Kim, Eunjoo Mary, *Women Preaching: theology and practice through the ages* (Cleveland: Pilgrim Press, 2004).
Kim, Seyoon, *Paul and the New Perspective: second thoughts on the origins of Paul's Gospel* (Grand Rapids: Eerdmans, 2002).
Kim, Seyoon, *The Origin of Paul's Gospel* (Grand Rapids: Eerdmans, 1983).
Kwilecki, Susan, 'Contemporary Pentecostal Clergywomen: Christian Leadership, Old Style', *Journal of Feminist Studies in Religion* 3.2 (Fall 1987), pp. 57–76.
Kyriaki Karidoyanes Fitzgerald (ed.) *Orthodox Women Speak: Discerning the 'Signs of the Times'*(Geneva: World Council of Churches, 1999).

Lee, Jarena, *Religious Experience and Journal of Mrs Jarena Lee, giving an account of her call to Preach the Gospel* (Philadelphia: Printed and published for the Author, 1849), 36,. http://digilib.nypl.org/dynaweb/digs/wwm9716/@Generic_BookView
Levy, Isaac, *The Synagogue: its History and Function* (London: Vallentine, Mitchell & Co Ltd., 1963).
Limouris, Gennadios (ed.), *The place of the woman in the Orthodox Church and the question of the ordination of women*: Report of the InterOrthodox Symposium, Rhodes, Greece, 30 October to 7 November 1988) (Katerini: Tertios, 1992).
Lischer, Richard, *Theories of Preaching: selected readings in the homiletical tradition* (Durham NC: Labyrinth Press, 1987).
Litfin, Duane A, *St Paul's theology of proclamation: 1 Corinthians 1–4 and Greco-Roman Rhetoric* (New York: CUP, 1994).
Loades, Ann (ed.), *Feminist Theology: A Reader* (London: SPCK, 1990).

MacHaffie, Barbara J, *Her Story: women in Christian tradition*, 2nd edn (Minneapolis: Fortress, 2006).
MacHaffie, Barbara J, *Her Story: women in Christian tradition*, 2nd edn (Minneapolis: Fortress, 2006).

BIBLIOGRAPHY

Mack, Burton L, *Rhetoric and the New Testament* (Minneapolis: Fortress, 1990).

Martin, R. P. *Worship in the Early Church* (London: Marshall, Morgan & Scott, 1964).

May, Melanie A., 'Tracking the Ways of Women in Religious Leadership', in Fiorenza, Elisabeth Schüssler (ed.), *The Non-Ordination of Women and the Politics of Power* (London: SCM Press, 1999), pp. 89–101.

Mbiti, John S., *African Religions and Philosophy* (Heinemann, Oxford, 1989).

McCarthy, Carol, 'Ordained and Female' *The Baptist Quarterly* 31.7 (July 1986) pp. 334–5.

McEwan, Dorothea and Myra Poole, *Making All Things New: Women's Ordination – A catalyst for changes in the Catholic Church* (Norwich: Canterbury Press, 2003).

Methodist Worship Book (Peterborough: Methodist Publishing House).

Miles, Rosalind, *The Women's History of the World* (London: Joseph, 1988).

Moltmann, Jürgen, *The Church in the Power of the Spirit: A Contribution to Messianic Ecclesiology* (London: SCM Press, 1977).

Moore, Zoe Bennett, *Introducing Feminist Perspectives on Pastoral Theology* (London: Sheffield Academic Press, 2002).

Morisy, Ann, *Journeying Out: A new Approach to Christian Mission* (London: Continuum, 2004).

Morley, Janet, *Celebrating Women* (London: Women in Theology & Movement for the Ordination of Women, 1989).

Moule, C. F. D., *Worship in the New Testament* (London: SCM Press, 1961).

Moynagh, Michael, *Changing World Changing Church* (London: Monarch Books, 2001).

Myers, B. L., *Walking With the Poor. Principles and Practices of Transformational Development* (Maryknoll: Orbis Books, 1999).

Nesbitt, Paula D., *Feminization of the Clergy in America: Occupational and Organizational Perspectives* (New York, Oxford: Oxford University Press, 1997).

Newman, Louise Michele (ed.), *Men's Ideas, Women's Realities: Popular Science, 1870 –1915* (New York and London: Pergamon Press, 1985).

Norrington, David C, *To Preach or not to Preach: the church's urgent question* (Carlisle: Paternoster, 1996).

Northcroft, D. M., *Women Free Church Ministers* (London: Edgar G. Dunstan & Co., 1929)

BIBLIOGRAPHY

O'Faolain, Julia & Laurel Martines (eds), *Not in God's Image: women in history from the Greeks to the Victorians* (New York: Harper & Row, 1973).

Palmer, Phoebe, *Promise of the Father; or, A Neglected Speciality of the Last Days* (New York: Garland, 1985)

Peel, David, *Reforming Theology* (London: United Reformed Church, 2002).

Peters, Marygrace, 'The Beguines: feminine piety derailed', in *Spirituality Today* 43 (1991), pp. 36–52 (available at http://www.spiritualitytoday.org/spir2day/91431peters.html).

Phiri, Isabel Apawo, Beverley Hadda and Madipoane Masenya (eds), *African Women, HIV/AIDS and Faith Communities* (Pietermaritzburg: Cluster Publications).

Piper, John and Wayne Grudem (eds.), *Recovering Biblical Manhood and Womanhood: A Response to Evangelical Feminism* (Wheaton, Illinois: Crossway Books, 1991).

Porter, Fran, *Changing Women, Changing Worlds: Evangelical Women in Church, Community and Politics* (Belfast: The Blackstaff Press, 2002).

Powers, Janet Everts, 'Recovering a woman's head with prophetic authority: a Pentecostal interpretation of 1 Cor 11:3–16' *Journal of Pentecostal Theology* 10.1 (2001).

Reports on the Working Parties on Ecumenical Instruments (London: British Council of Churches and Catholic Truth Society, 1987).

Robeck, Cecil M, *The Azusa Street Mission and Revival: the birth of the global Pentecostal movement* (Nashville: Thomas Nelson, 2006).

Royden, Maude, *The Church and Woman* (London: James Clarke & Co, 1924).

Ruether, Rosemary Radford and Rosemary Skinner Keller (eds), *In Our Own Voices: Four Centuries of American Women's Religious Writing* (San Francisco: HarperCollins, 1995).

Ruether, Rosemary Radford, *Sexism and God-talk: Towards a Feminist Theology* (London, SCM Press, 2nd edn, 2002).

Ruether, Rosemary Radford, *Women-Church: Theology and Practice of Feminist Liturgical Communities* (San Francisco, London: Harper & Row, 1985).

Russell, Letty M., *Church in the Round: Feminist Interpretation of the Church* (Westminster: John Knox Press, 1993).

Sahgal, Gita and Nira Yuval-Davis (eds.), *Refusing Holy Orders: Women and Fundamentalism in Britain* (London: Virago Press, 1992).

Saunders, Madge, 'The Challenge of Service', in the 10th anniversary brochure of the United Church of Jamaica and Grand Cayman (1965–1975), p. 5.

Saunders, Rev Marjorie, *Sojourn as a Missionary*, from the 25th anniversary brochure of the United church of Jamaica and Grand Cayman (1965–1990).

Scholer, David M, 'Women in Ministry', in *The Covenant Companion* 1 January 1984, p. 13.

Scholer, David *Selected Articles on Hermeneutics and Women in Ministry in the New Testament* (Pasadena: Fuller Seminary 2005), published as a reader for his course NS561, *Women, the Bible, and the Church*.

Smith, Pamela J. Olubunmi, 'Feminism in Cross-Cultural Perspective: Women in Africa', *Transformation: An International Dialogue of Evangelical Social Ethics* 6.2 (1989), p. 13.

Southern, R W, Western Society and the Church in the Middle Ages (New York: Viking, 1970).

Stanley, Susie C, *Holy Boldness: women preachers' autobiographies and the sanctified self* (Knoxville: University of Tennessee Press, 2002).

Statements of the Methodist Church on Faith and Order, 1933–1983 (Methodist Publishing House, 1984).

Stout, Harry, *The New England Soul: preaching and religious culture in colonial New England* (New York: OUP, 1986).

Strom, Andrew, *The 'Out-of-Church' Christians* at http://homepages.ihug.co.nz/~revival/oo-Out-Of-Church.html.

Taft, Zechariah, 'A Reply to an article inserted in the Methodist Magazine for April 1809 entitled, "Thoughts on Women's Preaching", extracted from Dr James Knight' (Leeds: printed at the Bible Office by G. Wilson near the Old Church, 1809).

Taft, Zechariah, *Biographical Sketches of the Lives and Public Ministries of Various Holy Women* (Peterborough: Methodist Publishing House, 1992), vol. 1.

The Methodist Worship Book (Peterborough: Methodist Publishing House, 1999).

The United Reformed Church 'The Basis of Union and Schedule D: A statement concerning the nature, faith and order of the United Reformed Church version 1 and 2', 1971

Thurian, Max (ed.), *Churches Respond to BEM*, vol. 1 and 2 (Geneva: WCC, 1986).

Tillich, Paul, *The Protestant Era* (Chicago: Chicago University Press, 1948).

Tillman, June Boyce and Janet Wootton (eds), *Reflecting Praise* (London: Stainer & Bell and Women in Theology, 1993).

Torjesen, Karen Jo, 'The early Christian *Orans*: an artistic representation of women's liturgical prayer and prophecy', in Kienzle, Beverly Mayne and Pamela J Walker (eds), *Women Preachers and Prophets through two millennia of Christianity* (Berkeley: University of California Press, 1998).

Townes, Emily M., 'Black Women From Slavery to Womanist Liberation,' in Ruether, Rosemary Radford and Rosemary Skinner Keller (eds), *In Our Own Voices: Four Centuries of American Women's Religious Writing* (San Francisco: HarperCollins, 1995).

Truth, Sojourner, 'Woman's Rights', in Guy-Sheftall, Beverly (ed.), *Words of Fire: An Anthology of African-American Thought* (New York: The New Press, 1995), p. 36.

Vickers, John, *The Schismatick Sifted*, quoted in O'Faolain, Julia & Laurel Martines (eds), *Not in God's Image: women in history from the Greeks to the Victorians* (New York: Harper & Row, 1973).

Walton, Heather and Susan Durber (eds), *Silence in Heaven: a Book of Women's Preaching* (London: SCM, 1994).

Ward, Hannah and Jennifer Wild (eds), *Human Rites: worship resources for an age of change* (London: Mowbray, 1995).

Ward, Hannah and Jennifer Wild, *Guard the Chaos: finding meaning in change* (London: Darton, Longman and Todd, 1995).

Warren, Robert, *Building Missionary Congregations* (London: Church House Publishing, 1995).

Watson, Natalie K., *Introducing Feminist Ecclesiology* (Sheffield: Sheffield Academic Press, 2002).

Webb, Pauline, *World Wide Webb* (Norwich: Canterbury Press, 2006).

Weidman, Judith L (ed.) *Women Ministers: How Women are Redefining Traditional Roles* (Harper & Row, 1985).

Wesley, John, *The Letters of the Rev. John Wesley, A.M.*, ed. John Telford (London: Epworth Press, 1931).

White, Deborah Gray, *Ar'n't I a Woman? Female slaves in the Plantation South* (New York: W.W. Norton,1985).

Wilson, Philip B, *Being Single: insights for tomorrow's church* (London: Darton Longman & Todd, 2005).

Wilson-Kastner, Patricia, 'The Once and Future Church: Women's Ordination in England', *The Christian Century* 100.7 (1983), pp. 214–216.

Wootton Janet, 'Books, Liturgical, Congregationalist', in Bradshaw, Paul F. (ed.), *The New SCM Dictionary of Liturgy and Worship* (London: SCM Press, 2002) pp. 77–79

Wootton, Janet (ed.) *Worship Live* (1994 to date)

Wootton, Janet, 'English Congregationalism and its Relation to Ownership of Property and Land', *International Congregational Journal* 2.2 (August 2002) pp. 179–200.

Wootton, Janet, 'The Priesthood of all Believers – Is This What You Want?', *Feminist Theology* 1 (Sept 1992) pp. 72–9.
Wootton, Janet, *Introducing a Practical Feminist Theology of Worship* (Sheffield: Sheffield Academic Press, 2000).
Wootton, Janet, *Introducing a Practical Feminist Theology of Worship* (Sheffield: Sheffield Academic Press, 2000).
Wootton, Janet, sermon preached at Westminster Abbey on the Sunday after Easter, 1988, published in Walton, Heather and Susan Durber (eds), *Silence in Heaven: a Book of Women's Preaching* (London: SCM, 1994), pp.143–6.

http://www.iona.org.uk
http://emergingchurch.info, http://www.freshexpressions.org.uk
http://en.wikipedia.org/wiki/Women_in_Sikhism
http://ww.quaker.org.uk/templates/internal.asp?nodeid=89729
http://www.churches-together.org.uk
http://www.icc.ac.uk/courses_desc.php?course_id=26
http://www.newfrontiers.xtn.org/magazine/volume2issue9
http://www.newfrontiers.xtn.org/our-mission/training1/module_index
http://www.sikhs.org/women_h.htm
http://www.spurgeons.ac.uk/site/pages/ui_courses_masters.aspx
http://www.watchwomen.com

Name and Subject Index

academy, *see also* education 19, 99, 107, 139, 156, 177–9
Africa 47, 68, 71–6, 143–4, 148, 160
Africa Inland Church 160–1
Alstyne, Frances van 5
Anglican Churches/Communion 13, 67 (n. 45), 113, 115–24, 145, 148
Anna 77
anointing 14, 22–3
apostolic succession 6
Athaliah 33
Attaway, Mrs 43, 55
authority 7, 17, 57, 76, 87, 101, 110, 152, 162

Bam, Brigalia 112
Bangladesh 184–6
Baptism, *see* sacraments
Baptists 2, 3, 20, 43, 46, 55, 56, 74, 86, 145, 167, 193
Barbauld, Anna Laetitia 6
Batten, Mrs C. R. 88
Bennett, Joyce 116
Berry, Jan 6
Bible, interpretation of, *see also* Jesus, 6, 14–15, 23–6, 32–9, 52–5, 58, 62, 71, 72, 75, 76–8, 84–5, 107, 109, 118, 120–121, 157–8, 169, 203
bishop, *see* leadership, senior
Black Majority Churches 2, 23, 47, 59, 145, 160–6, 193–5

Bliss, Kathleen 109
Body of Christ (church as) 13, 16, 26, 155
Booth, Catherine 18, 45, 59, 84
Booth, Evangeline Cora 46
Booth, William 18, 45, 59
Britain and Ireland School of Feminist Theology 99–100
British Council of Churches 2, 190
Brown, Antoinette 47
Burroughs, Nannie 86

Calder, Jane Scott 182
Calvary Holiness Church 59
Catholic Women's Ordination 121
Cavert, Mrs 109
Chakko, Sarah 109
Chamberlain, Elsie 94
charismatic movement 59–60, 169
Chidley, Katherine 43
Christian Survivors of Sexual Abuse 94
Chung, Hyung Kyung 111
Church, early 39–40, 54, 71, 78
emerging, 7, 65 (n. 4), 102, 140, 203
medieval 41–2, 52–4, 85
New Testament, 15, 38–9, 76–8, 203
Church in Wales 89
Church Life, *see also* Faith and Order 3

INDEX

Church Meeting 4, 6, 136, 171
Church of England 1, 21–2, 48, 87–91, 106, 107, 109, 111, 114–19, 120, 123–4, 145
Church of Scotland 106–7, 112, 143
Church of the Nazarene 59
Churches Together in Britain and Ireland 2, 194, 204
Churches Together in England 2, 194
Circle of Concerned African Women Theologians 7
Civil War, American 47
Civil War, English 43–4
colonialism 68, 72, 76, 204
Coltman, Constance 19, 43, 48, 106–7, 108
communion, *see* sacraments
Community of Women and Men in the Church 3, 107, 110, 113
congregationalism 2, 4, 6, 63, 86, 96, 99, 108, 112, 120, 167–71, 176, 181–4, 189
Council for World Mission 184, 191
Council of African and Caribbean Churches, 2
Council of Churches for Britain and Ireland, *see* Churches Together in Britain and Ireland
Countess of Huntingdon, Selina 45
Countess of Huntingdon's Connexion 2
Crawford, Janet 113–14
Crosby, Sarah 58
culture 7, 19, 24–5, 32, 42–4, 47, 63, 68–80, 85–9, 92, 98, 100–1, 106–7, 165, 167–9, 199, 201, 202–5

Daly, Mary 32
deacon, *see* leadership, local
deaconess 39–40, 107, 112, 183, 189, 190
Deborah 33, 75, 77, 78
Dicks, Elsa 18
dissent/er 1, 44, 85, 92
Dorcas 39
dress 17, 55, 79, 96
Driver, Judith 6
dualism 72, 79, 84, 86, 88

ecclesiology 4, 31, 46, 63, 67 (n. 45), 90, 96–9, 110, 114
Ecumenical Forum of European Christian Women 124
ecumenism 2, 21–2, 90, 105–15, 145, 148, 178, 180, 190, 199–200
education 14, 19, 50, 51, 61, 96, 107, 108, 130–1, 137, 143, 161–5, 168, 170, 174–6, 180–2, 184–6, 188–9, 197, 199–200, 203
elder, *see* leadership, local
equality 17, 57, 59, 69, 70, 86–8, 98, 101, 105, 107, 120–1, 190, 199, 204
Established Church 1, 89, 106–7
Esther 34
Eucharist, *see* sacraments
Europe 41, 99, 109, 116, 120, 124, 143–4, 148–9, 180–1
evangelical 1, 59, 186
Evangelical Alliance 194
Evangelical Revival 2, 3, 58, 73
evangelism, *see* mission
Eve 15, 84

Fageol, Suzanne 90
Faith and Order, *see also* Church Life 3, 113–14, 139, 148
family, *see* relationships
Fell, Margaret 18, 44, 55
feminist theology 7, 35, 78–9, 82–102, 111, 124, 169, 174–7, 203

217

INDEX

Finney, Charles 58
Fiorenza, Elisabeth Schüssler 32, 83, 95–9, 101
Fisher, Mary 44
Forrester, Margaret 112
Forster, Roger and Faith 24
Fox, George 44, 56
Free Church Federal Council 1–4
Free Church/es 1–11, 12–13, 18–19, 25, 30–1, 46, 48, 51, 59, 63–4, 92–93, 96, 107, 108, 118, 121
Fresh Expressions, *see* Church, Emerging
Friends, Society of 4, 44, 46–7, 56–7
Fry, Elizabeth 45
fundamentalism 59, 204

Gates, Edith 20
gender 14–15, 61–2, 69, 79, 85, 88, 94, 101, 106, 148, 156, 168, 171, 176, 178, 198, 200
General Secretary 5, 178, 194
gifting 13–14, 18–19, 22–5, 40, 53, 77–8, 87, 194
Girls Brigade 189
Gnanadason, Aruna 111, 113
Gnostics 40, 85
Goddess 83, 135
Gordon, Clementina 181
Gouldbourne, Ruth 20
Great Awakening, First, Second, *see* Evangelical Revival
Grey, Mary 158
Griffiths, Ann 44

Hagar 85
Hannah 34
headship 7, 23, 118, 195
Hild/a 41, 100
Hinduism 177
Holiness Movement 3, 47, 56, 59, 87, 98

Holy Spirit/Spirit 4, 14, 22–3, 31, 39, 40, 46–7, 53, 56, 58–9, 87, 110, 120, 123, 133, 139, 162, 169, 200
Hong Kong and Macao 115, 116
Hooten, Elizabeth 44, 56
Huldah 33, 77
Hurrel, Elizabeth 88
human rights, *see also* social concern, slavery, equality, feminism, , racism, poverty, temperance 3, 7, 46, 83, 85, 98, 105–6, 123–4, 147, 203
Hwang, Jane 116
hymns/books 5, 60, 202

Ichthus Christian Fellowship 24
inclusive language (of God) 42, 90–4, 98, 118, 179, 203
inclusive language (of humans) 6, 62, 90–4, 98, 99, 124, 177, 202
India 47, 68, 109
institution/alisation 18, 40, 44–5, 54, 56–57, 63, 79, 84–6, 97–8, 101
International Church of the Foursquare Gospel 59
Iona Community 36, 93
Ireland, 1
Islam 185–6

Jamaica 187–91, 193–5
Jamieson, Penny 116
Jesus 11, 13, 15, 31, 34, 35–8, 61, 70, 71–5, 76–9, 83–5, 94, 131, 141, 156–7, 169, 174, 203–4
Joan of Kent 43
Joanna 37–8
Judaism 181
Julian of Norwich 42–3, 183
Junia 39
justice, *see* human rights, social concern

INDEX

Kastner, Patricia Wilson 89–90
Kempe, Margery 42–3
Kiek, Winifred 85
Kim, Eunjoo Mary 62

laity/lay 7, 12, 20, 96, 176, 181, 199–200
leaders/hip local 4, 6, 19, 57, 136, 144, 152, 171, 177, 182–3
leaders/hip senior 2, 4, 18, 23, 27 (n. 17), 45–6, 108, 111, 116–23, 178–9, 194–5
leadership, style of 6–7, 177, 203
Lee, Jarena 62
Leuenberg Agreement 149
Levison, Mary 107, 112
Li Tim Oi 115–6
liberal theology 32, 97, 174, 176
liberation theology/ies, *see also* feminist, womanist, mujerista theology 7, 98, 100, 101–2, 169, 176, 203
Lutheran Churches 112, 116, 120, 149
Lydia 39, 77

MacPherson, Aimee Semple 59
Magnificat 34, 36
male models of ministry 94–6, 138
Mallet, Sarah 58
Margaret of Scotland 41
marriage, *see* relationships
Martha 37, 76
Mary Magdalene 6, 36, 38, 53, 83
Mary, mother of Jesus 34, 35–6, 135, 155
Mary of Bethany 37, 77
Mayland, Jean 202
McCarthy, Carol 3
McConnachie, Catherine 107
Mennonites 55
Methodism 2, 13, 21–2, 44, 45, 47, 61, 74, 87, 88, 92, 107, 120–1, 145, 148, 149, 150–9, 165, 196
Methodist Missionary Society 199–200
Mewhort, Grace 85
midwives, Hebrew 34
minister, *see* leadership, local
Ministry of Word and Sacrament 107, 113, 137, 142, 198, 199
Miriam 34, 77, 78, 94
mission/ary 9, 39, 45, 57, 60, 68, 73, 116, 132, 184–6, 187, 199
moderator, *see* leadership, senior
Moravians 55, 116, 145, 148
Movement for the Ordination of Women 99, 124, 200
Mujerista Theology 7, 82, 100

Naomi 34
National Free Church Women's Council 2, 88
New Frontiers 24–5
New Testament Assembly 2, 194–5
Nonconformist/ty 1, 4, 44, 56

Old Catholic Church 112
ordination 3, 9, 16, 46–7, 48, 64 (n. 4), 76, 86, 89, 91, 95–6, 107–13, 115–24, 150, 159, 160, 182, 194, 198, 204
Orthodox Churches 13, 90, 110, 111, 113, 114, 121–3

Palmer, Phoebe 47, 58
pastor, *see* leadership, local
pastoral care 93–4, 98, 132, 140, 146–8, 151, 154, 156
patriarchy/al 7, 32, 33, 70–1, 78–80, 83, 87, 95–6, 139, 20
Peart, Ann 90
Pentecostal Churches 2, 22–3, 56, 59, 87, 145, 193
persecution 1, 157, 184–5

219

INDEX

Petit, Elizabeth 44
Petzold, Gertrude von 106
Phoebe 39, 75, 78
Philip, daughters of 39, 77
Phiri, Isabel 7
politics 70, 85, 98, 106, 123, 147, 184, 185–6, 190, 198
postmodern/ity 101
poverty 3, 60, 85, 129
prayer 25, 40, 42, 57–8, 122–3, 131, 133, 151–2, 182, 197
prayer meetings, *see* women's meetings
preaching 5, 14, 43, 47, 50–64, 107, 140, 145, 146, 151, 152, 199
presbyter, *see* leadership, local
Presbyterian 4, 57, 120, 187–9
president, *see* leadership, senior
priest/ly/hood 6, 16, 35, 118, 123
priesthood of all believers 12–13, 17, 55, 63
Prisca/Priscilla 39, 75, 77
prophecy 15, 33–4, 39, 54, 57, 77–8, 202
Puritans 43, 98

race/ism 3, 68, 79, 101, 163, 189–91, 200
Rees, Christina 119
Reformation, 2, 3, 42–3, 55, 116, 149
Reformed Churches 112, 116, 120, 149
relationships 17, 19, 21, 27 (n. 13, 17), 42, 45, 47–8, 61, 69, 87, 110, 133–4, 136–8, 143, 149, 162–4, 170, 173–4, 176, 181, 183–4, 193–5, 196
religious communities 40–2, 53, 85, 181–3
Richardson, Baroness Kathleen 4
Roman Catholic Church 2, 90, 112, 114, 121, 135, 181–3, 186, 204
Roman Empire 17, 54, 79
Royden, Maud 84, 85, 106, 108
Ruether, Rosemary Radford 32, 86, 90, 96–9, 101
Ruth 34

sacraments 5, 6, 13, 16, 40, 56, 92–3, 122, 136, 139, 140, 145, 147, 151, 152–3, 154, 182, 195, 196
St Hilda Community 90–1, 101
Salvation Army 3, 18, 45–6, 59, 67 (n. 45), 87–8, 97, 129–34
Samaritan Woman 37–8, 83
Sarah 85, 94
Schori, Katherine Jefferts 117
Scotland 1, 41, 142, 188–9
sexuality 40, 61, 69, 85, 92–3, 157–8, 170, 177, 178
Sikhism 69–70, 78, 79, 80 (n. 3)
silence/ing 1, 3, 7, 31, 82, 84, 86, 90, 133, 141, 157, 179, 203–4
singleness, *see* relationships
slavery 47, 72–4, 188, 204
Smith, Amanda 47
social concern 45–6, 83, 129–34, 148, 184
Society for the Ministry of Women in the Church 99, 108, 123–4, 200
Stansgate, Margaret, Lady 108, 200
Stanton, Elizabeth Cady 32, 105
Stewart, Maria W. 74, 75
story, the importance of 7–8, 50, 61–2, 205
suffrage, women's 46, 85, 108, 123
Sunday School 60, 167, 178, 188–9, 194
Susanna 37–8
Syrophoenician woman 37

220

INDEX

Taft, Zechariah 84, 88
teaching 16, 43
temperance 46, 85
Tillman, June Boyce 6
Tonkin, Ada 85
tradition 15, 47, 97, 101, 113, 122, 165
training, *see* education
transformation of Church 7, 90, 97, 100, 124, 200, 205
  of leadership 7, 94–6, 140, 177, 205
  of society 7, 32, 35, 94, 97, 100, 190, 204
Trible, Phyllis 32
Truth, Sojourner 74
Tubman, Harriet 74

Unitarian 3, 86, 173–9
United Churches 149, 188–91
United Reformed Church 2, 87, 107, 108, 120–1, 135–41, 142–9
unity 3, 21–2, 114, 117, 120, 149, 200
USA 44, 46, 47, 56, 58, 59, 61, 62, 73–6, 86–91, 98–100, 109, 117, 119, 164, 200, 204

vocation 13, 19, 95, 130, 135–6, 142, 143, 150, 160, 165, 170, 174, 180, 182, 201, 203
voluntary work 97, 174, 194

Wales 1, 9, 44–5, 87, 89, 99

Webb, Pauline 202
Wedel, Cynthia 109
Wesley, Charles 5
Wesley, John 44, 54, 57, 199
Wesley, Susannah 57, 107
Wesleyan Reform Union 2
Whitefield, George 45, 58
widows, order of 40
Winkworth, Catherine 6
witchcraft 42, 101
woman who anointed Jesus 31
womanhood, cult of 75, 79, 88
Womanist Theology 7, 82, 100, 203
Women and the Church 119, 123
Women-Church 90, 97
Women in Theology 6, 89, 91, 99, 174
women's meetings 60, 86, 162, 178, 194
Women's Ordination Worldwide 121
Women's World Day of Prayer 199
World Council of Churches 12, 107, 108–15, 139, 180–1, 190, 201
World Council of Churches Decade 89, 91, 100, 111, 113–14, 204
Worship, 5, 90–4, 98, 110, 139, 145, 156, 177, 202–3

Zarephath, widow of 34

www.ingramcontent.com/pod-product-compliance
Lightning Source LLC
Chambersburg PA
CBHW070304230426
43664CB00014B/2637